VIRTUAL PRESENTING

Responding to the widespread and continued acceleration of virtual working practices in recent years, *Virtual Presenting* provides a clear guide to producing, presenting, and broadcasting in a remote context.

Unlike traditional studio production where a presenter is surrounded by a crew and cameras, the virtual presenter is often isolated or connected to a remote crew. *Virtual Presenting* explains how to make an authentic connection across great spaces, linked only via the Internet. Topics covered include how to build a virtual setup; how to appear on camera; how to appear confident and comfortable; and how to optimize your presentation voice. The authors demonstrate how to tell effective stories across the entire new media landscape of webcasting, webinars, livestreams, and virtual events. Finally, success stories and case studies from teachers, students, and professionals are interwoven to show how these guidelines translate into best practices.

Virtual Presenting will be a valuable resource for students of media production and remote broadcasting as well as professionals looking to become stronger communicators and visual presenters.

James (Jamie) Cohen is an Assistant Professor at CUNY Queens College teaching Media Studies. He is a digital culture expert and educator, as well as a writer, speaker, and producer. Jamie holds a PhD in Cultural and Media Studies specializing in Internet literacies and media making.

Michael (Mike) Sorrentino is a Producer and Entrepreneur. He founded Sorrentino Media in 2016 and has grown it into an industry leader in remote video production. His early career began in producing news and he has taken many of those methods and technologies into live-streaming content for global brands.

VIRTUAL PRESENTING

A Guide to Formats, Production, and Authentic Delivery

James Cohen and Michael Sorrentino

Routledge
Taylor & Francis Group
NEW YORK AND LONDON

Designed cover: bounward / DigitalVision Vectors via Getty Images

First published 2023
by Routledge
605 Third Avenue, New York, NY 10158

and by Routledge
4 Park Square, Milton Park, Abingdon, Oxon, OX14 4RN

Routledge is an imprint of the Taylor & Francis Group, an informa business

ISBN: 978-1-032-27185-9 (hbk)
ISBN: 978-1-032-25777-8 (pbk)
ISBN: 978-1-003-29171-8 (ebk)

DOI: 10.4324/9781003291718

Typeset in Bembo
by MPS Limited, Dehradun

Jamie—

To my wife Nickie, my constant and forever adventure partner, and my beautiful daughter Vera.

Michael—

To my wife and rock, Annie, and to our daughter Rose. Rose, I can't wait to see what amazing things you do in life.

CONTENTS

FIGURES

PREFACE

The Story

Once upon a time, we advanced to a point in history where we could produce video content, but not all be in the same place. We've had this ability for some time, but it, unfortunately, took a global pandemic to make it necessary. However, we had no preparation and we, well, sort of winged it.

But Media Production is a skill. It has rules, it has grammar, it has conventions, it has a long history.

In the world of remote media production, we still apply those concepts. How do we do it properly? How do we enhance our skills? How do we be better on camera and how to we help those who are *on camera* present as well as possible? What is the tech involved? What else can we use?

In this book, we'll take you **in order** through the steps to become better at virtual presenting - from you to the cameras that capture us.

First, we'll go over the basics of presentation, next we'll discover the nuance embedded in the way we appear on camera and how we can help those on camera learn those techniques (we'll also be incorporating the tech), next we'll introduce all the ways in which we engage with each other on all the different platforms and media distribution, both accessible (Zoom, Teams, etc.) and advanced (remote production kits). Finally, we get to put it all together in the form of productions, virtual events, livestreams, webinars, calls, and major productions.

It's also important we hear how **you did it.** We have a chapter that collects real case studies of remote production. There's a lot to learn from those with experience.

Soon, you too will be an expert.

ACKNOWLEDGMENTS

Michael Sorrentino

Much of my work in this book was written on Amtrak trains. From New York to Miami, Chicago to DC, and Emeryville, CA, to Chicago on the stunning California Zephyr, I had a productive 4,927 miles. For me, this was an amazing way to check off two major bucket list items, writing a book and traveling across the country by rail. I highly recommend it, you'll meet some great people, see amazing places, and understand first-hand how the journey really is the destination.

I thought I would spend my entire career in TV news. Ten years at the same network gave me stability and a line of sight to an upper-management future. Then I fell in love. My former co-worker had become a dear friend. We set one another up with our friends over the years but after about 10 years of friendship, realized that it was each other we were interested in. At that time, Annie Scranton had started Pace Public Relations and was in the process of growing it into the industry leader it is today.

Seeing her success, the freedom to travel and make her own life, inspired me. It was Annie that encouraged me to do media training on the side (I had been doing it as part of my full-time job). Without Annie's inspiration and encouragement, you wouldn't be reading this book and I would probably still be in an OK job, never knowing what else was possible. Annie has been my rock; the love she provides is the fuel to be a better human, husband, dad, son, brother, and CEO. No number of paragraphs in a textbook will do justice to the thanks and gratitude I hold for my beautiful bride.

When Jamie Cohen and I were having one of our many geek-outs about video production, the idea of writing a book developed organically. Jamie, having authored one of the best texts on New Media yet, was a natural partner and has been an amazing usher through this process. I cannot thank him enough for his friendship, guidance, and intelligent conversations.

When Jamie pitched the idea of having the "Voices from the Field" for Chapter 6, it turned out to be a rewarding venture where Jeff Miner, Ashesh Satvedi, and Gemma Toner (among others) all jumped at the chance to educate others and share their stories. It's not enough to thank them for helping with this book by sharing their insight, but for being spectacular partners over the years.

The entire team at Sorrentino Media is owed thanks for helping develop this book in some capacity. Our Director of Photography, Omar Lopez's partnership and genius have helped make our company successful, my work life easier, and helped form parts of this book, as you'll read in Chapter 4. Kristi Szczesny was a great help in researching materials and keeping me on task. To the rest of the team, Liz Weaver O'Keefe, Wade Shields, Ashley Vernola, Dave Shaw, Dan Baker, Dan Wolff, Jesse VandenBergh, Emily O'Keefe, and others, we are building something amazing together and I'm so lucky to be on your team.

When our proposal was accepted by Routledge and we had to actually start the book, I was in a tough place emotionally. My mother was very sick and later passed away from a rare mitochondrial disease. I'm not a very emotional person, so trying to handle that initial shock and grief while running a company and writing a book, I thought might be too much. Along the way, Jamie was there to encourage and guide me.

Riding the train solo for so many hours, I had plenty of time to write and to think. That experience of seeing the country and meeting strangers really helped. I think, in some ways, my mom was there with me, reminding me about what is important and what really matters - like my daughter, Rose. I want her to grow up and know that even when you think everything is too overwhelming, you can power through and do something good.

Whether they realize it or not, both Jamie and Annie showed me that we can channel the grief of that which we don't understand into something productive that will hopefully help others. That's what I hope this book does for you, that you can take some of our knowledge and experience and become a better producer to create content that will make the world just a little bit better.

Jamie Cohen

A little over a decade ago, I had been introduced to the concept of Massive Open Online Courses (with the uncomfortable acronym "MOOC") and became fascinated with online learning and remote media production. A decade later, the market is huge and expanded way farther than I ever imagined the original concept would go, stretching across education to private sectors. Everyone is now involved.

While I didn't write my portion of this text on trains, my mind fluttered around the world and through conversations with colleagues and co-workers, domestic and abroad. I was able to write in between travel and teaching and as it turned out, the lessons I'd learned years ago applied to the evolution of virtual presenting through the pandemic response and in the hybrid period that followed.

Everywhere I went for conferences, seminars, or even study abroad in Italy, the conversation leaned into what it was like to continue sharing our thoughts, our ideas, and our media during the stay-at-home period. Nearly everyone had a plan and strategies and wanted to talk about their experiences. I knew we were on the right path with this project.

Mike and I go way back, but working with him on this project was amazing and fulfilling. He and I have had brainstorming sessions for years upon years and I am ever grateful that Mike has given me the opportunity to produce for his company on occasion. While I mostly teach theory now, I feel educators should dabble in production or service now and then to recenter their pedagogy. Mike trusts me with my skills, and I trust him with his support and his incredible leadership.

Most importantly, I have to thank my wife Nickie who is my rock and biggest supporter—as I am hers. She gave me the space (sometimes quite literally in many parts of the house as I move around while I write) to put this piece together. Throughout the entire text-writing process, she was pregnant with our daughter, and we worked together to support each other. I'm excited to raise our daughter together.

Professionally, I'd like to thank some other people who have given me the opportunity to learn more about how production works and what creativity may come from it. In my time between the two institutions, I was fortunate to have been employed as a multimedia producer, leading a team to create amazing webinars, virtual events, and live streams. I'll thank my manager Joe Cruz who trusted me to develop a media department in a publishing company. I also need to thank my most trusted confidant at the publishing company, Liana Jabs, a truly spectacular remote media producer who radiates good energy and truly cares about how to connect with an audience.

It's important to thank our wonderful Broadcast Education Association Panelists Jennida Chase, Robb Montgomery, Andrew Conte, and Chris Strobel who really helped us think through some of the important parts of the project. Additionally, I'd like to thank Anastacia Kurylo, Dave Shaw, Kenneth Pendergast, and Martin Schlesinger. And a big thanks to Andrea Ranalli who has been a great guide in Italy and now an amazing remote media producer in Rome. I'd also like to thank my research partner Josh Chapdelaine who shares my belief that we should share our expertise and make it accessible.

Lastly, we'd like to thank Hannah McKeating and Lizzie Cox at Taylor and Francis for their support, trust, and collaboration throughout the process.

1 INTRODUCTION

The Shift to Virtual

The stress really began to build around June of 2020. Conferences and meetings and conventions were getting canceled; school plans for the fall were being reconsidered; entire industries were shifting to remote work scenarios. There were no rules, just an expectation that we were to use the tools out there to migrate into the virtual world. Surprisingly, most everyone met the challenge and figured out how to translate some real-world experiences into the digitally connected world.

In one instance, a journal publishing company that focused on genetic engineering started to plan their annual fall symposium. The plan that year was to create a digital conference, focusing on mRNA and how the COVID-19 vaccine (at the time in progress) was being developed and what we can learn from its science. Some of the top biotech key opinion leaders in the world were set to speak about it. Originally, they'd all planned on meeting in Cincinnati, Ohio, the location of the in-person event in September 2020 and since they still had those dates blocked out on their calendars, the choice to meet online was easy. However, this was a publishing company, not a media company.

The decision to go fully remote and do virtual presenting was daunting at first. When you plan an in-person event, you can hire an events company that does the planning, connects with the location to provide amenities like food and beverages, chairs and tables, booths and barriers, and everything you'd need to make the event work. It's a typical process at hotels and convention centers. What does the symposium conference look like online?

The publishing company quickly hired several multimedia professionals to lead the charge to develop the online virtual event. Costs for online events platforms varied greatly, and the writers and publishers really didn't have any idea what features would be necessary for the online conference to have. To be clear, neither

DOI: 10.4324/9781003291718-1

did many of the multimedia producers—it was all new territory. Most multimedia producers come from a traditional television background, working with larger cameras, lights, locations, and trained talent. Virtual production was going to be an exciting new endeavor.

Platforms were demonstrated for the company, and they settled on Accelevents, a virtual events platform that is robust and customizable. Because the pandemic had sent so many companies into the same exact predicament, Accelevents' platform was being updated in real time as well with new features coming online daily. The multimedia producers only had a few weeks to develop a production strategy for the event. They worked with the marketing team and hosts (who were the editors of journal) and ended up creating a 4-hour event with an opening keynote and closing keynote and simultaneous break-out rooms. It was scheduled just like the in-person event, but no travel necessary.

It wasn't without hiccups, these were still the very early days of remote media production and virtual presenting, and audiences were forgiving, but it worked and over 3,000 people attended live and enjoyed the show. Data was collected from the users and follow-ups were made with the attendees who interacted the most with the platform. The marketing team used the data to connect with the audience after the production with surveys and follow-up material.

The company would go on to create five more virtual events, more than there were actual conferences planned on location, because the ability to produce the online events had a greater return on investment. As the pandemic waned and people returned the office, the publishing company decided to lean into the multimedia projects, expanding their company into the virtual space permanently.

In another scenario, a large artificial intelligence company with a bevy of resources was doing the same. They had conference plans, but knew they had to accommodate the translation to online attendance. While virtual platforms were a good place to host their global meeting, the company knew that some of its audience could only use Zoom, not any browser-based application. In addition, the AI company wanted to express a high-quality feel for their virtual production. Rather than hire an events company, the AI company hired a multimedia boutique production company to produce their event.

The multimedia production company gladly accepted the challenge. On the fly, the producers invented new technologies and virtual presenting kits built into Pelican cases. The cases were sent to guests all over the world and inside, they found ring lights, iPhones, and specialized instructions on how to set up the gear and tips for presenting. Meanwhile, inside the AI company's main meeting space, the media producers set up cameras and small stages for some of the top-level executives to deliver their talks to the remote audience. Safe and masked, the multimedia crew and the AI company teamworked their magic, creating a virtual studio in their meeting space.

The next challenge was presenting. Most of the executives who were set to speak had only done so in front of live audiences or in interview settings. They now had to learn how to present effectively—and authentically—to a remote audience. The mood would be different, they would have to bring more energy to the virtual show and perform in a way that didn't seem forced. They had only a few days to learn techniques and the production team worked around the clock to make sure it all turned out well.

On the day of the show, the executives presented from their meeting space over Zoom and were able see their panelists on return monitors under the cameras. It looked like a conversation in real time. Even when everyone returned to the office a few years later, the yearly production still takes place in a hybrid format.

One of the most beautiful examples of how this switch changed the lives of the people who started using remote media production is a story of a mutual aid organization on the West Coast. During the pandemic, it was difficult for some disadvantaged people to get their groceries or find access to good education. The organization turned to webinars to help assist community members during the lockdown period. The company raised money and licensed a seat from On24, a browser-based webinar platform.

The director of the program created a guidebook for the volunteers on how to speak to the virtual audience. They had to make the content both accessible and meaningful *and* take advantage of all the technical tools the platform offered. The organization used the guidebook to learn how to speak on camera and how to use a playlisting feature on the On24 platform. They decided to go with a simulive approach, meaning they'd schedule the webinar for a specific time to air, but the media is all pre-recorded and edited. Along with their simulive approach, they could split the clips up so each segment allowed for different features to appear below the video.

The volunteers each recorded their segment on their home computer using their personal web cameras. The director helped stage direct their settings and made sure the lighting looked nice and the background looked neat but remained authentic. It was a lot of work, but they knew the show should be as high quality as possible. The goal was to record each part straight through so they didn't have to edit the footage. After each volunteer uploaded their clip to their shared drive, the director edited it and timed out the simulive production.

It took some time to figure out the timings and they practiced it several times on a duplicate version of the show. Being simulive, the volunteers had the opportunity to be present during the show and answer questions to the live chat that was scrolling up the side. The live chat made it feel personal and the community felt engaged. Everyone felt that the webinar was even more valuable than their traditional community meetings because the platform enabled surveys, resources, and live Q&A. The organization decided to sign a longer license and continues to produce their webinars.

These three anecdotes offer a look at some of the ways that virtual presenting, formats, production, and authentic delivery online and in hybrid formats can benefit companies, organizations, and producers looking to change the way we connect with audiences.

The Many Modes of Remote Media Production

We are interested in connecting remote media production and virtual presenting to the media production industry. In television news, producers have been doing live interviews from people's houses for decades and virtual events date back to the 1990s, but when the pandemic changed the way we collectively produced visual content, it changed the way we watched it as well. This shift is ongoing and will likely continue throughout the future of media production.

For one, technology has become more accessible, not just in the sense of its ease of use, but in cost and practicality. Web cameras, from small devices you can buy on Amazon to web cameras with artificial intelligence to follow you as you speak, are as abundant as computer mice. DSLRs and mirrorless cameras now have applications to enable the camera to connect directly to your computer so you can use a production quality camera as your web camera.

But most importantly, the way we interact with media has changed. For example, only a small percentage of people were avid consumers of YouTubers' content or livestreamers productions. When we wanted to learn more about something, occasionally we'd be interested in signing up for a webinar. Virtual events were built primarily for meetups among Internet-based groups that lacked mobility or budget to meet in person or host a conference. For the most part, academics preferred physical conferences to host their yearly meetings.

For nearly 2 years, most media shifted almost completely to the virtual space.

In an effort to slow the spread of COVID-19, news organizations helped crew and talent build small studios in their houses, Zoom became a tool for large scale events as well as meetings, platforms were developed rapidly to host thousands of guests, webinars and livestreams stood in for community meetings and gatherings. Amazingly, many of these things continue and will persist over the next many years. It turns out that remote production has some incredible benefits from helping mitigate climate change to protecting the health of participants to enabling international guests to appear as part of your production without the exorbitant travel expenses.

What We Learned from Going Virtual

In the anecdotes above, we saw that moving online meant that new skills had to be learned very quickly. Never before in media history did industries have to meet the need of a shift. Traditionally, shifts would take years: from radio to television, from television to YouTube, from YouTube to livestreaming. Traditionally it wasn't mandatory either, some moved, some didn't. But what we learn from every shift is that somewhere out there, someone is inventing the style that would become the framework for all future creators and producers.

Transitioning to virtual formats meant we learned things that we wouldn't have known otherwise about our audience and our production styles faster. In the first anecdote about the journal publishing company, they learned that the leads generated from the virtual event were far more valuable than any lead that they had traditionally received from their in-person events. Virtual event platforms collect a lot of data from users and if you know what you are looking for and what goals you are trying to achieve, the data is priceless.

In the second anecdote, the shift to virtual presenting meant that the media production company had to figure out how to achieve consistent production quality with virtual guests spread out all over the world. The reason media producers make television in studios and controlled sets is for consistency. When a client is interested in high quality on a web stream, the typical web camera may not be up to par for the demand. The kits in the case were invented for the project but are now part of many hybrid events and productions.

The third anecdote looks at how small, non-profit organizations can use virtual production to enhance community engagement. Aside from the ability to organize their resources in one tool, they were able to produce their talks in advance, giving them more confidence in presenting their content. The most important takeaway from the mutual-aid organization was discovered during the live chat offered while the simulive was airing. Because users were chat based, more interactivity was noticed, and more substantive questions and answers were provided. The community benefit from the amount of interactivity both streamed through video and through the platform.

There is still far more to learn about remote media production and virtual presenting. As we settle into the return to the office, whether hybrid or remote, we now have to consider virtual production will look like over the next decade. What new tools will be developed as we learn to connect in digital ways? How can we continue to combat "Zoom fatigue" and overuse of screens? What new ways will we learn to present to global audiences and hyper local communities? Who will become the creator of the best format of authentic screen delivery and how will we use it to our advantage?

So many people created their own guides during the pandemic and continue to update them as production methods evolve. There were guides about delivery, authentic communication, organic approaches, remote media setups, technical skills, and PowerPoint deck presentation. We believed it was time to compile much of this knowledge into one guidebook. In no way, can this book be comprehensive and total, digital media changes too often, but we do hope we covered enough ground to give you a great set of instructions for your next project, big or small.

We also wanted to provide you with enough context as to *why* virtual presenting and remote media production work. We delve into the histories of authentic delivery to histories of the technology you use to make these projects worth producing. As we are passionate about high-quality production and education, we wanted to be sure to give enough background to these processes, so they make sense. It's also helpful to explain to your teammates where some of these skills and technologies came from.

Why We Wrote This Book

The authors (Michael and Jamie) go way back. We went to college together and we both studied traditional television production and subsequently both became television producers for different projects and companies. From there though, we diverged a bit. Michael went on to work for major broadcasting companies, working up to producing live production in the field with experimental live stream technologies. Later, Michael invented (and holds the patent for) a smartphone case that keeps your lens clean and your privacy safe. Michael founded Sorrentino Media, a boutique production company that is mentioned in the second anecdote.

Jamie worked on a reality show that incorporated sponsored content and the experience inspired him to learn more about it from an academic perspective. Jamie went back to school, twice, and learned how the Internet is changing our everyday lives, studying YouTube and digital culture. In between both graduate degrees, Jamie founded an Internet studies degree at a small college and focused on making producing digital content more accessible.

The authors converged once again years later when Jamie temporarily left academia to pursue a return to video production. Michael hired Jamie to produce a few segments for Sorrentino Media and Jamie was fascinated by how much had changed in the years since his last work in traditional media. When the pandemic changed everything, Jamie was hired by the genetic engineering publishing company in the first anecdote. Jamie was tasked with developing an entirely new multimedia production division at the company and producing six virtual events and over three-dozen webinars in an 8-month period. The division has since scaled.

During the pandemic, Michael, as inventive as always, created the remote media kits that were sent to guests all over the world. They have now become standard for higher level virtual productions. Michael is an expert in media training and adapted his skills to the virtual world. Learning how to present authentically in the virtual world is daunting, but Michael made it accessible and interesting. Obviously, much of Michael's advice is included in this book.

PERSONAL STORIES

Hey, Michael (Mike) here. Throughout this text, Jamie and I are going to chime in with some examples and personal stories that might be helpful. These stories come from our real experiences and resonate among my peers, colleagues, and fellow producers. In these sidebars, I'll note some experiences that gave me the experience necessary to continue to excel as a multimedia producer, help people become better virtual presenters, and enhance remote media production. These personal stories help us be a bit more candid about some of the more niche experiences you may encounter. Enjoy!

During the pandemic period, both authors were doing remote media production and virtual presenting—on both sides of the camera! Over and over, clients, colleagues, friends, and other producers were talking about their guides and their hope that someday there'd be a book to collect all the tips and tricks and tools of the trade for anyone to access.

And that's what you're reading. We hope you learn a lot from what follows. We cover a lot of information.

What's in the Book?

This book is set up to increase in skills and depth as it goes on. We approached this text in a manner that we believe will satisfy everyone from students to professionals in the field to people looking to start producing virtual productions for the first time. While there's no way to cover 100% of the field, we did our best to cover the top-level necessities and the educational foundations that support them.

Our chapters focus on practical applications of skills training and historical context as to why the world of virtual presenting is so unique and important. We also provide a chapter on why presenting virtually exists. In educational settings, this background chapter helps faculty engage in conversation with students about *why* we need to connect history to the present. Context matters and helps us apply criticism to future projects and enables us to defend our decisions.

As the book progresses, it gets more technical, but we strove to make the information as accessible as possible. We start off with what it's like to be in front of the camera and move to the production skills necessary to produce phenomenal webinars and virtual events from behind the camera.

We open with Chapter 2, **Presentation Basics**, a chapter with the most important information to start building your skills for virtual presenting. Presenting in the digital world is unique from traditional media but happens to combine media skillsets from both traditional and online media. Presenting on camera has a history of more than eight decades and its evolution has typically come from the delivery system. The skills that we learned in our television careers apply to virtual presenting, but with several important modifications.

Throughout this chapter, we focus on delivery skills and how to make connections across the digital world. By learning about pitch, pace, posture, and passion, you'll enrich your skills almost immediately if you've been asked to be a guest on a webinar or livestream. This section enhances how well you use your voice to intone your points, how to give thoughtfulness to the timing of your talk, what you need to know about how to hold your body, and how to express your expertise memorably.

You'll learn that virtual presenting has an inherent issue of transmission loss—virtual audiences are not only fickle, but the small screen within a screen streaming style means you have to give a bit more to your approach than you would in real life or even on traditional media. We call this the "30% energy

FIGURE 1.1 Annie Scranton sits with her laptop ready to do a virtual presentation

principle" and it's been successful with all our clients and students. Chapter 2 will also focus on the more important—and often overlooked—details of virtual presenting, from reading the virtual room to checking in with yourself.

Finally, we delve into the importance of increasing your interview skills. Even before the move to remote interviews during the pandemic period, companies were using virtual interfaces to interview candidates. There's a lot to know about presentation basics that will help you find an edge among the competition (Figure 1.1). We leave you with the most important skills of them all: optimism, positivity, and a good attitude!

In Chapter 3, **What Is Authentic Delivery?**, we cover the history and application of authenticity and how on-camera delivery methods have evolved over the last century. When you present on camera to a virtual audience, there's a big contrast between how we've learned to watch and read video media. We're used to television and seeing people present in a certain way. When you present virtually, you are expected to be both professional and be yourself. It's a tight balance, but achievable.

Chapter 3 is part of this book because we believe having context to our methods is extremely important for classrooms and educational settings, but also helps you as a producer or on-camera talent understand *why* you are doing what you do. Everything comes from somewhere and learning the background makes us more competent. We start with a framework and utilize Erving Goffman's important text *The Presentation of Self in Everyday Life* from the 1950s. Goffman's text delves into the dissection of our multitudes of presentation styles.

We present differently to everyone we meet and in every setting we encounter and becoming more aware of this makes us better actors—and we don't just mean stage actor, we mean agency. Agency is your ability to act, to make choices, and to be an agent of change. We make impressions on other people around us and our impressions can change depending how much effort we put into our presentations. It becomes more complicated when we mediate those presentations. What was once on a stage, is now on a screen.

Going through the history of new media presenters, from radio to television to YouTube, shows us why we watch media the way we do. How do we know how to talk to an audience over the air? How do we know when to look into the camera? How do we know we're doing it correctly? By studying the figures that helped create the formats, we get a sense how messaging works over the last century. But then, the Internet changed everything.

The Internet democratized media access, enabling anybody with a camera to post themselves online for the world to see. Originally, media presenting was for the very few to talk to the very many. Now, the very many talk to literally everyone! Because virtual presenting takes place using digital tools, we explore how different YouTubers, TikTok users, and Livestreamers have found success. The most important part is to understand how we can be ourselves and be authentic to others.

Finally, the chapter ends with a short guide on how to set up your space for presenting authentically. If you are a producer, this is especially helpful for your guests and talent so you can give them the best opportunity to be memorable on screen.

In the following chapter, we get into the technical aspects and skills necessary to produce quality media and virtual presentations. Chapter 4, **Multi-Platform Preparation and Pre-Production**, is a behind the scenes look at how the media industry operates—from television to webinars. Learning how to create remote productions is the core of this book. Chapter 4 can get technical, but we hope to make some of the more specific details accessible in your work.

First, we believe there is no such thing as production without pre-production. Learning technical skills is part of that process. You may hear words like "codec" or "streaming," but do you really know what they mean? These are terms used by remote media producers dozens of times per day, and for good reason—it's how it all works. From a technical standpoint, it may help you make better choices when it comes to picking a platform or setting up a studio.

There are also many roles on a remote production, and we help you see the difference between a big production and a personal set-up. We help you understand who does what and why, so if you are just starting out, you know who to task with each responsibility. The personnel of your production, whether that be a team of ten people or just you and a friend, have specific jobs to do to make the production successful. Your clients will be very appreciative of your knowledge.

Chapter 4's main goal is to help you learn the more advanced techniques of pre-production, from lighting and framing to shooting with traditional cameras to producing with cell phones. We also spend time focusing on how you can use remote media production in an educational context. Not just in what we've learned, but how to teach courses or run workshops with the camera gear you have. We give you tips on how to position the camera, how to incorporate camera switching, how to increase your audio quality for your students.

Finally, the chapter concludes with an important, easy to use guide that synthesizes what we learned. It's the part of the chapter you'll want to dog-ear and return to over and over. It's what we hope you use in your setups every time you start thinking of doing a remote media production.

Finally, this book culminates in a robust chapter on producing a remote show and building out the perfect setup for virtual presenting. Chapter 5, **Virtual Events, Webinars, Livestreams, and Calls**, puts together everything we've learned so far about presenting, authenticity, and pre-production and goes into important details to consider when building your projects. Over time, we've realized there are some standards to include on nearly every production whereas there are some details that are platform specific.

In general, you'll learn how important registration data and user tracking are to your production. Remote media production differs from traditional media mainly by the way data is incorporated into your work. Unlike traditional media, digital media enables *you to see* how users interact with your project—where they go, how much time they spend on a site, how much they interact. This data helps you do everything from configure the user interface to create marketing leads for your team. This tracking comes with an important caveat: compliance. We go over the importance of privacy and tracking as well.

At the producer's level, you'll also be responsible for making sure your on-screen talent, keynote speakers, and key opinion leaders are comfortable, presentable, knowledgeable, and authentic. There's so much to keep in mind when you first contact your talent, so we've assembled a detailed checklist for you to consider when preparing your speakers for virtual presenting. Some of our advice is interpersonal (how to interact with executive assistants) and some is very technical (permissions for web camera use) but all of the details have been used in our work.

Chapter 5 also discusses important details like global production time and when to go live to an international audience. The remote media production industry is digital and global, and your audience may not be where you are producing your show. We recommend discussions with your team to prepare an airtime and make room for interactivity. It's a big world and there's a lot of possibilities to gain new audiences in regions you don't traditionally connect to. From there, we get into producing.

From medium-sized productions like livestreams and webinars to huge productions like virtual events, there's more to learn than most realize. Platforms differ in tools and offering, but for the most part, there are consistencies with what you can prepare for. We go into detail on several platforms, prioritizing Zoom and Vimeo Pro, two products we use consistently, but tools that we know are used frequently. When producing a webinar, a choice needs to be made whether to use a browser-based platform or an application and there are reasons for each choice. We hope you enjoy our explanations.

Our breakdown of webinars—both live and simulive—are designed to make sure that you have a good guide in your top drawer to refer to when producing your content. Our goal is to make sure you take a holistic view of producing into your project preparation and this section covers a lot of ground.

Finally, the chapter concludes with an exploration of virtual events, the largest scale production in our book. Virtual events can resemble in person conferences, or they can be completely unique virtual environments with avatars and immersive meeting rooms. Producing a virtual event is as close to producing traditional television as possible, but because the audience is *part of the show*, you need to incorporate attendee needs directly into your production. For example, networking is one of the most sought out features of a virtual events platform.

With that in mind, Chapter 5 leaves you with a section about what safety you can implement into your platform. We've learned a lot about trust and safety over the years and have had our own setbacks and learned from other producers' errors. People want to connect with oneanother across the vast digital networks and you're responsible for their success!

In Chapter 6, **Voices from the Field**, we've asked producers from all over the globe some questions about what they've learned and their thoughts on the future of remote and hybrid media production. Their stories are added to this book not only to substantiate what we've put together for you, but also to provide diverse opinions on their experiences. Each contribution is wonderful, and we thank them for adding their thoughts to this book. We hope you enjoy what they've written for you.

How to Use This Book

This book has been written so you may read each chapter separately, or in order. We recommend reading the book in order because we make assumptions of your knowledge in later chapters. The early chapters provide the foundation for the knowledge. However, this book is aimed at a wide range of audiences from high school to college production courses to working professionals making virtual presentation part of their job.

Each chapter gives context to each of our technical additions and occasionally you'll see sidebars with additional information that contains digital media literacies and our personal stories. You may find these sidebars helpful for filling in the blanks of your knowledge.

We also provide a basic glossary in the back of the book to cover some of our more technical terms. Throughout the text, we define the terms in context, but the glossary gives a quick glance at terms that are used most often and in the context in which the book uses the terms. Technical terms—like the word "key" for example—are used to describe many things. The glossary helps to minimize the variations and clarify our approach.

This book could be a useful guide to keep on your desk or your shelf. We hope you reach for it every time you have a question about what production steps are useful in your project. We are certain that remote media production, hybrid production, and virtual presenting will be around for the rest of your career, so this foundational guide can be used for years to come.

Thank you for being here with us as we cover *Virtual Presenting: A Guide to Formats, Production and Authentic Delivery!*

2

PRESENTATION BASICS

Building Your Skills Is Like Architecture

Before we begin, let's remember that every on-camera presenter, from a first-time guest to a seasoned anchor, must use a similar framework to connect with the audience. Those who've never been on camera before need to "walk before they can run." We encourage first timers to remember that there are steps to take, that you cannot just go on camera the first time and become a superstar. It takes a lot of time and practice to build a relationship with the audience. We may use the example of a building and its many levels to explain this.

Any building, from a high-rise apartment building to a single-family home, relies on a solid foundation to remain standing. Cracks in the foundation or improper planning can make the structure weak and susceptible to collapse. Think of your on-camera persona as a building. Each level cannot exist without mastering the one below it. Think of these four levels as steps in your journey toward being a fantastic on-camera presenter.

FOUNDATION: Understanding what your message is, who the audience will be, and the platform that you'll be communicating with. Here, you're focused on just getting your facts straight, to speak clearly and concisely, and to avoid messing up. The foundational level is all about having basic conversational speaking skills, knowing what your message is and how you can relate it to the audience.

Floor 1: You've got the audience; you know what to say … but *how* do you say it and cut through the noise? Here, we focus on mastering the four Ps. As you'll learn in this chapter, there are four Ps (Pace, Posture, Pitch, and Passion) that need to be understood and honed in on to effectively break through the many barriers that are the audience's attention span.

DOI: 10.4324/9781003291718-2

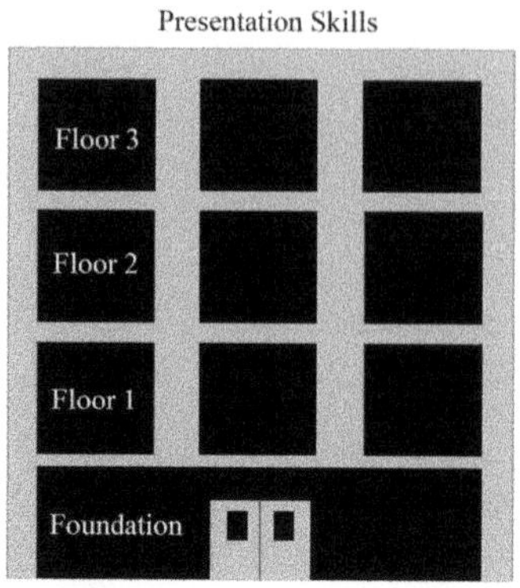

FIGURE 2.1 The floors of presentation success

Floor 2: You're an effective speaker, and you've been in front of this group before (or they've heard about you). On this level, you can work on building on your relationship with the audience. Here is where you can start getting creative in your production methods and show some of your personality. Don't get too ambitious, though. The audience might know who you are, but you still have work to do to become a household name.

Floor 3: This is the penthouse. You're a regular on-camera presenter, the audience knows you and has a clear opinion of your work. If they like you, they are fans. If they don't (and be prepared for some "haters" out there), that's ok too. You can't win them all. On this level, you can start adding humor. The audience and the host know you and your style. Here, it's OK to make some jokes, open up a bit about your personal life (if you choose), and be a bit more vulnerable.

Presentation Skills in Virtual Production

Media Training Meets Non-Traditional

We tend to focus on the equipment, the process, and the applications that we plan to use in our remote production set up. However, we often easily overlook the person in front of the camera, which is more important than the camera equipment and software. We're going to go through some basics of presentation skills. These can apply to everything from a video conference to a pitch or presentation in front of a large or small group, a panel discussion that you might take part in front of an audience, or even just one-on-one communication when you're in a professional environment and want to command the attention of your audience. Let's start with conversational speaking.

In the early days of mass media, it was common to have a person on the other end of your screen talking *to you* or *at you*. The world was a lot smaller almost a century ago when broadcasters could reach just about every household. Newscasters like Walter Cronkite would sit behind a desk and tell us what was happening in the world through an authoritative tone and polished script. News used to be a public service required by TV networks.

Things are very different now. News and broadcasting have proven to be tremendously profitable. Hundreds of media companies now compete for attention with countless news organizations delivering the same story from a hundred different angles. Audience attention spans are waning and, more significantly, we've become more cynical about the person delivering the message because we are aware that in some way, they are trying to sell us something, whether it be a product, a service, or their own personal brand.

In the age of online presenting and social media, we've all become voices on a screen, but just because the camera and the screen exist, doesn't mean these skills come naturally. There are lots to learn and we'll take you through the steps.

WERE THE GOOD OLD DAYS REALLY AS GOOD AS THEY SAY?

If you ask a handful of random people on the street how much they trust a particular journalist or news agency, you're likely to get varying responses from 0 to 100. In the early days of television news, there were only a few newscasters at the national level. When people that lived in that era look back, it's not uncommon for them to reflect positively on a time when people trusted the news and there was no "spin." That might not necessarily be the case.

A poll in 1972 was conducted by Oliver Quale,[1] a public opinion poll specialist, that focused on trustworthiness of political candidates. The poll was conducted in the Bronx section of New York City and asked whether respondents trusted a figure or not. Among the public figures were six names, four were political figures, one was the newscaster Walter Cronkite, and another was a made-up name. Cronkite's name was considered trustworthy by 68% of respondents, well above the others (the next highest ranking being 54%). Since then, this poll has been referenced in countless articles and marketing materials listing Cronkite as the most trusted man in America.

According to the study, Cronkite certainly was more trustworthy than the other options. However, the poll did not compare the iconic newscaster to any other journalists, only politicians and a made-up person. Some consider this statement to be flawed, considering he was up against polarizing political figures and another person that didn't exist.

What do we take away from this example? Simply that even during what many considered to be the golden age of objective broadcast news, the audience most certainly had its level of skepticism. Today, our news diet consists of information that fits our personal biases. Trustworthiness is earned by catering to the audience, rather than giving a dose of what the presenter may consider reality or hard facts.

What can we learn from this? Even though the platforms and personalities change, the audience is smart. The viewer knows that facts can be distorted, cherry-picked, and the message delivery can be slanted. It is up to you, the presenter, to cut right to the chase and be your true and honest self. Anything else, and the audience will see right through you.

Conversational Delivery

To connect with today's savvy and cynical audience, we must understand one thing: authenticity is rewarded. While we'll dive deeper into that in the next chapter, the first step in authentic delivery is to use a conversational style in your speaking.

TV news personalities tend to write in a way that the audience can get bored very quickly. For example, a lot of journalists will write something like "officials say that no arrests have been made yet in the case." Sure, that sentence makes perfect sense. The problem here is that no one actually speaks like that. When you're sitting down with a friend and having a cup of coffee, talking about something in the news, you would never say, "officials say that no arrests have been made yet in the case." Of course not. You would most likely say something like, "the police haven't arrested anyone yet."

This is a perfect example of the conversational barrier in news. We have to write like we talk. This applies to everything from a news report to a speech or a presentation to a small group. As mentioned earlier, the audience is a lot more cynical today than used to be. So is a viewer, you want to get your information from someone that you feel is a relatable and likable person. It is important that we remember that the audience is made up of humans who want to hear from a human, not a robot.

Doing a presentation in front of people in the same industry might allow you to use a lot of jargon. However, the most effective presentations are those that can appeal to a wider audience of people who understand the terminology that you are using. In short, whether it's written or ad-libbed, use words that everyone will understand and talk like **you**. Strip away jargon or "industry speak." If you must use certain terminology, explain it briefly so that anyone watching will know what you are talking about.

Even if you're giving a presentation to a very niche audience, it is very common that presentations are recorded or streamed live. There is always a chance that your work might be viewed by someone who is not as in tune with the topic. By crafting your material in a clear, concise, and conversational way, you are opening the door to educate others and give information to people who you might not have even thought would be watching.

PERSONAL STORY

Mike here!

In my early days of producing news, I was working with a group of very talented young journalists. My job was to train them to be comfortable reporting on the national stage. One of them in particular had this amazing star quality and, in fact, is now a quite successful correspondent for a national news organization in the US. Unbelievable to many of his colleagues today, on one of his first practice live shots, this reporter gave a very poor delivery in his stand-up. It was hard to comprehend this poor presentation because he had done a lot of terrific videos leading up to this. I pulled him aside to ask him what went wrong. He wasn't sure. I asked him what he had done differently in writing his script this time that he had not done previously. He replied that when he was writing his script, he was almost pretending to be the voice of another anchor whom he admired. This was the problem. He was writing for someone else's voice and not his own. It's nice to admire a great talent, but he has to be himself.

We worked together to take all the important data and facts from his old script and just write it like he talks. On the next attempt at a practice, he knocked it out of the park.

Presentation Skills 101

Imagine This

Here you are, you have been invited to participate in a very exclusive streamed panel discussion. You've done your homework, you thought up some clever facts and figures, and you put yourself in a quiet room and knock this out of the park. Your webcam light turns green, you are now live with some of the industry's top experts. Your responses are witty, you are engaging, but for some reason you are just not seeing the facial reactions from the other panelists and attendees that you expected. What could be wrong? When the event is over, you ask for feedback and the moderator says "Well, to be honest, you looked disinterested, pre-occupied, and unprepared." "But how," you ask, "I prepared for weeks!" She explains that your monotone delivery combined with terrible posture and no eye contact made it seem like you were distracted and confused. She suggests you watch the presentation back to see it for yourself.

The Four Ps of Presentation Skills

Using the example you just read, let's go over the four Ps of presentation skills: Pitch, Pace, Posture, and Passion.

Pitch

One of the first things you notice when watching your presentation video is that you sound a bit unsure of your own answers and data. It's almost as if the end of your explanations has a higher pitch as if every sentence ended in a question mark. This is called up-talking. The term was coined in a 1993 *New York Times* article by NYU School of Journalism Professor, James Gorman, and it's very common.[2] When doing media training with a lot of corporate executives, it is very common that entrepreneurs and people who work in very technical fields tend to "uptalk" when explaining something highly complex.

Uptalking can happen when we want to avoid intimidating the audience, so we might use a softer and more deliberate approach. The problem is uptalking does the opposite of what you may intend; it sounds like you are talking *down* to the audience. Sometimes people might unconsciously uptalk because that is how they often hear others speak. Uptalking can also happen when we aren't as confident in ourselves.

Confidence is at the core of solid presentation skills. There is a reason that the term con artist refers to people who can get others to buy into what they're talking about. They can talk about anything with confidence. However, we implore you to use this power for good. Tap into the confidence you have for the expertise you were providing and channel it into an authoritative delivery. It is imperative that when delivering a presentation, end your sentences with periods or exclamation points and not a question mark. After watching your video, your first note to yourself is to make sure to put periods or exclamation points on your outline so that you speak in declarative statements.

UPTALK

Uptalk is nothing new. It's been around for a long time and will likely only become more common in modern speaking.

The term "uptalk" was first used in New York University Professor James Gordon's 1993 *New York Times* article titled "ON LANGUAGE; Like, Uptalk?" In his article, which is a great read by the way and still holds up well, Gordon explains that he first started noticing the "intonation contour" change when his "students had this rising intonation thing? It was particularly noticeable on telephone messages. 'Hello? Professor Gorman? This is Albert? From feature writing?'"[3]

The rise in pitch at the end of a sentence traditionally indicates a question. When you hear someone giving orders or directions, the listener wants them to speak with authority. Gordon's article references an airline pilot and how a passenger might not love the idea of their pilot sounding unsure of their announcements. This is a symptom of uptalking.

In a 1990 dissertation for her PHD, Cynthia Ann McLemore described her findings from studying a sorority at the University of Texas. The paper is quite entertaining, as it lists various exchanges within the group regarding mundane topics. In one example, a member is announcing an upcoming career advancement workshop. Her tone is heavy with uptalk, and the transcript shows those uptalking sentences ending in question marks:

> "y'all
> Can I ask y'all something real quick
> I'm sorry
> They told me I could make an announcement and it's real important
> 'Cause I worked on it all summer long?
> an'
> I'm really stressing about it?
> I have interview? Workshop?
> It's a program put on by the business council?
> an' it's Wednesday night?
> It's the sa- it's like before our party?
> It's from four to six?
> An'
> I know all ya'll need it." (http://itre.cis.upenn.edu/myl/surprise/llog/CAM_Interpretation.pdf)

As you probably interpreted while reading, this announcer doesn't come across as authoritative as she could. In fact, the transcript makes it seem as if she's perturbed or unsure of herself. Some members of her study argue that the tone is "a communicative strategy for realizing the group's stated values of participation, involvement, and inclusion." As far as research papers go, McLemore's is worth a glance.

The problem with uptalking is that it does not convey confidence. It might convey several other things, but confidence is not at the top of that list. In fact, to some it conveys the opposite. In a Guardian article titled "Word up," author Matt Seaton asks presentation expert Diane DiResta, the author of *Knockout Presentations: How to Deliver Your Message with Power, Punch and Pizzazz* about uptalking. DiResta says of uptalking, "It's as if a person's tentative tone allows them to retract the statement if it is met with criticism or disapproval. People are afraid to take a stand." (https://www.theguardian.com/books/2001/sep/21/referenceandlanguages.mattseaton)

Since confidence is the core of public speaking, it's important to be mindful of uptalking. The audience might not be intimidated by you, but they are less likely to absorb your message if you speak using uptalk. Ok?

Pace

The next thing you notice when watching your presentation video is that you tend to say "um" or "ah" a lot. There are a few places where you say the word "like" too many times, and there are a few places where you linger on the word "sooooo …" long enough that to the viewer sees it's obvious that you are trying to collect your thoughts. This use of so-called filler words is also incredibly common.

When filler words are overused, it is usually the result of simply talking too fast. If you are talking faster than you can think, your brain can't process what you were talking about. It's that simple. The key here is to just slow it down.

Think about the environment that you are in when you're delivering a presentation. There might be a lot of people watching you and there might be a lot of logistics involved in preparing; maybe there are a lot of bright lights and cameras around, and frankly you might be a little nervous. Who wouldn't be? When we are nervous, we take shorter breaths. When we take shorter breaths, we get less oxygen into our lungs. As a result, there is less oxygen in your bloodstream and ultimately, your brain and then we are not firing on all cylinders.

One of the best things you can do before a presentation is to simply take some deep breaths. Three deep breaths in through the nose and out through the mouth can do wonders, it allows you to level yourself out. Now, this doesn't mean that by simply taking three deep breaths that your pace will magically be perfect—of course not, but breathing is an important part of talking. If you are reading a scripted presentation, you should mark in your script places where you can stop, take a breath, and collect your thoughts. If you are ad-libbing your presentation, use any opportunity you can to pause for half a second, take a breath, and slow yourself down.

Your next note to yourself is to mark up your bullet points on your next presentation to include a note to "Take a breath!"

BREATHING: IT'S SIMPLE AND FREE!

Anxiety, am I right? Hopefully in the class you're taking or the seminar you are attending, you don't have too much of it. You can always tell your professor that the authors told you it's ok to have a little less homework. However, we know that less homework, money, the right job, award, or social status is not the cure for anxiety. We all have it, and the best we can do is manage it.

As mentioned in this chapter, when we are stressed, our breathing is impacted. Our brain becomes accustomed to what it feels like to be happy (longer, consistent breathing) or anxious (shorter, less consistent breaths). When we are stressed or nervous, you cannot just flip a switch for it to go away. We need to almost reboot ourselves. The first step here is slow and consistent breathing. This sends signals to the brain that your body is relaxing, and your brain will begin the process of switching over from stress mode to happy mode.

In a *Harvard Business Review* article titled "Research: Why Breathing Is So Effective at Reducing Stress," authors Emma Seppälä, Christina Bradley, and Michael R. Goldstein write:

> *Changing the rhythm of your breath can signal relaxation, slowing your heart rate and stimulating the vagus nerve, which runs from the brain stem to the abdomen, and is part of the parasympathetic nervous system, which is responsible for the body's "rest and digest" activities (in contrast to the sympathetic nervous system, which regulates many of our "fight or flight" responses). Triggering your parasympathetic nervous system helps you start to calm down. You feel better. And your ability to think rationally returns.*[4]

Breathing is incredibly simple, and you can start for free! Just a few even breaths in and out, it's not that complicated. Of course, there are a million different methods of breathing and meditation out there and a lot of them are terrific. In fact, guided meditation and breathing exercises are an excellent way to slow yourself down and reset. Just be mindful that there are also a lot of programs for sale that you might not need.

Posture

You continue to watch your video and look for ways that you can improve. What you noticed next is something that your mother would not be proud of. You are not sitting up straight. One of the most obvious ways that a presenter can look disinterested or unorganized is by simply having bad posture. Posture goes beyond just what the audience will perceive. When we are sitting up straight our oxygen and blood flows best. By sitting up straight and having your head up straight, you are setting yourself up for success.

The next thing you know is that *your* eyes tend to drift away from the camera. When one of the other panelists is talking, you notice that you are looking away from your webcam. When you are talking, you notice that you are looking down from your webcam. Now that you are the audience, you can see how this makes you look distracted and disinterested. You go back into your home office to investigate what happened and looking at your desk, you realize that you have your notes on the screen below your webcam, this explains why you were looking down when you are talking. You then realize that your notepad is next to the computer on your desk. When the other panelists are talking, you are looking away from your screen and webcam.

Eye contact is one of the most crucial parts of effective communication. In presenting to an audience, it is very important to look around the room and make eye contact with those watching your presentation. One-on-one, it is a little more obvious that you should make eye contact with the person you're talking to. Virtual and remote presentations are no different, but it's much harder to manage. What makes it more difficult in virtual presentations is that webcam placement is never ideal. You, the speaker, may have notes or you might also want to look at the facial expressions of the people attending. Unfortunately, this gives the viewer the impression that you are not looking at them.

As technology improves and webcams are embedded behind computer screens, this will hopefully become less of an issue. Until then, it is important that when you are talking, you must look into the webcam. The webcam represents the eyes of the audience. By looking into your webcam, you are saying to the audience that you are talking to them and they can make eye contact with you. It is very unnatural, yet very important. You make a note to yourself to put your notes very close to your webcam, or memorize what you can for the next presentation.

FIGURE 2.2 Jesse VandenBergh demonstrates Correct Posture

FIGURE 2.3 Correct Posture. Notice the shoulders and space between the seat and back

Passion

The last thing that you notice when watching your presentation video is that your vocal delivery is very monotone. You remember that the moderator had mentioned this in her feedback to you.

Let's take a step back from the environment of a presentation. Let's think about why we are doing this presentation or any presentation. For the most part, you are trying to explain, educate, or inspire others with your presentation. Ultimately, you are selling something. Of course this is not sales in the traditional sense, this is selling an idea. This doesn't mean you are looking for money, you are not tricking anyone, but you need to get the audience to "buy into" whatever you are saying.

This applies to all presentations. Remember, you are the expert, people came to listen to you. You were invited. Anyone can watch somebody read a paper about whatever topic you were talking about, but an effective presenter is somebody that is animated and is a more projected and polished version of themselves. Your final note to yourself is to remember to call on the passion you have for the subject matter and show that to the audience—to not hold anything back.

PERSONAL STORY

Mike here.

One of my very first jobs in high school was working as a floor salesman for an electronics retailer. Passionate about technology, I was so excited to work in the computer or television department. I quickly learned, though, that the commission on these devices was nowhere near as lucrative as appliances. After speaking with a manager, I was given the opportunity to try the appliance section for a week. My first day was terrible. I did not sell a single refrigerator, microwave, or dishwasher. Demoralized, I was encouraged by the manager to observe one of the more senior saleswomen. Watching her was like watching an artist at work. How could she be given the same information and have access to the same tools, but sell so many appliances? The answer was surprisingly simple. She cared. When she talked to customers, she listened. She was able to pair them with something that they truly needed, and when she talked she was so animated because she loved all of the intricate technologies involved with modern appliances. I, however, had almost no interest in home appliances. The lesson was clear, confident and passionate delivery inspires others.

The simple act of "hamming it up" as well as increasing my energy level when talking to customers about appliances caused my sales to start rolling in. When people care about something, it is obvious. For the audience, we want to listen to people who are passionate. That is the bottom line.

The 30% Energy Principle

There's an old adage in traditional television broadcasting that "the camera adds 10 pounds." This refers to the effect of "barrel distortion," which is when a zoom lens can create a slight barrel-shaped distortion of the image thus making the subject look slightly wider in the center. Some good news though is that modern cameras incorporate a digital zoom or artificial intelligence that can compensate for this. Regardless, the idea is to encourage wardrobe and lighting experts to compensate for the barrel distortion effect. In presenting for virtual environments, we must consider a similar phenomenon as it relates to your energy level.

As you'll learn in chapter 3, presenting on camera is not a one-to-one translation from physical presentation styles to digital. Think about all the "layers" involved: you are speaking to a camera, the camera is converting light into electric signal and digital code, that code is streamed to multiple points along the way to the viewer. These points on the stream path might be a video control room, a web conference platform, or a social media platform. At each point along the way, the video is being decoded and re-encoded for the purposes of having a stable and watchable video stream to the end user.

Because of this, your video experiences a level of "transmission loss" on the journey from your studio to the viewer. Transmission loss is a term that describes the decrease of intensity of an electronic signal on its path. With modern video streaming, we experience a similar effect called "packet loss." Packet loss is a similar phenomenon in the digital space, where packets of information are lost due to unstable network connectivity or a weak wireless internet connection. On the technical end, this means that the video may drop frames, or reduce quality to keep the video running without lag and in as much real time as possible.

Fortunately, technology is constantly evolving to adapt to this, sometimes filling in those gaps of lost data using artificial intelligence. Regardless of your connection, you should assume that just as the camera adds 10 pounds, it will lose about 30% of your energy level. Think further about the viewer—they may be watching on a phone, a tablet, or a screen on the wall and they may be listening on that device's internal speakers that may not be the most dynamic sounding. Therefore, you must assume that the audience is watching your presentation from a distance, both figuratively and literally.

To make up for this virtual loss in energy, you must overcompensate with a dialed-up delivery that almost feels as if you are overdoing it. The way to gauge this is to record yourself and watch it back. In media training sessions, this is a common practice of recording and watching back a presenter's delivery over and over. This is a way to dial-in on just the right level of energy. Remember the 30% energy principle as it applies to your passionate delivery. When you think you're at 100%, bring it up to 130. Record yourself and watch it back—you might be surprised that, to the viewer, you are not overdoing it.

Check in with Yourself

Someone once gave an interesting anecdote about sailing from Los Angeles to Hawaii. He said that it is a direct route, but if you are just 2 degrees off course, you end up in the middle of the ocean. When you are sailing in the open sea with miles of ocean around you, it is important to constantly check your bearings. This applies as well to public speaking. It is important to constantly check in with yourself; take a breath and remind yourself of the four Ps. These are opportunities to reset your posture, slow your speech rate, and collect yourself. Presentations are like a marathon; you can stop once in a while (for just a split-second) and check your bearings.

You are probably asking, "How am I supposed to check in with myself in the middle of a presentation?" The answer is a lot simpler than you think. For example, perhaps when the moderator of a panel is introducing all the guests, this is a great opportunity for you to take deep breath, think about what you are going to say next, and to check in with yourself. How is my posture? Am I talking too fast? Maybe host of an interview is asking you a long-winded question and another opportunity to check in with yourself appears. Moments like this will happen not only on live broadcasts but in person events. It is crucial to remember that you are not going to nail it every time. Allow yourself to make mistakes; remember that authenticity is rewarded. If a speaker is too polished or too perfect, the audience can see right through that. It is going to work to your benefit for your presentation to be conversational and therefore relatable.

Always On

You may have heard of the common phrase "hot mic moment." This is where a celebrity or politician it's caught off-guard saying something they shouldn't have said out loud and it is recorded or broadcast live for the whole world to see. Sometimes funny, usually embarrassing, but always interesting. Hot mic moments are fun to watch but you never want that to be you. Hot moments are an obvious and simple example of someone being caught off-guard. However, this is not the only way that you can get caught off guard. There are many ways in which you can become too comfortable when you think the audience isn't paying attention.

DON'T GET CAUGHT OFF GUARD

When presenting, you need to think of yourself as "always on." If you are doing an in-person presentation, you are on from the second you walk in the building. If you are on live television, you are on from the second you walk into the studio. If you are on a virtual event, you are on from the second you click "join." All too often we get lulled into a false sense of security that no one is watching us when we are not the one talking. That is never the case.

The audience will often take their cues from someone participating in a panel or event that is not actively speaking at the moment. For example, one panelist might be disinterested in another panelist if they are looking away or have a negative reaction in their facial expression—the audience can see that. Not only will the audience see that, this nonverbal cue tells the audience member that they also do not need to be interested in the subject. Thus begins a downward spiral of attention on the part of the audience.

Reading the Room

The term "reading the room" refers to being able to observe audience reaction and nonverbal cues in real time. It's imperative to see how the audience is responding to your presentation. A great communicator knows how to read the room without being distracted. It can be quite difficult to do, being that you have enough to think and stress about as it is but, with practice, it will get easier. It doesn't matter if you're talking to one person or 10,000 people, getting a read on the audience and their level of interest is core to reaching them with your message. The "room" looks very different today than it did just a few years ago. For example, the "room" is not always a physical space, it might be a virtual environment like a web conference or VR space.

An engaged audience is looking at you or the other speakers, they are not looking away from the speaker or screen, they are nodding an affirmation and it generally looks like they're enjoying what they are watching.

Disinterested audiences also can have obvious signs. We look for things like wandering eye contact, tense or confused facial reactions, folded or fidgety arms, or general distraction like looking at a phone or something happening out of the view of their web camera.

CODE SWITCHING

A great amount of people on this planet are raised to speak two or more languages. The English language holds a hegemony, or dominance, over much of the international communications space, but many native languages contain nuance, lexicon, slang, and dialects that can only truly be understood by fluency. When we switch between languages, depending on the crowd or conversation we are in, the term is called "code-switching." While the term is primarily used in regard to languages, it can also mean how we switch our style of expressing ourselves in different conversational groups or settings.[5]

Whether we realize it or not, we shift our conversation style depending on who we are talking to. Usually, we do this depending on our comfort level. As we'll learn next chapter, we perform differently in different settings. In the case of code-switching, keep in mind that when you are in a community of presenters, you are speaking differently than when you are with your friends.

When you are with different groups of friends, you may change your speech patterns to reflect theirs. We may do this to fit in, to persuade, or to properly express a thought.

When you are on a livestream, check in with yourself every so often to see if you are losing the audience or connecting with them better. It's nice to switch to reflect them, but your presentation is yours and they are there to see you. Keep an open mind and listen to yourself. It takes practice, but the more aware, the better we are of our presentation skills.

Imagine This

You are standing in front of an audience of almost 100 people at a conference where you've only dreamed of being a speaker. You have prepared a presentation that you just know is going to "wow" them. You've studied your facts, you've prepared your slides, you've rehearsed your delivery a million times. You are ready.

You open with a very strong introduction, and the audience generally seems interested. They are smiling and nodding. Your confidence soars, but you're only five slides into a 55 slide presentation. You're going to have to work for it. On slide 23, you take the opportunity to read the room during a slide that has a short video. You see people looking at their phones, a couple is having a conversation in the back, there are less people in the crowd now than when you started.

So … you've lost your audience. Can you find the way back to their attention? It is very tricky. the methods vary case-by-case, but certainly it is possible. You think quickly on your feet, so you decide to shock them a bit. On the next slide, you clap your hands and raise your voice significantly when pointing out a key fact. Everyone in the room stops for a second and looks back up at you. You've got them back, but now you have to keep them.

Getting the audience back can be relatively easy, keeping that attention is the real heavy lift.

To grab attention, you could do something as simple as raising your voice suddenly, asserting yourself so that they must listen to what you are saying. From this point, you must dial it up significantly because you have to work harder to maintain that attention. Remember you are the expert. If you have lost them, it means your passionate delivery is not as passionate as it needs to be.

Using the Space

Delivery is not just the words that you say for the gestures that you make. Whether you are presenting in person or on camera you must make use of the space you are given: if on stage, use the stage. If on camera, use the frame that you are given. A caveat, though, is to be mindful of overdoing it. Move with purpose. Here are some examples of effective use of space.

On Stage

Many times, when speaking on stage, presenters tend to want to stay behind the podium. It's almost like a safety blanket that you can hide behind. You feel comfortable knowing that your notes are right there, and frankly it is a place where you are less likely to fall, trip, or make a mistake. The only mistake you will be making though is that you are not effectively working to pull the attention from the audience. If you have a stage, use the stage. Walk and talk, use your hands, look around the room. By making the audience follow you, you're making them work just hard enough that they, subconsciously, will be invested in what you are saying and therefore less likely to tune out. A slow pace (occasionally) from one side of the stage to the other will make a big difference. As mentioned above, don't overdo it. Walk with purpose and intention, don't channel your nerves, and run around the stage. A confident stride is yet another nonverbal cue to the audience that you care, you did the homework, and are passionate about the topic.

In a Small Room

A lot of the same rules apply to a small room that would apply to a stage. If you are in a conference room, try to use the space you are given. If you are standing, take a few steps here and there at a slow and confident pace. If you don't want to end up out of frame, you can always take a step back and a step forward, lean in, and lean back. Movement helps but remember your audio source as well.

FIGURE 2.4 Jamie using his small office space with a wide angle camera

On Camera

Movement on camera can be tricky. Too little movement is boring. Too much movement it's distracting. The first thing to evaluate is the framing of your shot. If you have a "medium shot" for example (this would be from the belly button to just above the top of your head), use your hands to gesticulate. Gesticulation is when you make gestures with your hands while speaking.

In TV, a common phrase for a boring shot of a person talking into the camera is "talking head." When TV news producers prepare a clip of someone talking to air on a newscast, many times they will cover the boring "talking head" shot with footage relevant to the topic. This is called B-Roll. The reason newscasters often covers a "talking head" with "B-Roll" is because it is boring, and the attention span of the average viewer only gets shorter every day. Therefore, the more animated a speaker is on camera, the more airtime they will get. Therefore gesticulation is important and will help you in delivering your message to the viewer.

As with the above, be mindful to not overdo it. Gesticulate with purpose. A good trick to avoid overdoing your hand gestures is to keep your elbows to the side. Now, you don't need to lock them in place, but by keeping elbows to the side you are able to use your hands without flailing your arms too widely. Hands and arms should be kept within the frame of the camera, and movements should be slow and intentional.

Interviews

Coming Out of the Gate Strong

Try to think of a moment where you had to put your best foot forward. Think of a job interview. As the manager waits for you to walk down the hall toward their office, they're able to see you and whether you like it or not they are taking a read on your presentation before you even say a word. For example, how is your posture? Are you fidgeting on your phone? Are you making eye contact as you walk toward them? Do you walk with a confident stride? Are you smiling? Are you reaching out your hand to initiate a handshake? These are all nonverbal cues that the manager is looking at to determine if you are confident and can present well. After all, they are looking to hire someone who can present well to clients and peers within the company.

When you are on camera, you don't get that luxury. The second your camera is visible to the audience they are taking a read on your confidence level. As silly as it may seem, a warm inviting smile goes a long way. Posture also plays a role here. Sitting up with your head straight, looking directly into the camera tells the audience that you are confident and prepared. You are telling them non-verbally that you are someone that deserves attention and that they should listen to you. Here we will focus on some key things to remember in order to come out of the gate strong on an interview and to make sure you use that time wisely.

THE POWER OF A SIMPLE SMILE

Smile, you're on camera! When we take a photo, we ask everyone to smile. Why is that? Well, the foremost reason is that people generally look better when they smile rather than frown or have an unpleasant resting face. Additionally, when we smile the rest of our body tends to follow suit and loosen up a bit. Smiling is contagious—when someone sees you smile, they will generally smile back—even if they are looking at a video or photo.

Kindness in general can cause a chain reaction. If you are having a bad day and someone does a random act of kindness like buying a coffee, opening a door, or just smiling and saying hello, it will usually brighten that day even if for just a few seconds.

Not only is smiling contagious, but positivity and happiness go a long way. James Fowler and Nicholas Christakis, researchers at Harvard University and the University of California, San Diego concluded in a study that "people's happiness depends on the happiness of others with whom they are connected. This provides further justification for seeing happiness, like health, as a collective phenomenon."[6]

Look, we all have those days and no one can be happy all the time, but smiling in presentations are tools to get your message across. If you're prepping to go on camera for a presentation and are not having the best of days, think about putting on a smile. "Behavioral Ecology Theory suggests that all smiles are tools used in social interactions; that theory claims that cheerfulness is neither necessary nor sufficient for smiling." according to Dr. Harry Witchel, Discipline Leader in Physiology in a 2018 study by the Brighton and Sussex Medical School (BSMS).[7] In plain language, you don't have to be genuinely happy for a smile to do its job, it's just as effective to actively smile and not only your audience will have the emotional response you're looking for, but you might just feel a little better.

In an interview with NBC News,[8] Dr. Isha Gupta a neurologist from IGEA Brain and Spine explains the chemical reaction wherein a smile releases the feel-good dopamine and serotonin hormones in your brain, "Dopamine increases our feelings of happiness. Serotonin release is associated with reduced stress." This is because our brain is programmed to associate a smile with this chemical reaction, so when you smile you are effectively turning on a happy switch in your brain. Try smiling right now, you'll feel just a little bit better.

Imagine This

You have been booked as a guest on a prominent news broadcast. Your excitement is soaring. You have done your research, you have prepped yourself on great delivery, and you are ready to go. Making your way to the studio, you remember that you are always on. You enter the studio big smile end are full of enthusiasm for a great interview. The tech manager gets you all set up for your interview in the studio. The anchor speaks directly into your earpiece (called an ifb) to introduce themself. You have a nice dialog and feel comfortable. The show is currently in commercial break, you are live as soon as they come back from that commercial break.

The host introduces you and welcomes you to the show. You are smiling, you give a warm greeting, and the interview starts. The host asks you the first question, and it's an easy one. You handle the response with ease. You can't wait to get to that one question that you know is coming because you have prepared the perfect response. Suddenly, the host can be seen listening to their earpiece—there is breaking news. The host then interrupts the interview to turn the broadcast from your subject to the breaking news. The host thanks you and says that they would love to have you back another time, but that this news is big and the broadcast must shift to covering this important story.

Unfortunately, this happens all too often. Breaking news trumps everything. This is why it is important to use every second you have to get the message across because you never know what is going to happen.

Don't Save the Best for Last

If you have a great piece of information, a clever anecdote, or a compelling one-liner—don't sit on it. As you've seen above, breaking news can change everything. On a broadcast, whether it be on live television or a virtual event, anything can happen. Get your best information out right at the beginning. The difference in presenting versus a written article or story is that you don't have time. In broadcasting, you don't have the luxury of setting up your message with deep context. You have to just get the facts out right away.

Let the Host Do the Work

This book is more than just about live television. In the world of virtual production, live events can be streamed to the masses, or they can be to a small group or individual. In either scenario, when you are the guest there will always be a host or moderator. Remember that they also have a job to do. Your job is to deliver the facts and information that you were invited to share. Their job is to pull that information from you in an orderly fashion and to structure the interview in a way that is compelling and digestible to the audience.

Let the host do the work. This is a simple way of saying that you don't need to talk too much. In general, responses to questions should be short and sweet. That does not mean a simple yes or no but a thoughtful and concise response. Your job is to answer the questions without over explaining. When the host asks a straightforward question, give a straightforward response. If the host feels that more context or a follow-up question is required, they will ask it. Think of the host as someone who is speaking on behalf of the audience. Make your point, but if the anchor wants you to elaborate, they will ask you!

Remember that the audience has an attention span that decreases every single day. If you feel that more context is required, you can suggest to the host that this is something you would need much longer to explain. This is actually a great opportunity to promote your website or research—inviting the audience to dive deeper on another platform (outside of the broadcast).

PERSONAL STORY

Jamie here!

When I was a television producer and digital journalist, I had to consistently utilize the "silent laugh." The silent laugh is when I wanted to react to the interviewee, but I didn't want my own audio to get mashed into the audio of the other person. Mics are sensitive, and we do our best to get clean audio to the editor or sound mixer. Sometimes, your interviewee says something that's funny or requires a response to show you are interested in their story. Occasionally, you need more than a smile to keep the energy going.

This is where the silent laugh comes in. To the interviewee, it looks like you're laughing, but there is no audio. The easiest way to do this is to breathe in rather than breathe out when you laugh, but you can just practice laughing quietly. This technique is important for interviews, but exceptionally important on livestreams. On many platforms, the video switches to the person making a sound. Your response laugh may be well-timed and authentic, but if you are the interviewer, you may not want to interrupt the stream.

It's a choice you'll make when the time comes whether you want to laugh out loud or just laugh silently, but you should respond to your interviewee in a way that is appropriate to their statement. It'll save a lot of time with post-production and sound editing and transcripts.

Appearing on Camera for the First Time

If you are guest, you may be sitting behind the scenes before the host brings you onto the stage. Some platforms just require you to turn on your camera and you appear; others have backstage environments. Hopefully you've been afforded the opportunity for a rehearsal, but if not, try your best to match the framing of the host or panelist on screen before you. Always make sure you are using the rule of thirds for your composition (which we'll get to in Chapter 4), but also don't be so distinct from others on screen. It's jarring to the audience if you end up on a split screen with the host and your head is three times bigger than the host.

If they are sitting further back, try to mimic that position at first. When you are brought on camera, you'll look like you are sharing the virtual space. You can then slowly move in or change your frame but be aware of the first moment you appear on screen.

As mentioned earlier, you're "always on" and you can't really predict when the host will bring you on or you may click that camera button too early. It's not the time to be fixing your hair or makeup or taking a drink of water at that exact moment. The first impression is important.

Plugging

You may have heard the phrase "plug." A plug is when someone promotes their brand or materials on a broadcast. Sometimes a plug is obvious and unwarranted and inauthentic. That is not effective. An effective plug is when the conversation organically allows for it, and you can promote your brand or research in a way that enhances the interview and encourages the audience to act.

It is sometimes good to think of broadcasting as sales. Ultimately you are trying to promote a message or brand. You are looking for the audience to act and either buy your product, visit your website, or become interested in your message. An effective presenter can "sell" their message to the audience in a way that is authentic and doesn't make the viewer feel like they are being "sold" something, but rather encouraged to learn more. Conversational delivery and passionate presentation are how you will get the audience on your side and sell your message. We'll continue this discussion in the next chapter.

Resting Position

If you're taking part in a panel discussion, whether it be virtually or in person, one thing to be mindful of is your resting position. What is your posture like? Are you smiling? Where are you looking? A good trick to remember is to "smile and nod" when others are talking. This lets the audience, the host, and other panelists know that you were interested in what they are saying and that you were actively participating in the conversation.

It is common that when another person is talking, your face will react to what they're saying. Sometimes people say something that you might disagree with. It is very important to remember to have a peaceful "resting face." Resting face is the expression you have on your face when not talking. Generally, a half-smile will do the job.

PERSONAL STORY

Mike here.

I was hired by the CEO of a tech company for media training. When I first met this client, I didn't know what he would need from me because he was so accomplished and seemingly a great presenter. In our first session together, he explained that he hired me because he was not presenting well on the panels. I asked him for some footage of recent panel discussions that he was a part of so that I could do my research.

What I saw in reviewing the footage of his panel work was that he looked disinterested while other panelists were talking. His focus was wondering. At times he would look at his shoe or look around the room. It was almost as if he was bored. While the fix was rather simple, it took quite a while to reinforce that he needed to stay focused on what the others were saying. Old habits are hard to break. Here was a successful tech CEO that could pitch to any Venture Capital firm but fell flat on his performance on industry panels. His peers would get annoyed by his apparent lack of interest. Moderators thought he was a weak panelist.

The audience takes their cues from the speakers, even when not speaking. Once he dialed in his focus, other panelists took him more seriously and audiences more receptive.

Eye Contact

One of the very first questions that comes up in media training sessions is "where do I look?" It can be hard, especially when presenting on a webcam. In short, the answer is to look at the audience. What does that mean when the audience is not in the same room as you? The camera is the audience. The camera is how the audience sees you. Look into the camera as if it were the person you are talking to. This is much easier said than done, especially because webcams are usually above the screen, where you are looking at the audience members, slides, or your notes.

When in a television Studio, if you are on set with an anchor or host, look at them. An easy way to remember this is if you are on set with another human being, look at that human being. If you are in an empty Studio and the host is across the country in another Studio, look at the camera. It is very common and Studios to have a lot of distractions like monitors below the camera or above. You have to divert your attention from those distractions and stay laser focused on the camera's lens. Sometimes you can ask the technician in the studio dim or turn off those distracting monitors.

In a virtual event, it is very common to be on a web chat platform where you see several audience members in Grid View. As we talked about earlier you want to read the room. How can you read the room and not look at the audience? Just as if you were presenting in a small conference room oh, you need to look at the audience and then glanced at your notes for slides when necessary. When presenting in a virtual event, 90% of your eye contact should be into the camera. The other 10% of the time, you can look down and get a quick glimpse of the audience to read the room or check your notes or slides.

A famous 1968 study really sums up the importance of eye contact. In this study by Ellsworth and Carlsmith (1968),[9] an interviewer looked either directly into the subject's eyes or off to the left or right side. Participants in the study that had direct eye contact viewed the experience and the interviewer more positively. Those that didn't get direct eye contact evaluated the experience more negatively.

Always think from the audience's perspective. If they are watching you on the screen and you are looking at them, they will feel as if you are talking to them. Also remember that it's okay to give yourself a break in glance away occasionally.

Handling Surprises

If you're the guest on an interview, believe it or not YOU actually control the interview. The host can ask anything they want, but you don't have to answer their question if it is misleading or trying to put you into a negative light. The key to this is having solid "talking points." We'll dive more into preparing your talking points in Chapter 4. But for now, the idea is that your talking points are the key bullet points that you've prepared for the discussion. These are well thought out data points and messaging that you want to get across in your interview.

PERSONAL STORY: PICK YOUR BATTLES

Mike here.

I've worked with countless hosts, from prominent television newscasters to first-time moderators of a virtual event panel. Most spend a good amount of time preparing for the interview and are looking out for the audience and genuinely want to educate and inform. There are always bad apples, and some hosts are only looking out for themselves. I've known TV anchors that don't read any of the research their producers have worked hard to prepare. I've also seen hosts that have a clear agenda and only want to create moments that become a viral video clip.

In media training, I always tell clients to pick their battles. Some things are worth it, and most are just not worth your time. For example, a host might not have asked how to properly pronounce your name and when introducing you to the audience they botch your name. I encourage clients to not correct them unless it's really off or misleading (like someone else's name and title). In many cases, your name and title will be on the screen in the form of a "lower third" banner at the bottom of the screen or on a slide presentation.

Remember, an interview is always going to be shorter than you expect, and you don't want to have your best materials get lost in the shuffle. Stay focused and keep the interview positive.

Keep the Glass Half-Full

There's a common phrase that refers to overly optimistic people as "glass half full" folks that lean toward the positive, as opposed to "glass half empty" people that tend to look at the negative aspect of the same situation. If you are being interviewed, think of the exchange as a glass of water. You don't have to give them everything, but you have to give them something. If the host asks you a question that you don't know the answer to, or don't feel comfortable answering, you don't owe them anything other than airtime. Therefore, you have to give a response that is somewhat related to the original question but could be a bit of a departure and more in line with your original talking points. The key here is to keep the conversation positive and never get caught in an adversarial relationship with your host. Stay positive and always be a "glass half full" mentality with your presentation.

When you can't give them a straight answer, try to give them *something*. Even if it's semi-related and is in line with your talking points. This is where those talking points come into play—they are your safety blanket. If you don't have the specific answer, you can always use an answer that you already know. It's important to keep smiling and say positive, *always*. Remember that you never want to get into an adversarial relationship with the host. Even if the host becomes rude and pushes you into a corner, never back down. You are in control of the interview, and you don't have to do or say anything you don't feel comfortable with. If you stay positive and keep on the "high ground," you will prevail, and the audience will respect you more for it.

Never lie. If you don't know something, that is ok. Remember, authenticity is rewarded. You can be honest with the host that you don't know or aren't the right person to answer. "I need to look into that more carefully BUT …," or "I may not be the best person to answer that BUT …," or "I can't speak to that exactly, BUT …"

Imagine This

You're the Vice President of Communications for a major non-profit. You've been invited to talk about your latest energy-saving initiative. You have some apprehension about agreeing to the interview, because the host of this particular program leans very heavily against the current President and their administration's policies.

The interview starts out well. You're asked about the mission of the non-profit. The host seems to be treading lightly on politics, but you feel a "gotcha" question coming. Then … they hit you with it—you are asked a politically motivated question that is clearly designed to get you to pick a side. However, your mission is to be apolitical and promote your non-profit's mission. You're not here to alienate half the audience.

"So, what's your take on the President's latest push to heavily regulate this type of work? Wouldn't that be a bad move for Americans?" the host asks.

You respond, "Well, I can't speak to the president's political motivation here, but what I can tell you is that our organization is the leader in this field, and we will always work with the current administration to make the world a safer place for all."

The host pushes back, "You're dodging my question here. I'm asking if you think this will be bad for your organization and its cause."

You graciously respond, "Thank you, it's a good question. With that said, I think we still have to see what exactly is in the details of the President's plan before we can make that assessment. I would be happy to dive deeper into this and come back on when I can prepare a thoughtful response that you and the audience deserves."

The host realizes they aren't getting you to take the bait. There are only 2 minutes left in the interview, and they move onto the next question.

PERSONAL STORY: LOSING MY PLACE

Mike here.

When I was a Field Producer working in TV news, I was often put right in the middle of a disaster zone. Two examples from the same year, 2010, are the Deepwater Horizon oil spill or when I was in Haiti just after a massive earthquake took the lives of well over 100,000 people and leveled the main city of Port-au-Prince. In that time, I relied heavily on my smartphone to take photos and videos of the events happening around me. After having to constantly wipe dirt or debris from my lens, I realized that there had to be a better solution.

I invented a smartphone case called the "EyePatch Case" that essentially had a lens cap. A sliding switch would both cover the camera lenses on the phone and wipe dirt away. After some time on the market, the product started gaining popularity and I was invited to go onto a television show to pitch my product to a studio audience in hopes that they would vote for me over another inventor to win prize money.

The process of casting a network television show is a daunting one. Producers must comb through sometimes thousands of applicants, picking the most likely to succeed. Then an audition tape is made to show the on-camera persona. This is done to gauge the likability of the subject as well as their performance. Remember, it's a show—the audience wants to be entertained! From there, the producers will select their pool of finalists and "cast" the ones they deem fit for the broadcast.

When I was cast on this network show, I was both excited and nervous. Being a producer myself, I figured I would also make for a great guest (after all, I do train people for this very thing in my career). I was assigned to work with a team of two producers that worked with me almost weekly in the months leading up to the taping of the show in Los Angeles. Each virtual meeting with the producers was a rehearsal of the pitch I was going to do on stage in front of an audience of about 100 people plus a very well-known host and another inventor that I was competing against for the prize money. Every rehearsal involved slight tweaks to improve the entertainment factor of the pitch and to keep it within the time given.

I was a ball of nerves on the day of filming. Waiting in the "green room," I had several hours to do breathing exercises and meditation to calm my nerves, focus, and of course—practice my pitch. When I was called to the stage, I entered a studio full of lights, sounds, and lots and lots of people ... just watching me. Waiting for me to "wow" them or fail gloriously in front of their eyes. I strut on stage with a courageous bounce in my step, smiling all the way to my "mark" on the stage where I was to stand.

The host did a brief introduction and cued me to begin my pitch. Having done this hundreds of times, there was no reason for what happened next. I froze.

One and a half minutes into my 3 minutes of precious pre-recorded network TV time, I completely lost my place in my heavily scripted pitch. For about 10 seconds, I just looked around at the audience, the host, back to the audience, back to the host, to the other inventor ... I couldn't believe what was happening. These 10 seconds felt like a solid hour of embarrassment and disappointment—all the work, the travel, and the trust people put in me to get to that place; and here I was, just standing there with nothing to say. My memory simply escaped me at the worst possible moment.

A few seconds later, I recalled a key phrase from the scripted pitch and was able to continue. I finished my pitch, and the host came over for a couple of minutes of interaction with his classic comedic style to liven things up. When the time came to vote on the winner, I was not picked. Losing out on the money was only a minor setback. Losing the opportunity to really get the word out on my invention was the true failure. No matter what, even with clever editing, I was not at my best and the real loser was my invention that didn't get the passionate pitch it deserved.

I remember walking away from that experience thinking that I was a terrible example of a presenter. How could I train on-camera guests and hosts to do something that I clearly had failed miserably at? I took about six months off from my media training before I realized: my failure was a tremendous lesson in what *not* to do. I overly scripted my pitch, I was trying to be someone I wasn't, and I gave myself too much room to fail.

Having dissected this moment over and over since, I have realized that the best thing to do in these moments is to keep smiling and deflect. Had I just said something—perhaps calling attention to something else in the room, or even admitting that I lost my place in an endearing manner—the audience would identify with me, rather than just sit there wondering what was happening.

The biggest lesson I have learned from that experience is that you always have to be ready to "tap dance," which means that you have to always have "filler" content. To say something is better than nothing at all. We all have moments where we will stumble, though I hope for your sake it's not in front of a live audience but remember that it's a learning experience.

Since then, two great things have come from this. The first is that I have a great story to tell my media training clients as an example of what can happen. By telling them this vulnerable moment, I find that people can relate to me even more—knowing that I'm not pretending to be "Mr. Perfect." In the end, I have more good performances on camera than bad. The second good thing is that my episode of that show never aired and, unfortunately for the staff and crew of that show, the series was canceled after one season. So, luckily for me, no one (including me) will likely ever see that footage.

The Green Room and Being Green

The green room is a waiting room for on-camera talent. The origin of the name has two versions, one is that understudies or actors that were backup for the lead cast would wait in a room in case something happened to the main actor. The room was called a "green" room, here "green" referring to the fact that these understudies were typically less experienced. (The other origin story is much simpler: the room was traditionally painted green.)

When you are starting your career, or just starting out with a new project, you may lack experience with the specific skills. You will, of course, learn these, but at the beginning you'll be green. The reason it's called being green, is that you are still like a little tree, yet to grow your protective bark. At first, you look like every other seedling, but over time, you grow big, strong and provide help for seedlings around you.

When on a livestream, you may be in a virtual green room, which could be a space where you are watching the show live but not on camera. And we can't stress it enough, you could appear on camera at any time in this virtual setting.

Positivity Matters

Do you notice a trend with all of these examples on what to do when you're caught off-guard? Be positive! Always maintain your composure, avoid getting into an adversarial situation, and keep smiling! You'd be surprised how far a smile will go.

The Temporary Narcissist

In this chapter, you've learned that confidence sells. The reason any of us go on camera is usually to promote a mission, message, or brand. Whether you like it or not, when you are on camera you are in sales. You are selling your message and the best salespeople are incredibly confident in their product.

Think of a politician, even one you don't like. They are all famous for being able to talk about almost anything on TV news, whether they are telling the truth or not, with 100% confidence that what they are saying is correct. Although, we all know—that's very often not the case.

Now think of a pitchman on a late night TV infomercial. The product they are selling may very well be overpriced and poorly made, sometimes even useless. However, they impress viewers with remarkable demonstrations on camera, with a passionate delivery that this product will change your life. These pitchmen know exactly what they are doing. Most people assume *they couldn't say it if it weren't true.* That's partly true. In fact, many infomercials are carefully written so that they don't go all the way to guarantee something but simply make it sound like they are doing so. They use phrases like "proven to help solve" the problem. Notice they say "help solve" the problem, rather than just "proven to solve" the problem. See what they did there?

There's a term for this, "con artist." Con here refers to "confidence." These bad actors use false confidence to basically lie to people. We can turn that around, though, and use those powers for good.

It's incredibly common that con artists and politicians possess narcissistic behavior. Webster's dictionary defines a narcissist as someone with "an extremely self-centered person who has an exaggerated sense of self-importance." You know these types—the politician that is never wrong, the athlete that is the "best in the world," by their own definition. This behavior is not authentic and is not healthy for an individual or society, but what can we learn from this?

Let's go back to your moment in the spotlight—you're about to go on camera for a big interview. The lights, the camera, the content … your insecurities begin to weigh heavily, and this is where self-doubt comes in. Many people refer to this as "imposter syndrome," this is when your mind starts telling you that you don't belong or aren't good enough. We all have that insecurity and it's healthy to have a minimal amount of doubt, otherwise you'd be exhibiting narcissism. However, excessive self-doubt can derail your entire delivery and spread like a virus through your mind.

When you're on camera for an interview or a presentation, remember that it's only a finite period of time—sometimes a few minutes to an hour or so. For that brief period, try to turn off that self-doubt and remember that you were invited. YOU are the expert that was asked to speak on the topic. You've done your homework and you deserve to be there. That's where the term "temporary narcissist" comes into play.

For the few short moments that you are on camera, pretend that you're a narcissist. Pretend that you are the ultimate expert on the subject—to a degree. You certainly want to balance that with authenticity (don't lie, don't answer a question if you don't know the answer) and with a level of humility. The point here is that you need to just overcompensate for your self-doubt with a little bit of extra confidence. We call that temporary narcissism.

This is a power that needs to be exercised with awareness and caution. Remember, authenticity is rewarded—don't be anyone other than yourself. The message here is that YOU are good enough and YOU are the expert. The trick here is to use this only the first handful of times until you develop a true confidence of self.

Think of a snowy hill where kids are sledding. One friend goes down on her sled and makes a path in the snow. Another friend follows suit, and the sled naturally finds its way into the same path. Eventually, the path in the snow is so deeply carved that it's hard to sled outside that path. That is exactly what happens in our mind with habits and believe it or not, you can make good habits. It may sound a bit childish, but it comes down to pretending. If you are someone that has a lot of self-doubt, you have to *pretend* that you're a bit of a narcissistic person for that period of time that you are on camera. Stay true to yourself, but just tap into that passion and pretend that you're more confident. After a few presentations, you'll find that you don't have to pretend anymore, that the paths in your brain have been re-carved and that you believe in yourself, even if just a bit more.

Bad actors who take advantage of vulnerable people will always be around and they will use confidence to lie to their audience. What we can learn from them is that confidence sells—it's an incredibly powerful tool, and one that should be used for good. That's a big part of why this book was written, to empower good people to convey their message to audiences. That's why you're here, and hopefully you now have some tools in your belt to win in the messaging war.

NEUROPLASTICITY

What are your bad habits? We all have traits about our personality or behavior that are either counterproductive or even destructive. Did you know that you can potentially train your brain to change that behavior? This concept is called neuroplasticity. This is basically the same concept that smiling (mentioned earlier) can cheer you up.

The Encyclopedia Britannica refers to neuroplasticity as the "capacity of neurons and neural networks in the brain to change their connections and behavior in response to new information, sensory stimulation, development, damage, or dysfunction." To be clear, this does not apply to all behaviors, as some are truly chemical imbalances, and you'd need much more than a video production textbook to fix.

When two nerve cells start communicating, they create a connection called a synapse. These synapses are basically pathways for electronic impulses to travel on between the two nerve cells. When you hear, see, touch, taste, or smell something, your nerves send a signal to your brain, which then reacts to it. The path of that signal impacts the way you react. If you can change that path, it is possible to change your impulse reaction.

If you really want to boil down neuroplasticity, it comes down to the concept that "practice makes perfect." The brain is like a muscle, in that the more you exercise these changes the stronger they get. Studies have shown that stroke survivors who go through repetitive exercises and continually have more challenging ones are more likely to regain functions. The same goes for something less life-threatening, like learning to play the guitar. Your brain is used to doing certain combinations of finger gestures and movements for sports, hobbies, typing, etc. With enough practice, you can create new "muscle memory" by learning the guitar by repeating the same movements and making it a little harder on yourself each time.

How do you apply this to emotion or behavior? Acting! Just as we referenced the temporary narcissist to combat low confidence and how you just need to play the role of one for the short time you are "on," the same goes for other emotions. In order to truly create change within your neuro pathways, you have to give it your "all."

A psychologist with the University of Utah, Megan Call, writes in her paper, "Neuroplasticity: How to Use Your Brain's Malleability to Improve Your Well-being" that you must act with intention, repetition, increased intensity, and over time.[10] This will take a while, it's not an overnight change—most people won't cure their stage fright overnight like they do in the movies. However, with practice and attention—this is possible.

We find this with people who tend to use filler words such as "um" or "like." Using this example, let's tackle this issue by breaking it into steps:

Identify the Root of the Problem

In many cases, the speaker often is speaking too fast. The filler words allow the brain a little extra filler time to process what the speaker is trying to say.

Create a Solution Plan

The speaker needs to slow it down. We'll work with them to practice their presentation at a slower pace, then do it again, maybe record it and watch back, keep repeating. Each time, we raise the bar a little.

Take Action on Your Plan

Start practicing and take note of the filler words in everyday conversation. Record the speaker and let them analyze themself.

Repeat. Repeat. Repeat.

Remember the example earlier referring to the snowy hill and carving a fresh path? That is basically what is happening here. New paths between nerve cells in the brain are being "carved" and therefore literally opening a whole new way of thinking or feeling.

The Basics, in Sum

We cover a lot in this chapter, but in conclusion, we hope that you practice your presentation often. Getting better at virtual presentation requires confidence and the four Ps: Pitch, Pace, Posture, and Passion, but also a knowledge of how to utilize your body and space. It's not easy, but confidence builds with each iteration and each production you manage to complete. Regardless of whether or not your first appearance on camera went well, don't give up! Continue to make presentation basics part of your everyday life and soon, you'll find that your expertise, no matter how niche, is important. Speak and share with confidence and bridge that virtual gap.

Notes

1 Reeves, Richard. "The City Politic: The More Things Change …" *New York Magazine*, 22 Jan. 1973, pp. 8–9.
2 Gorman, James. "ON LANGUAGE; Like, Uptalk?" *The New York Times*, 15 Aug. 1993. *NYTimes.com*, https://www.nytimes.com/1993/08/15/magazine/on-language-like-uptalk.html.
3 ibid.
4 Seppälä, Emma, et al. "Research: Why Breathing Is So Effective at Reducing Stress." *Harvard Business Review*, 29 Sept. 2020. *hbr.org*, https://hbr.org/2020/09/research-why-breathing-is-so-effective-at-reducing-stress.
5 Thompson, Matt. "Five Reasons Why People Code-Switch." *NPR*, 13 Apr. 2013. *NPR*, https://www.npr.org/sections/codeswitch/2013/04/13/177126294/five-reasons-why-people-code-switch.
6 Fowler, J. H., and N. A. Christakis. "Dynamic Spread of Happiness in a Large Social Network: Longitudinal Analysis over 20 Years in the Framingham Heart Study." *BMJ*, vol. 337, no. dec04 2, Dec. 2008, pp. a2338–a2338. *DOI.org (Crossref)*, https://doi.org/10.1136/bmj.a2338.
7 "Psychology to Grin About: The Benefits of Smiling and Laughter." *UWA Online*, 6 June 2019, https://online.uwa.edu/news/benefits-of-smiling-and-laughter/.
8 Spector, Nicole. "Smiling Can Trick Your Brain into Happiness—and Boost Your Health." *NBC News*, https://www.nbcnews.com/better/health/smiling-can-trick-your-brain-happiness-boost-your-health-ncna822591. Accessed 30 Aug. 2022.
9 Ellsworth, Phoebe C., and J. Merrill Carlsmith. "Effects of Eye Contact and Verbal Content on Affective Response to a Dyadic Interaction." *Journal of Personality and Social Psychology*, vol. 10, no. 1, 1968, pp. 15–20. *DOI.org (Crossref)*, https://doi.org/10.1037/h0026385.
10 Call, Megan. *Neuroplasticity: How to Use Your Brain's Malleability to Improve Your Well-Being*. http://accelerate.uofuhealth.utah.edu/resilience/neuroplasticity-how-to-use-your-brain-s-malleability-to-improve-your-well-being. Accessed 30 Aug. 2022.

3

WHAT IS AUTHENTIC DELIVERY?

Imagine this:

> You're standing two or three feet behind a curtain on a large stage. You hear the rustling of the audience in the cavernous theater, people are getting into their seats. You peak out from the curtain, but you can barely see them because the lights are so bright, but you know it's a sold-out crowd. The stage manager taps you on the shoulder—"Two minutes ..."

Your heart starts to race, but you go over what you know about presenting. You take some deep breaths, take in the senses of the environment around you, practice in your mind the opening lines of your talk. You remind yourself, make sure to make eye contact with someone in the audience for several seconds before looking at someone else. Look through the bright lights, make human connections. Be authentic.

You feel a bit of sweat on your forehead, but quickly dab it away. You hear the music swell and the audience hushes and the host steps out to introduce you. It's brief, but you have a few seconds to get ready. "And, please, let's give a big round of applause ..."

"You're up!" the host says as they walk by you, ushering you onto the stage. You walk out, look straight ahead, the clapping slows down. You draw a deep breath and ...

You look directly into the green dot on the top of your laptop and begin your talk.

Authentic Virtual Presenting

It's a completely different experience to present in the world of virtual media production. You have to bring the big stage version of yourself to a tiny square on

DOI: 10.4324/9781003291718-3

a screen with the loss of over 90% of the feedback you'd normally receive—whether visual, audible, or non-verbal. It's just you and the tiny camera and your imagination as to how many people are in the audience. In this chapter, we're going to expand upon our presentation basics and delve into authentic delivery. How do you put your best version of yourself on-screen? What are some ways to be simultaneously reflective while also presenting? How can we tune that voice in your head to work faster than what you're saying out loud?

When we present on camera, especially in terms of public speaking, it is not a one-to-one translation from physical presentation styles to digital. Working in the remote world means to sort of consider yourself from the viewpoint of the spectator, knowing they are watching you differently than they would if you were in person. It's really a completely new environment.

Over the last several years, especially in the height of the pandemic, hundreds of pieces were written that aimed to help presenters get a better understanding of how this new remote world works. While we'll be combining and synthesizing much of that here, we'll be going a step further to discuss what "authenticity" means and how you can better engage with your audience than ever before.

We'll be doing some comparisons to on-air personalities in traditional media broadcasting, but our primary focus will be to compare the virtual producer to the ones that perfected the model: online influencers, vloggers, and YouTubers. Why them you may ask? Well, unlike on-air talent, their income comes from a deep understanding of how to produce media content to an audience they cannot see. They've created the models of authentic delivery in new media settings. Many, many books have been written about presenting on traditional media formats, but when we focus on the digital, we need to highlight the superstars and their techniques.

When YouTube launched, there was already about a decade of content that had been produced as web-native, meaning made for the internet, media. From the mid-90s to 2005, those with a fast enough internet connection could experiment with new methods of personalized presentation and delivery. When YouTube launched in 2005, it was soon after that the vloggers occupied the creative space, inventing new media production styles (jumpcuts, music, framing, setting) that helped set the stage for our new virtual media presentation world. Since then, we've come to recognize the YouTube influencer aesthetic as the authentic, the authoritative, and the watchable.

But how did they know what they were doing? Did they just experiment and see if it worked? Well, yeah, that is sort of what they did. These early influencers had far lower stakes than traditional media on-camera talent as they were creating the space in real time. They had a huge advantage over the old paradigm though: visible view counts and the comments section.

We'll be using some of their techniques to explain how authenticity works, where it comes from, and how you can better amplify your expertise for your audience.

This chapter will first frame out the history of presentation and authentic delivery and work our way up through traditional and new media authentic styles. With practice—and you should always practice—you'll find that virtual presentations, whether on a webinar, a call, a virtual event, or in a meeting, can be fun and creative *and* get us to better learn about ourselves.

Brief History of Authenticity Theory

"All the world's a stage," says the melancholy Jacques in William Shakespeare's *As You Like It* (1623), "and one man in his time plays many parts." Shakespeare uses Jacques to explain how as we grow, we put on different personalities and performances, each reflecting who we are at that age and what our experiences bring to the audience. As a piece of meta-reflection on Shakespeare's own work, he was focusing on what makes us unique as a presenter. More importantly, he reflects on the idea that we have to remember that we'll continue to learn and grow too. We don't just stop learning, we keep going.

Three hundred and thirty-three years later, the American sociologist Erving Goffman wrote *The Presentation of Self in Everyday Life*, a text analyzing dramaturgy and symbolic interaction. To Goffman, these studies were a powerful contemporary commentary on how we do "impression management," or, the ability to see how we make connections with others, especially through our presentation styles. Goffman's text furthers Shakespeare's point more exactly: "All the world is not, of course, a stage, but the crucial ways in which it isn't are not easy to specify."[1]

Goffman's book recognizes how much we are in the environment of presenting nearly all the time. It's been essential reading and formative for public speakers, but especially important in terms of how timeless some of Goffman's observations have stood the test of time, even into the digital age. Some of the most important influencers, celebrities, sports figures, and businesspeople engage in impression management whether they know Goffman's work or not. It's important to contextualize how we're going to be covering what it means to present and *be present* throughout remote media production and virtual presenting. For your benefit, having a general background of why and how we use impression management will make you a better producer, director, and on-screen talent.

What We Can Learn from Erving Goffman

There's no doubt that at some point in your life you heard the phrase "you never get a second chance to make a first impression." Often attributed to either Will Rogers or Oscar Wilde, the phrase appears after Erving Goffman's book, but reflects the sentiment expressed in Goffman's text. Erving Goffman was a sociologist and studied how actors and performers on stage interacted with their audience and their fellow performers. In his book, he translates the act of performing into how we live and act in our everyday lives. The book covers how our behavior affects our teammates, why character matters, and most importantly, the art of impression management.

What Does It Mean to Manage Our Impression?

Let's start at the beginning.

You have the wonderful ability to make your own choices, express yourself, and translate your thoughts into actions. We call this agency. Your agency is sometimes what we call "free will," but for the sake of this book, we'll be using in terms of how we "act." We use the term "actor" not as someone who may be on stage, but rather in the same sense Goffman used in the sociological context: how we engage with others within our social structure.

Being an "actor" means having autonomy, but it also means having awareness of those around you and how you are being "perceived" by others. In physical space, there are a lot of things to take into consideration in social settings, and very often, physical space privileged those who are able over those that may have disabilities. This form of exclusivity is reduced in the digital world, but then we come up against the digital divide of access. In other words, how we "act" in physical spaces differs from screen-based performances, but we should know how much impression management matters.

First, Goffman reminds us that there are several performances that occur in our everyday life. First, how we present ourselves in private, second, to those close to us, and third, to an audience (to strangers for example). We're always putting on some sort of performance, even when we look in the mirror. We prepare ourselves and put on makeup, comb our hair, and put on fashionable clothes. In most cases, we do this for ourselves, but we're thinking about who will see us and how we'll come off to them.

Goffman spends a fair amount of time focusing on gestures in his book. This is because most of what we say is not even verbal, it's non-verbal, displayed in micro-expressions from our face, the way we move our body, whether we fidget or stay stoic, and how we make eye contact.

The trick is to become aware of all of this, but not let it be a distraction. Think of it like playing an instrument or working with tools. At first, the instrument and the tool is all you can think about. Are you holding it right? Is it working efficiently? But over time, with practice, you no longer think about it, it sort of disappears. You become an expert by knowing how to use the instrument or tool, but you don't think about it any longer—at least not in the front of your mind.

Your agency and performance are like that. At first, when you start thinking about how much goes into impression management, it's really all you can think about. But then, as time goes on, it becomes more invisible. When you get *really* good at it, you may even be able to think at the same time you are speaking, almost creating two channels of thought at the same time.

In much of the professional world from LinkedIn connections to office meetings, we find ourselves caring deeply about impression management. In most guides for job interviews, school functions, networking events, resume making, website design, and social media, there's usually always a section on how you are perceived by followers. In the age of digital communication, one where we can see each other in live video settings, we created a new layer of impression management—one that combines the professionalism of real-time meetings with digital presence.

At some point, someone has to be the first to create the format for any type of presentation. For thousands of years, the method of oral presentation and stage presence was perfected. The tools of the ancient orators, from Ancient Greece and Rome to the present, had important things to do for the audience: Present and be memorable, speak and share knowledge, express and be powerful.

Then, very rapidly, the world shifted when technology burst open after the industrial revolution.

There's a good anecdote to keep in mind that helps put history into perspective: George Washington and Julius Caesar moved at the same speed and had the same tools for stage presenting. However, the biggest advantage Washington had in his time was mass media in the form of printed media. In the 1800 years between Caesar and Washington, the press was the big difference. In the last 150 years, we've jumped wildly ahead from the telegraph to radio to the modern internet. We take for granted many of these technologies, but they are very new media.

This book is a result of the extremely rapid shift during the pandemic that caused much of the connected world to combine many presentations and technology literacies into one format. And it only took two years to learn how to normalize a completely new standard of presenting and make it foundational to future presentation styles.

Let's take a look at the pioneers of the modern visual presentation space to see how we came to understand television as a visual medium of presentation. By learning from the techniques of the past, we can figure out how to apply the successful methods of the past to our connected present.

Technology and Mass Media

In the mid-1400s, a German man named Johann Gutenberg upgraded an old technology and accelerated all of humanity into a completely new paradigm of connectivity. The printing press, first developed in the early 1st century, could only make one print at a time. It was a time-consuming process—someone had to carve a block in reverse, coat it in ink, and stamp it on paper (which also had to be made). Gutenberg's invention was called "movable type." It used smaller blocks made of metal with carved letters or commonly used words which could be slid into a large press. Instead of carving each sheet, a custom layout could be created each time and printed. Just like that, we jumped into the modern age.

In an incredibly short period of time, literacy spread throughout the world and the printing press changed the way we communicate with the masses. Famously, the first text to be mass-produced was the Bible. Often overlooked was the short-form content that was produced at the same time. A German priest named Martin Luther took advantage of the new technology to create smaller and shorter media, today we'd call them pamphlets or brochures. In the early 1500s, Martin Luther was ordained and soon after, called for a discussion of the major church practices and started the Protestant Reformation. Across the world, the printing press enabled people to share information, create news, tell stories, spread information, formalize language, and change power dynamics.

Information, and especially how we share it, is vital to keeping people educated, knowledgeable, and ready to participate in civic life. Imagine for a second that for all your life you've received information in print, even if it was delivered by Morse code from a telegraph machine. You couldn't access media in real time, you had to wait until it was received, set up on the printer and printed. You were disconnected from the event by a variable outside your control.

Then, all of sudden, it accelerated rapidly. In the late 1800s, telegraph lines connected people over even further distances, but they were tied to specific locations and literally where the wires could reach, often connecting big cities, but excluding smaller towns.

With the telegraph lines, this new invention enabled people to hear things in *real time* and experience information as it was happening. It was called the telephone.

The telephone is a one-to-one medium, but it changed how we communicate. We had to use tones in our voice to transmit sounds and intonation that would help the person on the other end of the line know what we meant, how we felt, share urgency, or just connect with one another. But importantly, we knew who was on the other end of the receiver.

Soon after, an Italian engineer named Guglielmo Marconi began experimenting with using telephony (that's what they called it), electricity and electromagnetic conduction to push waves into airspace. The waves contained sounds that could be received by another device that was tuned to the wattage that was in the air. Radio was born.

Just a little over a century ago, people were given the opportunity to hear radio and consumed events in real time.

How did radio broadcasters know what they were doing? It was a new media, there were no rules. Up until radio, you presented to the public in rooms where the audience was visible. In text, you translated the media to be read, hopefully offering enough context for the information to stand freely on its own. But now, if you wanted to speak to people in real time, across vast amount of space, you had to come up with a presentation method. It was experimental at first, just as every new media.

Radio and the New Presenters

In Tim Wu's book, *The Master Switch: The Rise and Fall of Information Empires* (2010),[2] Wu goes into detail about each new media had its start. According to Wu, in 1921, a man named Andrew White did something extraordinary at a boxing match that changed the world. At a boxing match in Jersey City, New Jersey, White, who worked for the Radio Corporation of America, RCA, used a telephone with a very long cable attached to a transmitter to announce a boxing match. According to Wu, White announced the boxing match to 61 cities into "radio halls" where people could hear the match in real time. Andrew White had become the first radio announcer.

Radio, up until that moment, was used as a military technology (as you'll also see with the internet), so White's intervention changed how the medium was used.

As Wu argues through his text, many of the first broadcasters on new, real-time new media were amateurs trying to figure out how it worked. Andrew White knew how to announce a fight to a live crowd, but when you are transmitting to thousands of people who are disconnected from the visuals, you have to add color—meaning visual commentary. What's going on? How does it look? What's the mood? More importantly, how does your presentation impact the storytelling?

When the pandemic caused hundreds of thousands of people to become overnight broadcasters, we were all amateurs in a field that was well-established for the last century. The fortunate part of our present was that we had examples to work from, we weren't broadcasting for the very first time, we were mimicking those who had come before us. From Andrew White to Edward R. Murrow to Barbara Walters to Jenna Marbles, we were using the techniques of all the new media.

In the world of audio, podcasting increased its popularity during the same time virtual presenting and remote media production became more prevalent. There are many books on audio production and podcast producing and we highly encourage you to look into those as well to learn the aspects of virtual presenting in audio formats. From here forward, we want to focus on visual media and multimedia production.

From the Television Tube to YouTube

Television is technically an extension of radio technology, but the key difference is the visual production and camera settings. Most importantly, television changed how we connected with authority, which converted our primary format of rhetorical delivery from the stage—which for the last 5000 years has been our primary method—to the flickering box in the living room. We no longer need to *see* the presenter in real life, but we do have to *trust them* to be the authority. They know this too and employ their authentic delivery techniques.

Like Andrew White inventing the methods of radio broadcasting, several notable historical figures invented the origin of the television broadcast. While television was invented in the late 1920s, it wasn't until the 1938 World's Fair when it would be introduced to the world. It would be another decade before it became an affordable technology that could be in people's living rooms.

After World War II, suburbia was burgeoning in towns across the United States eventually spreading to other parts of the world. The suburbs were houses that were further spread apart than in cities, but didn't have their own farmland and extensive properties. People had neighbors, but at a distance. The television became the connective device for these houses and people wanted to see what was happening in the world.

In the late 1940s, CBS executive William S. Paley hired Edward R. Murrow to be an on-air broadcaster for a radio show called *Hear It Now*. Murrow was a recognizable voice on the airwaves. He had a knack for presenting information in a way that the audience would keep listening. When he reported from London, he would open his broadcast with "*This* is London," accentuating the "This" at the beginning of his sentence. He knew that a tonal catchphrase would help him be recognizable among the many voices that were occupying the radio space.

In the early 1950s, consumers started buying televisions at an incredibly fast rate. In a few short years, televisions became a necessary part of the household. In 1951, *Hear It Now* transitioned to the new medium and was renamed *See It Now*. Murrow became a well-known and well-trusted authority on the news. He used the new medium in a way that would create the method of television broadcasting that would influence future visual media presenters.

Today, Murrow is most famous for his broadcasts between 1953 and 1954 that pushed back against Joseph McCarthy's attack on US citizens who may have been sympathetic to communism. Murrow, along with his producer Fred Friendly, used the television to broadcast Joseph McCarthy's inconsistent messaging to dismantle McCarthyism. The film *Good Night and Good Luck* (2005), named after Murrow's sign-off, dramatizes the events of that period and shows how poignant and trusted Murrow was as an on-air personality.

However, things changed quickly for television. Game shows, comedies, and entertainment quickly replaced the popularity of news. New technologies enabled multiple camera productions, budgets became bigger, advertisers had a distinct say in how productions would succeed or fail.

Television's influence only persisted. From the 1960 televised debate between John F. Kennedy and Richard Nixon to Walter Cronkite's coverage of the Vietnam War, visual media became the dominant medium for people to get their news. This continues today, with over two-thirds of the public relying on television to be the main part of their media diet.

But we're still talking about an exclusive medium, one that only broadcasted professionals hired by major companies who were chosen to be the face of the news or the star of the show. The days of the amateur inventing the new broadcast methods are a distant memory. Television, as a medium and a technology, was structured so that only a few could be on the screen.

Then, the next leap forward happened in the 1980s that switched the power dynamic forever: The internet and reality television.

THE BIAS SYSTEM IN PLAY

It's important to mention that we recognize the inherent bias in traditional media formats—and new media formats as well. All the names that have been mentioned thus far who have held the role of inventor, presenter, anchor, or founder are men. The system of inventions, whether that be television or social media, is unbalanced.

In the history of media, white men have often dominated the space over time. Media is a hegemony, meaning a large system, and often relies on previously designed power structures. Whenever someone gains power, someone else may lose it. Power is not equally distributed. What's missing from many histories of media are the contributions from woman, people of color, and those with different abilities. Even in our present, the system is still unbalanced, but we urge you to think about the fact that much of what we use is designed by a select few.

Though the past cannot be returned to, we have the responsibility of changing the future and empowering those who have been missed in the history books.

The Power to the People

If you were to figure out a year where you can identify the beginning of the world we live in today, its origins would be in the 1980s.

The early 1980s introduced the camcorder to the public. While originally extremely bulky (you often had to carry a pack with the VHS tape in it), it allowed regular, everyday people to access visual media production tools at a personal level. Being able to produce video without having to access a studio or know a professional in the industry resulted in a change in mindset about what constitutes authority.

But if we're looking for the origins of modern authenticity, we should focus on 1989, the year that introduced two of the biggest culture shifts in modern history.

That year, two major events would change the world and shift us into our connected era and change the power dynamics of on-screen presenting: the invention of the World Wide Web and *America's Funniest Videos*. While these seemed completely distinct at the time, you can argue that YouTube is the ultimate combination of these two inventions and that our world we adopted when we use remote media production is completely downstream from these events.

First, let's talk about the World Wide Web. The World Wide Web is the user part of the internet. The internet is the infrastructure that supports pretty much everything we interact with on a daily basis, from our news, to purchasing, to shipping, to our phones, banking, and of course, social media and websites.

The internet was originally developed as a government tool in the 1950s and 1960s as part of the Defense Advanced Research Projects Agency, known as DARPA. The intention of the internet was to connect educational institutions with government agencies and military centers so that scientists and creators weren't duplicating research. (Technically, the internet was built as sort of a weapon, but that's a story for another book.)

At the dawn of the space race, the internet rapidly developed into new technology that would allow multiple users to connect to one server, a process known as time-sharing. This is really important to how we do remote production today as we still consider time-sharing and watch hours in a similar way that we did in the 1960s. When technology advanced, ARPANet became the Internet. To get technical, this includes the thousands of miles of cables stretched around the globe that keep us connected.

THE ACTUAL INTERNET

We connect to each other seemingly by magic. But there's a ton of infrastructure that sustains our connected world. To the surprise of many people, the Internet is composed of two very basic technologies: wires and radio.

The internet is connected globally by wires, most of which span the oceans and connected to hubs around the globe. Huge ships stretch cables across the sea, connecting continents to each other with fiber optic cables (meaning the signal moves at the speed of light) which then move on land to internet hubs and internet service providers (ISPs) such as Verizon, Optimum, Cox, and hundreds more.

When you connect to the internet in your home, you likely connect through a modem that's attached to a cable coming from your television provider. The internet is using the same technology the television uses. When it gets to your modem, you may be connecting through ethernet cables to a router which converts the wired signal into a radio signal and broadcasts it on a frequency that your computers and phones can pick up called WiFi (wireless fidelity). WiFi, and even Bluetooth, is just radio signal.

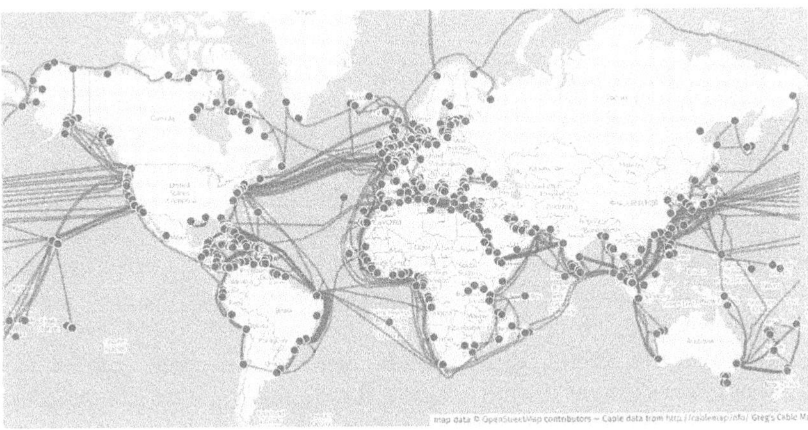

FIGURE 3.1 Undersea cable map (2015)—http://www.cablemap.info (cable data by Greg Mahlknecht released under GPLv3)

In the late 1980s, toward the end of the Cold War, a new digital language was created to get people to be able to use the internet in a more personal manner. People had been connecting via IRQ and IRC and even sending emails in the 1980s, but they were limited to text-only communication, long lag times, and an inability to really participate in the way the internet worked.

A team of engineers wanted to create a digital language that could be accessible by amateurs and enable people to have their own space on the internet. The World Wide Web introduced a new technology called the browser which used a new language called "hypertext markup language," or HTML. Markup refers to the way we can alter text like **bold** or *italics* as well as hypertext, meaning text that could be clicked on that leads to another spot on the web.

The browser used an easy system to translate code from hypertext to visual text on screen. It's called the "hypertext transfer protocol"—which is why "http" is the beginning of every web address.

Soon after, everyone could access HTML and have their own webpage. Authority shifted almost immediately as people could create media for thousands, if not millions of people to access.

The other shift in power dynamics was *America's Funniest Videos* (now called *AFV*). While television all over the world had been giving the common person a place on screen for decades with game shows and news reports, *America's Funniest Videos* introduced the world to DIY media production that rewarded the funniest submissions with cash prizes. For the first several years, *AFV* was a treasure trove of authentic video content.

For the first time in history, access to technology was opened up to millions more people than before. The camcorder became one of the primary ways we came to see people just being themselves—which is the core of authenticity.

The Shift to Internet Video

Of course, because media scales in ways we cannot predict, a few years passed before the introduction of reality television, a genre of television meant to portray people being themselves, but with something a bit more plot-driven. Starting with shows on MTV and then later on network television, reality television takes common people and allows them to be the "star" of a production for the episode or series. The more authentic a reality show contestant seems, the more successful they are with the audience.

In the 1990s, the World Wide Web also began to host video content. It was like a brand new world of sharing media. It flipped the world on its head. One of the earliest video websites was Pseudo.com, a site that had many channels for people to broadcast themselves. But then the dot com bubble burst and many of the earliest video sites disappeared.

One of the biggest weaknesses of online video is its bandwidth. Bandwidth refers to the size of the video as it makes its way across the internet. Video files are big, like really big. Think of it this way: your phone takes photos and each still image is about 3–5 megabytes depending on how much color is embedded in the image. So if that's just one frame, imagine how much is in 30 frames. You need to keep file sizes in mind when you create web video because the internet is not limitless.

When we stream content, the receiver has to use their own data to receive the media. One of the ways around this is through video compression which we'll discuss in depth in the next chapter.

The world had to wait until the right time for internet video to become a primary mode of delivery. Today, nearly all media we consume is delivered through internet-based systems and it happened very quickly.

To recap, for most of human history, media was one-to-few. Community-based performances were scalable only to the size of the arena in which the performance could be displayed. Only a little over 500 years ago, the moveable type printing press made media mass produceable, introducing a quicker way of getting access to information and enabling people to become more knowledgeable. From that moment of modernity, another several 100 years passed before the steam engine was invented that created two major leaps forward: the train engine, thereby enabling interstate and international wires to connect distances, and the steam printing press, which mass produced news.

After those wires were set up, the telephone and telegraph connected voice and information. Then radio pushed audio into the air! People had to learn how to be the authority to thousands. One-to-many production was invented. Just a few decades later, the television was inside people's houses and then the internet was developed followed by the World Wide Web, websites, and web video.

If you were to take all of human history and stretch it across a football field, digital media would occupy the space only the size of head of a pin at the end of field. And here we are. It's important to understand the history of this, because as you'll see in the next section, being successful as a digital media expert means you are sitting on the shoulders of giants. To be authentic may be a skill to learn, but it didn't just happen in a vacuum. It's connected to everything and everyone before us who decided to try something new to try to help the audience understand information in new and exciting ways.

In a moment, we became the producers of new media and the responsibility is to create the world for the next generation of media producers who may be using tools that we cannot even conceive of at this moment.

Authenticity Matters

What makes you authentic? And how can you achieve authenticity when you're on video? How can the audience tell you're being authentic? Well, it's actually kind of complicated, but once we learn what it really means, then we'll be able to use video to our advantage.

The most important thing to keep in mind is that when we use a video camera or are in front of a video camera, we're acting differently than we would in a non-mediated sense. Recording someone on camera gives the person holding the camera power. The director of the image oversees how someone *else* may see the content. Whether we know it or not, we shift power dynamics when we put a camera on someone else, whether it be an iPhone camera, a web cam, or a twenty-thousand-dollar professional camera.

On the other side of lens, we act differently as well. We put on a performance because we are aware of an audience, even if we don't know when or how the video will be seen. Today, there's much more of an immediate awareness of video destination, but when we used video tape and it took time to watch the video again, we were aware that at some point, someone who we may not be familiar with may watch the video. Somewhere in the back of our minds we activate a sense of ourselves that is performing for this unknown audience.

Authenticity is at the core of ourselves. It's who *we really are.*

According to Professor Stephen Joseph, "Authenticity is about being true to yourself in each and every moment." Dr. Joseph is a psychologist who studies how humans flourish—meaning grow and advance through wonder and life development. He explores authenticity in his book *Authentic: How to Be Yourself and Why It Matters* (2016).[3]

Dr. Joseph proposes that living authentically leads to living a more positive life, being real to yourself, and finding trust in what you do. In this section, we're going to talk about how to be authentic on camera, as a presenter, and what you can do to make sure the *real you* makes it across the screen to the audience, but is also compelling, authoritative, and positive.

To get there, we're going to give a bit more context as to how to accomplish this by referring to the more modern digital broadcasters, YouTubers, and digital screen stars and their techniques before getting into the very in-depth checklist of presentation basics.

Screen Authenticity

While the specific number is unconfirmed, there's an online legend that states, before YouTube, there were 17,000 YouTubes.[4] In the early 2000s, everyone wanted to be the home of web video. In 2005, it was YouTube ended up becoming the site that now defines online video. What makes YouTube the dominant video site on the internet? When Google purchased YouTube in 2006, it could easily have made its own product, Google Video, the replacement for YouTube. Google had the money and the technology to develop something more powerful, but they didn't. The reason wasn't about technology, but rather about community.

YouTube is a social network. It allows people an easy, low barrier to participate and upload video content and the ability to comment on the videos. When Google purchased the platform, they weren't buying the technology, they were buying the community.

In the first few years of YouTube, people starting using the site as a place to leave their video diary entries. No one defined how to use YouTube, so it was up to the users. Not since the days of Andrew White experimenting with radio broadcasting were everyday people able to try brand new methods of talking to an unseen audience.

Like Edward R. Murrow developing the techniques for visual broadcasting, YouTubers (at the time called vloggers for video bloggers) were developing successful methods of how to speak and present on the small screen.

What makes YouTube and remote media production a unique experience by comparison to mainstream video content is the way the audience receives the media. Most people watch YouTube on small screens, whether that be a computer monitor, laptop, mobile device, or tablet. This changes the way we have to think about media. Originally, televisions were quite small, so producers and directors of early content knew they had to focus more on close-ups. But as televisions grew in size, the small screen literally created a new method of video production distinct from big screen media.

Being an Authentic New Media Personality

Imagine this:

> You're a freshman at college and you really miss your friends. You could call them, but it's 2007 and your cellphone only has so many minutes left for the month. Texting actually costs money per text, so that's out of the question. Your friends really like how you tell stories, so you come across a new website that helps people connect with one another using video clips. You used to journal online quite often, so how different could it be to produce video journal entries. So you log on and make some videos for your friends, but, soon after, you find out that strangers are watching your videos … and they like them!

When Tyler Oakley started his freshman year at Michigan State University, he really missed his friends. Lonely in his dorm, he used YouTube to connect with his friends at home. Without thinking too much, he made personal video messages to them and posted them online. In the early days of YouTube humans were tasked with organizing the front page of the site. (Now that job is done by algorithms.) After Tyler uploaded his sixth video, someone at YouTube took notice of Tyler's sincere authenticity and posted it on the front page.

He was approachable and sweet and sincerely authentic. He wasn't creating a show or developing a personality, he was just being himself. Tyler's seemingly personal videos received hundreds of views. What Tyler realized is that his method of authentic video production was pleasing to strangers he'd never met before. He was just being himself, sharing his personal thoughts with his friends, but random people found his video appealing.

Tyler Oakley became one of the people who helped developed the style of small-screen authentic presentation. This case study will help you understand how YouTubers adopted an aesthetic that was collectively developed, but amplified by just a few personalities. At the time, YouTube's slogan was "Broadcast Yourself" which was both a play on the DIY aesthetic necessary to self-produce content and a verb for the fact you were now a broadcaster. Tyler was in the right place at the right time to be one of the leaders of a new media production aesthetic.

Takeaways from Tyler Oakley

Tyler's seventh video, titled "Raindrops,"[5] was the first video he made to an unknown audience. The video is awkward by today's standards, but you can see the formation of a new aesthetic and video production method that was distinct from traditional media.

The first 20 seconds of the video consist of Tyler making faces at the camera with a pleasant, open-source music track playing in the background. He uses jumpcuts to compress time in the video. When he starts talking, he expresses his emotions without feeling burdened by standard television censorship. The story he tells about going to class in the rain is short, but compelling. He makes direct eye contact with the camera and shares the story and ends with a note of gratitude.

In traditional media, reporters usually make direct eye contact with the camera as they are expressing authority. Interview subjects often look off camera at the news reporter when they are on camera, giving the audience a sense that someone is listening to them. To directly address the camera means that you are making a connection to someone who you cannot see on the other side while simultaneously being the authority of your content. (This also has some weird effects with the audience that we'll discuss in a bit.)

Tyler further uses the jumpcuts to compress time, editing out the common presentation interjections like "ums" or "uhs" or "like" that many of us by accident when we present to the public. Adding music helps hide the edits, but also motivates the content going forward.

Interestingly, YouTubers like Tyler Oakley use a verbal trick to keep the attention of viewers throughout their videos. The trick is called the "schwa" and it sounds like a dull "euh" noise. You can hear it in many YouTubers' voices and is the foundation of the sound that's made when YouTubers start their video with "Hey Guys" in that sing-songy voice. The "euh" is a swing of the words that causes people to pay attention. It's part of the authentic delivery method many new media professionals use when they are on screen talking for a bit.

Finally, another important part of Tyler's video is the setting and the framing. Later, we're going to go over how important it is to create a setting that tells a story about you without you saying it. Whether it be your bedroom, your office, or if you use a virtual background, the stage in which you present tells things to the audience. In Tyler's video, he's sitting in his dorm room. Even without sound, you know who he is and where he is. This is an important feature of remote video production.

The new aesthetic that Tyler was using helped define the YouTuber aesthetic still used today. It differentiates the content from traditional media.

Someone has to create the new style and Tyler Oakley helped build the universe for thousands of YouTubers over the next 15 years. For over a decade, Tyler Oakley was considered one of the most important YouTubers, spanning from the early days until the late 2010s. His authenticity helped him become endorsed (the primary way YouTubers make money) by several companies including Audible, Target, Bud Light Lime, and Disney.

As the years went on, video quality improved and so did Tyler's production style. He matured along with the technology. As later episodes show, he used better cameras and audio, set up better backgrounds, and became memorable as one of the most authentic YouTubers to be on the site.

Even though he was performing to millions of viewers, he did his best to be himself. He would read comments and connect with fans and listen to their feedback. He strove to be transparent in his process and explained quite often how strange it is to be a YouTuber and to be a virtual presenter. YouTubers are their own category now and defined by how they look on the platform. They're now distinct from traditional media personalities and new media personalities like TikTok stars.

When the pandemic moved many people into the digital space, college instructors, lecturers, public speakers, and field experts used YouTube to deliver their messages. They used the techniques that people like Tyler Oakley had developed 15 years previous to create compelling content that students, attendees, and interested audiences would appreciate.

But most importantly, people knew they had to be authentic if they wanted to make it work and make the time valuable.

PERSONAL STORY

Jamie here!

In the early 2010s, I finished my graduate studies where I focused on YouTube, vloggers, and webseries creators. It was an exciting time, but also somewhat scary. The industry appeared so quickly. It went from grainy videos and DIY television series to major Hollywood studios producing content in a three-year time period. I felt it was important that we take internet studies seriously and thankfully, so did some of my academic peers.

Later, I founded a New Media major at a small college. It was a bit of an uphill battle as most people in 2012 (and even today), consider the internet to be a sandbox and a playspace, not a space for serious critique and application of media theory. Regardless, the state saw its value and I launched an internet studies degree.

Students had a variety of courses, but the most difficult course was "Video Storytelling for the Web," a course designed around creating and supporting your own YouTube channel. Most people think that vlogging is an easy gig—it isn't! Just producing a few videos is a time-consuming process and on top of that, you have to promote your page, grow your following, and continue to come up with new material.

The program succeeds and continues to flourish because people recognized it isn't just about recording video and talking to a camera, but knowing that all of what they learn is founded on decades, if not centuries, of presentation techniques. I was always very proud of my students who succeeded in the web space. It takes a lot of courage to put yourself on camera for the world to see. Some of my former students continue to be influencers on Instagram and YouTube and I enjoy seeing their updates constantly.

Maybe the next big influencer can be you?

What We Can Learn from Influencers

We can't all be Tyler Oakley, Charlie D'Amelio, Jackie Aina, or Khaby Lame—heck, if you even know who all these influencers are, that means you're pretty tuned into social media. In this last section about the history of authenticity, we'd like to do a bit of a deep dive on how small screen influencers developed their method and what you can learn from them in your process of preparing how to be a great virtual presenter now and into the future.

After Tyler Oakley and his cohort developed the aesthetic that online influencers would come to use, platforms pivoted away from narrative content to focus more on individuals. According to Sarah Frier in her book *No Filter: The Inside Story of Instagram* (2020), influencers rose to fame because of the limitations of small-screen video.[6] The term "influencer" has its origins in the Instagram application and originally referred to "salespeople" or "celebrity endorsers."

Instagram is a low barrier to entry application and originally was designed to mimic the authenticity of analog content like Polaroid images. Users would take photos on Instagram and add filters (you may remember this!) and do their best to create a version of reality that was somewhat stylized beyond what it really looked like. Soon, the "Instagram aesthetic" was born and people flocked to the app to share their most mundane moments with the world with a tinge of color or upgrade to the appearance with filters like "Clarendon" or "Lark" (pre-built filters in the app).

The goal of the Instagram app was to turn anyone into someone who could influence someone else. Influencers are people who gain enough trust through their authenticity to help someone else make an actionable decision from liking or commenting to making a consumer purchase. It's like peer pressure with a filter.

What made Instagram distinct from other social media was its focus on images and the celebration of the mundane. At the time of Instagram's launch in 2010, Facebook and Twitter were the dominant social media. They were technically platforms of mixed media posting. Twitter was just a microblogging platform that barely prioritized images. (At the time, Twitter used a third-party app to include pictures in posts.)

Instagram's launch changed how we used social media and how we interpret what it means to be memorable on video. Over on YouTube, famous vloggers began to be called "creators" or YouTubers and entered YouTube's partner program where they could share revenue from their views and subscribers. On Instagram, founder Kevin Systrom had to figure out how to get people to participate more than posting images of their lunch, but he was also nervous that the platform would get clustered with tacky content.

Sarah Frier writes, "Systrom didn't want Instagram to turn into a collection of unsightly roadside billboards. When users posted about brands, instead of being so obvious, it would be best if they acted like they were letting their audience in on a life secret, or if they put the product in a spread of other beautiful things, or if they told a story."[7]

Think about how invisible influencers are to us when they are promoting a product. This is a strategy of online celebrities that use authentic methods to connect with us on a pseudo-personal level. Remember, the Kardashians are using the same exact app you are when you open Instagram. It levels the playing field.

Compare this to our examples about television and radio. Those mediums were exclusive to those who had access to the tools of big media. Even after *America's Funniest Videos* and reality television uplifted common people, they still didn't have the influence of a traditional media personality. When you use social media, celebrities don't get a different tool than you do, it's the same application for everyone. (However, influencers do get access to advanced metrics and a better dashboard than the average user.)

For several years, Instagram, the platform, helped the new influencers develop the style and aesthetic of the small-screen influencer. Images worked well, but they became very formulaic and users could start to identify an influencer post in their feed, sometimes glossing over the post. Something new had to be integrated.

The Beginning of Social Video

In 2012, Mark Zuckerberg decided to buy Instagram and add it to the company's offerings. The app was doing very well and Zuckerberg saw the long-term benefit of adding the product to Meta's (née Facebook) technologies. In the background, there were a handful of smaller apps that were prioritizing video as their main outlet. If Facebook was really about texts and multimedia posts and Twitter was about short-form text and Instagram was about still photos, then other apps knew they could promote video as their main focus.

YouTube's birth and overwhelming success in 2005 was a result of both the community and the fact that the audience now had access to faster internet bandwidth that would support the streaming of their media. This wasn't as easy on mobile devices. While you could use ethernet connections or Wi-Fi at home, broadband on mobile devices came at a cost—data downloads and available cell signal. It was (and still is) costly to use too much cellular data (since cell data shares its broadband spectrum with radio) and there is high charges for data limits.

If you were an app designer, the goal was to create video that would be more streamable and smaller. Short-form videos and compressed videos were the answer. Apps such as Viddy, Socialcam, and Klip were all video-sharing platforms, but the most famous success story was Vine.

Vine is one of the most important parts of modern internet history. Vine limited users to six-second videos and there was no going around the rules. The application changed the language of video production. Vine was like a sentence in the grammar of video. It had no choice but to be an authentic outlet. The limitation was its success.

At the time that Instagram was acquired by Facebook, Jack Dorsey at Twitter purchased Vine. Now it was up to Instagram and Facebook to figure out how to compete with social video. Vine proved that video was going to be the new way people would be interacting with social content and Kevin Systrom wanted to get into it as well. Within six weeks of Twitter's acquisition of Vine, Instagram launched its video tool allowing users to create 15-second video that would appear on the Instagram feed.

Very quickly, video posts became popular and audiences who liked Vine clips also liked Instagram video clips. Instagram learned that video posts were not anything like their still photo counterparts, but rather a completely new part of the eco-system that showed snippets of authentic life. According to Sarah Frier, one of the Instagram engineers had followed a dog account for many years and was pleased to hear the owner's voice for the first time ever when Instagram video was launched.

Now everyone was getting in the game. Snapchat introduced video to its platform and any social media that added the technology noticed users felt less stress to create curated content and post more unedited and raw content to their feeds.

PEER PRESSURE, FOMO, AND THE ALGORITHM

Social media, specifically Instagram, has a pressure problem. On the surface, adding a filter to mundane everyday things you want to post online seems like good fun, but that's not how social media works.

Everything you post is part of an ecosystem that ranks the success of your content. In traditional media, this is called ratings and executives make decisions based on these metrics. On social media, we see our metrics every time we post, but so does everyone else. When you post a picture or a video, you're competing in the attention economy and trying to get people to interact with what you posted. When your post does well, you release a small amount of dopamine which makes you want to post again.

One of the things Instagram excelled at was helping users create an imagined reality of their day. You don't typically post *everything* on Instagram, you only post the *best parts* that you want people to see. Sometimes, you create a performance of your everyday life. Goffman predicted this back in the 1950s, but he didn't have the ability to see that we would use digital ranking systems to keep up with.

Instagram's digital feed curation tool is operated by an algorithm that pushes exciting content to your feed rather than banal material. The goal is to make you feel left out of something exciting that your friends were doing or show you scenes from an event you may not have been invited to. This causes a problem called "Fear of Missing Out" or FOMO, and sometimes makes us feel bad.

In a leak of Facebook documents in 2021, people became aware that Facebook was well aware of the significant pressure young people feel when they use Instagram. Young women in particular were affected by the unreality prioritized by the Instagram algorithm. While this book focuses on media production and virtual presenting, it's important to be aware that the systems that organize our feeds don't always have our best feelings in mind when they operate.

Social media is, after all, a large advertising platform and marketing is part of the system that sustains the platforms. Remember, these platforms are free for a reason.

The Authenticity of Live and Vertical Video

At the same time platforms were experimenting with feed-based video, YouTube started experimenting with live streaming. In 2012, a gaming site called Twitch boasted it was reaching over 20 million users per month. People were interested in a new form of video production—live, side-by-side commentary of video game play-throughs. YouTube was already a place for this genre content called "Let's Play" where YouTubers would play a game and comment on it. It would help gamer figure out how to play the game, but also get the unique experience of sitting with a personality that would narrate the experience from their point of view.

Twitch is a platform that is primarily dedicated to game play streaming. Users can incorporate multi-streaming technologies like OBS (a software streamers use) and use graphics cards to connect their consoles or stream their computer games along with their live video. Live video has a level of authenticity that is much more real than that of the performative video of Instagram or Vine. Liveness meant realness and unexpected outcomes—although this was also a content moderator's nightmare.

The popularity of online video was beginning to define the 2010s. Video has a remarkable ability to add context and color to anything that's going on. When it comes to authentic video production, audiences were becoming addicted to these personalities, watching them religiously, and keeping tuned into their productions whenever they would happen. On the other hand, some online personalities used these platforms in negative ways and influenced young people to fall down dangerous rabbit holes.

But video persisted and many platforms began to prioritize the format. Instagram found new ways to incorporate video competitively and uniquely from YouTube and Twitch. They saw inspiration in the way Snapchat was able to keep young people on the platform. They noticed that Snapchat's native production style, meaning the way it was designed for the platform, was a popular way of delivering authentic media to the audience. Vertical video was a new way of framing media shots and sped up the content recording and delivery on mobile devices.

We hold our mobile devices vertically. It takes a second or two to change the orientation, so why not just keep the video vertical—and temporary.

In 2013, Instagram introduced Stories, a product similar to Snapchat's technology. Snapchat basically created the concept of mobile authenticity by allowing users to create vertical content that would automatically delete after 24 hours. The willingness to post your everyday life with the awareness that it would simply disappear, opened the door for more authentic storytelling by each user. Instagram Stories were extremely similar as they would also automatically delete a day later.

One thing that Instagram did differently than Snapchat was create a system that allowed users to tune into a new Story in chronological order. When someone posted to their stories, it would appear in a separate area and in the order in which it was posted. It made real time far more accessible to people and revealed a second layer to what people would consider part of their social posting method.

It was designed to be quick and inspired more spur of the moment type of recording, but most importantly, Stories wanted people to share themselves with less preparation and with far less concern over the filters or presentation. The presentation of yourself in your everyday life was now a social media feature.

PARASOCIAL RELATIONSHIPS

One key difference in virtual presenting is about how we make eye contact with the audience. As established by YouTubers and perpetuated by online influencers, the act of making direct eye contact is a sign of authority. When we are producing content for remote production, we're simultaneously behind and in front of the camera and we're looking into that tiny little lens to talk to our audience.

If you are authentic enough, the audience feels like they are communicating with you personally. One of the most important tricks in actual presenting or interviewing is to make direct eye contact with the person in the audience or across from us. It makes us vulnerable and lets us connect with people more personally.

Because people watch online personalities with much more proximity on their mobile device or close to their computer monitor, we feel like we're close to the person on the screen. This can lead to a side-effect of authentic production called "Parasocial relationships" and it's not always a good thing.

Parasocial relationships originated in the 1950s when people became really attached to actors' storylines on soap operas. The audience became attached, much the way you would if you read a book series and fall in love with one of the characters. Their fictional lives are compelling to your own life. While some people became attached to their favorite news personality, the concept of authority, or power over the audience, is different from how we watch online influencers.

The goal of authentic production is to make the person on the other side of the screen believe you are talking to them *personally,* not to the little green dot or lens. As a presenter, you have to pretend they are there *with you.* Unfortunately, sometimes that becomes *too personal.*

Parasocial relationships are when the audience connects with the online personality in a way that is more than a viewer, but a fan that feels like they're part of the production themselves. Though rare, at scale it can get weird. Many YouTubers feel that some of their fans become too close. (The word "Stan" is often used for this which comes from Eminem's song "Stan" that mixed the words fan and stalker.)

You have a lot of power when you are on camera and making eye contact is one of the most important things you can do to be an authentic and compelling presenter, but you should know about the side effects that occur when people watch personalities passionately. People who attend virtual productions or webinars feel a connection they likely would not have normally felt if it was a traditional television broadcast. Many online personalities take parasocial relationships as a compliment, but it does get weird sometimes when people see you in real life and want to say hello even though they've only seen you on a screen.

A true breakthrough appeared for consumers in 2016 when the company Bytedance purchased a music sing-along app called Musical.ly and named it TikTok. TikTok not only featured vertical video as a native format but includes a host of video editing tools to encourage people to make professional video content that worked beyond the record button. As of this writing, TikTok is the most downloaded social media app, hosting dozens of well-recognized influencers and over one billion users.

TikTok inspires people to connect with one another through sharing their expertise and their talent in a stylized way. TikTok has its own aesthetic and its own delivery method and the videos that do well have people speaking more clearly and methodically. The presentation methods introduced by TikTok are fairly useable in remote media production and virtual presenting in professional settings. While many TikTok influencers use viral dances or challenges to maintain popularity, we'll focus on some of the more educational channels that inform in creative ways.

The usefulness of TikTok as an educational platform is exciting. In one-to-three-minute clips (though the app is currently experimenting with longer form content), people have to deliver their content.

Authentic Expertise Delivered Digitally

Imagine this:

> You are the expert in the niche scientific subject matter focused on antibody research and your friend asks you for help on their biology exam. You decide to use the opportunity to show off your digital skills by telling the story about different antibodies by using musical artist Megan Thee Stallion's "Body" song and replace the lyric with your educational expertise.

Well, this is what Dr. Raven Baxter, better known at Raven the Science Maven, did in 2020 and her video went viral on TikTok. Dr. Baxter is a molecular biologist, and at the time, she was in graduate school. During the pandemic, she knew that telling stories the traditional way would no longer garner the same attention when new media styles were so prevalent. TikTok inspires people to take part in remixes by prioritizing musical tracks that can be re-used on each video. In many ways, TikTok is a musical remix factory because many users pick the music track first before they make their videos.

Dr. Baxter downloaded Megan Thee Stallion's track and did a version of karaoke over Megan Thee Stallions lyrics. Dr. Baxter's track is called "Antibodyody Antibody Song" and she replaced the artist's words with "Antibodies, IgM, IgA, IgM, IgE, IgG, IgE" to the beat of the music. At the same time, Dr. Baxter used the screen to point to the different molecular combinations.[8]

The video is extremely helpful because it explains how our body uses antibodies provided in the Covid-19 vaccine to protect our immune systems. "Antibodies make the haters see the bright light" Dr. Baxter sings, explaining that the virus can be stopped with the vaccine that builds up our adaptive immunities.

While it may seem weird to think that a molecular biologist may use TikTok to explain such a serious part of science, this case study should empower you to be creative in the world of virtual presenting. We are no longer tethered to the traditional formats of media storytelling—we can do anything!

Dr. Baxter's viral TikTok helped thousands of people learn about antibodies and vaccine safety and can teach us a lot about how different we can be authentic in this new media world.

What TikTok and Vertical Video Can Teach Us

If you are tasked with producing a webinar or livestream, think outside the box. This doesn't mean you have to download the latest viral music track to remix or change the orientation of your video, but you should consider that the audience isn't watching a Zoom the same way they are watching television.

As we went over in the previous chapter, there are presentation basics that you should most certainly incorporate in your work, but don't be afraid to consider how much storytelling you can do with what you have on hand. Virtual functionalities and screen sharing open new ways of using the screen when your guest is presenting. People are most interested in the person on screen but adding small flourishes can change the success of our project.

Here's a couple of things we can incorporate from the skills of a TikTok personality.

Think About Who You Are Talking To

When Raven was making her video about antibodies, she was creating the content for her former student. The student needed help and she was able to create a visually exciting video that incorporated a trendy song.

Each time you participate in a webinar or livestream, the audience is going to be far more niche than general programming. The audience is there for a specific purpose, and it will be beneficial to think small rather than general.

TikTok personalities, from cooks to beekeepers to wood carvers to molecular biologists, make an assumption that the audience is either there for the subject matter or tuned it based on similar videos. (The TikTok algorithm is a completely different conversation, but works on a content-aware system, meaning that videos that look like other videos are often put in the feed in some sort of order.)

Make Your Presentation Feel *Different*

It's easy to use Google Slides or PowerPoint to build your deck and presentation, but we also have other tools at our disposal. It could be good to incorporate moving pictures like gifs into our presentations to provide additional context. The slides can also be formatted differently than a basic webinar and could include features that are compelling. TikTok personalities do this by using the green screen feature and on Zoom, this can be done by pre-loading an interesting virtual background or using slides as part of the background. (We'll explain how to do this later.)

Make Your Audience Comfortable

Use language that is approachable with your audience and provide context as much as possible. The best thing to do is think about how high-level your presentation may be. While your audience is likely niche and specific, having context is important. Most TikTok explainers set up context before breaking down a theme or a story. If you are going to talk about space telescopes or space photography, you should give a bit of context as to why we even want to talk about outer space.

A brief, several second contexts will make the audience feel more participatory and engaged and they're likely to feel more comfortable with the content that's about to come across their screen.

Unlike TikTok, most virtual presenting will give you more time than 1 minute to get the entirety of your point across, but practice for the short form anyway.

The Collective Shift to Remote Production

In this final part of this chapter, we'll delve into the modern-day use of authentic presentation as we were collectively put in a situation outside our control, but during a period time where we had increasing access to the technologies that could keep us connected in real time.

It was, and continues to be, an interesting time to live through. The Covid-19 pandemic spread so rapidly and globally; it was hard to mitigate its spread. It's a disease that is really harmful and in order to reduce the number of casualties, we figured out that we could keep the world going remotely. Companies that had the ability to have their employees work at home utilized Zoom, Microsoft Teams, Skype, WebEx, and other platforms to host meetings, video conference one another, and collaborate at work from our homes.

On the educational side, schools were put in the awkward situation of converting in-person class into remote education. Access is not equitable or evenly distributed and in the first few months—the end of the Spring 2020 school year—was quite chaotic for many young people and teachers. While some faculty were trained for remote learning, it's an entirely different skillset for educators. For students, the pivot was stressful. Not every young person has access to broadband internet or even a computer with a web camera or a laptop. Many made due with public facilities or libraries.

(Some of the tips in the following chapters are focused on giving educators some advice on how to improve their virtual presenting or adapt some pedagogies for a hybrid world. Our hope is that we don't ever have to spend over a year remotely learning again, but we should be prepared regardless.)

Whether at work or at school, one thing became strikingly obvious, we had no choice but to be authentic. Very few of us have private offices or sections of our house that can act as a defacto home classroom or meeting room or virtual television set. Our colleagues, friends, peers, and classmates could see right into our private spaces. We opened windows onto our real spaces and pushed back our judgement. Thankfully for many, most of our streaming software applications enable the virtual background and we were able to blur out our private spaces.

We're sure many students were happy to go back to in-person education after broadcasting from their bedrooms. When it came to work, many employers continued a hybrid working plan, allowing workers to be in the office only for part of the week.

The Business of Remote Media Production

Aside from the business of remote work and streaming meetings and classes, the industry of virtual events, webinars, and livestreams became a segment of many non-video industries. Experts, professionals, public speakers, and specialists put a temporary halt to their travel and public appearances. An opportunity appeared to create new media in non-media spaces. Webinars and virtual events were incorporated into publishing companies, medical facilities, banking companies, state parks, and museums to name only a few of many dozens of examples.

These companies leaned into virtual presenting to keep their audiences engaged throughout the pandemic and supply substitute programming for their lack of in-person events. The downside: there were no rulebooks on how to do this! Now you're holding one, but at the time, most of the work was experimental or crowdsourced from helpful online communities or built by media professionals brought into the companies to assist with the new industry.

The most amazing part of the pandemic period of experimental remote production is that it was, for the most part, really successful programming for many businesses. Even after people returned to the office and public speakers began to buy plane tickets again, the webinars and virtual events continued. (As we'll discuss in Chapter 5, these events have an added benefit aside from convenience, they provide a ton of data and leads to many of these companies.)

In this hybrid world, we can do anything and make it look amazing. The goal is to continue making the productions high quality and operate in distinction from traditional media structures. We need to continue to think authentically and present as best as we can.

Overcoming the Fear of Presenting

There's just a few more things we want to cover before we go into the important tools and pieces of advice that we need to use when we are presenting.

Most of us are not born presenters. It took us years to hone our skills to publicly speak and even longer to be confident on camera. Being on camera is an act of bravery. Speaking to that little green dot at the top of the laptop monitor or speaking into a web camera or into the lens of a DSLR is daunting. Who is looking back? What are they thinking?

And then it hits you—the invasive thoughts creep in. "Am I fraud?" "Why am I the one who is about to talk?" "Oh no, they're going to judge everything I say!"

This is called "imposter syndrome" and it's extremely common. It's when we feel like we're a fraud even though we're the expert in our own thing.

According to the American Psychological Association, imposter syndrome is very common.[9] Due to the dominantly patriarchal system that exists, originally the syndrome was associated with women, but over time, it turns out that it's very common among anyone who may feel "the pressure to achieve."

Graduate students, people of color, minority groups, women, and LGBTQ people may feel more anxiety when presenting because the systems of authority are skewed a certain way. But that's where remote media production may level the playing field. Everyone has similar tools to use and with an internet connection and a camera, the subject is the authority.

It's normal to have feelings of self-doubt or self-consciousness when you are about to present. But this is where we believe remote media production creates an advantage—you should be yourself. No one is perfect and we should be proud of our achievements. Whether we're presenting our paper from class or speaking about a subject we're passionate about, you don't have to achieve perfection.

The most important thing to keep in mind when virtually presenting is that it's ok to make mistakes. Perfect is boring.

As we learned, authenticity is a process about learning to be yourself in front of others, pushing through the self-doubt that occurs when we overthink our awareness of the camera, the audience and the production. We want to make clear that remote media production relies more heavily on authentic presentation styles than traditional media formats. Webinars, virtual events, simulcasts, livestreams, and podcasts are produced by a range of talent, from the beginner to the professional. As this book unfolds, you'll be prepared to do this work professionally, but digital production should still be unique and distinct from the professional media sectors of broadcast television and film.

In the world of remote media production, audiences are interested in connecting in real time to you to hear your expertise, but they're looking for an earnest explanation of your work and what you bring to the production. If the audience cannot relate, they won't be able to make a connection with you.

Remote media production is an earnest and authentic format. Most attendees are viewing the content on their personal computer and are proximately close to the screen. Typically, you wouldn't watch a webinar in the same way you would watch a television show. Webinars and Zoom meetings are designed to be a collective experience where at any moment, someone from the audience may share a screen.

It's always important to practice your work (and we'll get into that in the next section), but you should keep in mind that people are hoping to see a human on the screen. When you are speaking, you are the authority. When you are on screen, you are the expert.

Look at it this way: When you were in school or you attended an in-person seminar, you automatically assumed that the person speaking was the authority. You didn't question it, you just knew that the person in front of the room commanded some power that was distinct from the audience. During a TED Talk, you usually focus on the speaker, not the audience members. In the environment of remote media production, this style is skewed because the audience is sometimes given equal access to the tools. (This is different in webinars and virtual events where the audience is relegated to text-only communication.)

Being Believable Means Being Imperfect

Authenticity relies on our ability to embrace ourselves and what we believe may be our shortcomings. If you are like everyone else, then you won't be memorable. The Zoom screen looks the same for nearly every production and most people don't remember the digital tool that they watch on the screen, they remember the people and the presentations they watched. If you want to make an impact, the authentic you is the one they'll remember days later.

The best presentations we remember feel more "real" than something that was over rehearsed or polished. They're the ones where we saw the presenter seem a little vulnerable, a little self-conscious, but still brave enough to push through and share their thoughts with the audience.

MEMORY AND THE SCREEN

If you're reading this book, you're likely interested in continuing a production style that you may have learned during the pandemic. If you're like us, you also have a weird sense of when things happened during that period of time and your memory has difficulty picking out certain days or when something occurred.

When we make memories, we require variety and difference to map onto our brains. When we spend day in and day out looking at the same screen sitting in the same seat, our brain has difficulty creating new memories. As far as our mind is concerned, it's the same day over and over again.

But we do remember things we saw and speakers we listened to, but only when they seem memorable from others. We use the term content in nearly a derogatory way, a reduction of media down to its most boring behavior, like it's just "stuff" on the screen. In order to make the audience remember even when the setting is the same, we need to create media that isn't content, but memorable segments.

Remotely Authentic

Douglas Rushkoff is an author of over two dozen books, the host of the popular *Team Human* podcast, and a well-known public speaker. Rushkoff gets asked to speak all over the world about the intersection of technology and society so when the pandemic hit, he was one of the first to speak out about the rapid shift we all had to take to learn how to speak inside the computer screen instead of in-person. When the world paused before vaccines were available, we turned to social distancing and remote media production.

For that first moment, all of us were thrust into the world of remote media production. "Video conferencing is really no substitute for live engagement," Rushkoff wrote in March 2020, just days after school shifted to online learning.[10] "Real, face-to-face encounters engage a host of painstakingly evolved social mechanisms for establishing rapport." Rushkoff has a theatre background and finds himself at home in the public speaking space. That's far different than the way most of us feel in front of crowds, but he offered some great advice that still holds now about how to be authentic on the screen. "Act as if you are really there," Rushkoff boldly states.

In the previous chapter, we learned many of the basics of presenting: Pitch, Pace, Posture, and Passion. Here, we'll delve into some of the presentation techniques that became necessary when the pandemic leveled the playing field and we all became on-screen personalities all at once.

As previously noted, one of the biggest contrasts to in-person speaking is the lack of human energy that comes from speaking in public. Since we're missing the view of the audience's bodies, we can't really know if people are synching up with what we are saying. Just like the audience sees our upper body when we're presenting, the same view is for the presenter. Sure, they may seem interested, but how can you really know?

There are some really good methods that many public speakers have provided that help us be unique and authentic on screen.

First, imagine what you look like from the audience's perspective. In a typical in-person talk, you may be able to speak for some time, but on a screen, it's pretty much the same shot the entire time. Look away and come back and you're probably seeing the same view from a few minutes ago. We all get distracted all the time. We have too many devices, we have too many tabs open, we have things to do that are right on our desk and just off-screen. We can get away with not paying attention. It's not fair to the presenter, but you know you do that too and you hope, even unrealistically, that the audience will be different for you.

Dress for Authenticity

"Dress for the job you want, not the job you have" is a phrase that comes up often when people are trying to help each other achieve career success. Well, this doesn't exactly hold true any longer, so this bit of advice gets a bit more complicated in a remote setting. Even before the era of remote and hybrid work environments, more casual dress and styles had entered the office. Comfort and style were prioritized over formal dresswear and a standard dress code. Things have changed and this aphorism may not be as healthy as universal advice as it used to be.[11]

And who would have ever guessed that you could go to work without any formal pant on?!

Virtual presenting means doing some research to know what to wear. You want to appear authentic to others in your appearance, but your visual impression on the screen should match the environment. In an interview setting, you may wish to check the company's dress code on their website. Some informational emails will contain some information on how to dress as well.

You don't really want to dress too formally for a setting that is more casual—your clothes say a lot about you. Fashion is personal and expresses your authenticity before you even say a word. Our recommendation is to wear what you would to a networking event for your specific industry. You know your industry best, and this helps because if you imagine a networking event, it helps you dress for success.

Who you are needs to come through the screen and if you are wearing clothes that make you uncomfortable, it will show on the screen. In the end, be comfortable, be you, and be your version of stylish.

The Authentic Setting

"For most of us, life happens against a backdrop of intersecting off-white walls," Paul Ford writes in his 2014 essay "The American Room."[12] Ford and some of his fellow researchers analyzed hundreds of YouTube videos and noticed something peculiar about most of the videos: the background was incredibly plain. Just a beige or off-white wall with maybe a generic piece of art or a boring bookshelf.

This is because the great majority of these YouTube clips were posted in haste or the focus was on the action, not the room. From the "Numa Numa" viral video to clips of people playing instruments in their basements, the backgrounds of many videos were fairly unremarkable. To be honest, it really didn't matter at the time because these videos were not intended to be seen in context of a presentation or remembered this way. They had no idea that Paul Ford would be analyzing them when they uploaded their clip.

Returning to the idea of broadcasting from your bedroom or personal space, we want to take a moment to talk about what we can do to create our own space and what people think when they see into our personal worlds. First, let's talk about the virtual backgrounds. The use of virtual backgrounds is still a good idea and as we talked about in Chapter 2, you should invest in good lighting and a more appropriate (meaning smooth and consistently lit) green screen. The "cleaner" the key (the term used for creating the computer graphics layer that separates you from the background) the better you'll look on screen.

Your virtual background should also include some basic information about you. Many public speakers include their social media handles or their company logo on their virtual background. It helps the audience aware of who you are and locate places to find you. In the case of a livestream or live virtual event, users can find you on social media and mention you as you are talking about your subject. From a host perspective, the main event's hashtag should be provided on the virtual background as well so the audience can tag both the event and the speaker.

Consistency is key, so if you are producing a virtual event, you should either supply your guests with virtual backgrounds that are customizable or create a spreadsheet that holds their information so you can create virtual backgrounds for all the guests on screen.

If you aren't using a virtual background, it gets a little more complicated because people are used to watching the news and YouTubers. People who have on-camera careers are very intentional about their setting and their background. We are going to take their advice and talk about what you can do to upgrade your experience for the online and remote audience.

The Background Authentic

Next time you are in your bedroom or most used living space, take a look around. What choices were made in decorations, plants, furniture, or electronics? Why did you set them up in the way you did? What story are you trying to tell a visitor who may come into that space?

Screenwriters and authors think about the personal space very often when they are developing a character that can be realistic and relatable to an audience. To tell a story effectively, the character has to make sense even when they are not acting. For example, when you watch popular shows like *The Big Bang Theory* or *Seinfeld* or *Friends*, we get used the set and what objects the characters keep in the background. Set dressing is important because it helps us understand the character. From Jerry Seinfeld's cereal boxes to the tchotchkes all over Sheldon and Leonard's room, we know more about the character than what is on the script.

Now, we have to apply that to our own character presentation for the online audience because our eyes wander when we're spending too much time on a screen. Even when you are watching television, you'll sometimes check your phone or multitask with multiple screens. When you're connecting over Zoom, Teams, or WebEx, sometimes you sneak in an alt-tab to switch programs or click one of your many open tabs while you're in a meeting, hoping the person on the other side doesn't see the lighting change. We love distraction and we drift. It's not your fault, it happens to everyone. On the other hand, some people pay too much attention to your setting and over analyze everything on the screen.

Unlike YouTubers who use jumpcuts to motivate the pace or break up the shots, a livestream or Zoom is just one continuous shot for an extended period of time. For the audience members that are really tuned in, remember that they are most definitely looking around the background of the shot. For those of use that don't have the privilege of setting up a custom studio for our live productions, we're likely going to be broadcasting from a fairly intimate space like a bedroom or shared space. The pressure to create a compelling background was somewhat influenced by the Room Rater Twitter account (https://twitter.com/ratemyskyperoom).

Photographer Claude Taylor created the account to judge—sometimes unevenly or unfairly—people's remote settings. Along with his rating, he'll also add some notes as to why the background received the rating it did. This can range from the brick walls to the books to the plants to artwork. For most recipients of a rating, it can be helpful, but to many, it could add to the stress of personal broadcasting. Regardless of how we feel about the @ratemyskyperoom account, we too feel that the background is an important part of the remote production experience.

Aside from the proper shot composition we introduced in the previous chapter, the following are some important tips and suggestions for maintaining an exciting background for your shot. Our main advice is to invest in a quality web camera or connect a DSLR or mirrorless camera with a lens to your computer if you plan on producing virtual presentations more often. The professional camera will give you the ability to control the focus and blur the background nicely without a virtual background. Controlling the out-of-focus parts of the shot is called the "bokeh" and without doing too much work, really upgrades the production quality of your shot.

Like many, you may not have access to a higher-end camera or the technical gear to make it work. In that case, you can build yourself a really nice background.

Books and Bookshelves

What do your books say about you? If you have a collection of books, do you show them on screen? Do people know you well enough to know if a bookshelf is authentic? If you choose to put books in the background, you need to know that if you put the book spines close enough to be read, the viewer will absolutely read what books you have there. Like with traditional television, people will read the text on a screen even if it has nothing to do with the production. When it comes to your personal books, displaying them helps paint a clearer picture of who you are and what you read.

If you really want to make an authentic impression, you should consider what the books say about you. A bunch of fiction books are great because it shows your taste in a certain genre. Non-fiction is a bit of risk because very often people have pre-conceived bias against some authors or the subject matter of the book. We're not saying you should just stick to recognizable books but focus on books that draw out more of who you are.

One advanced tip is to change the books for each unique presentation. This might sound unnecessary but think about it like your resume. When you apply to a job, you should customize your resume to each opportunity as it makes you a far stronger candidate. When it comes to virtual interviews, presentations, or events, the books should reflect the subject matter of content of the production or enable the interview to know more about you. Having books in the shot also helps create conversation opportunities during your interview.

Plants and Flowers

A very easy upgrade for your shot is to add a plant or put a larger potted plant in the background. Plants or flowers break up the shot and make the image more "painterly" and posed. Like an artist making a still life, added a well-placed plant or flower upgrades the shot and adds comfort for the viewer. Plants and flowers, especially healthy ones, tell the audience that you care and have patience. If they are flowers in a vase, it shows how much you care about what's being shown on screen. There's an added level of intentionality that the audience appreciates.

Plants like the fiddle leaf fig became somewhat of a trope during the pandemic because they have large leaves and are fairly easy to take care of (as long as you don't move them too much). Another good choice are adding succulents or flowering cacti to the shot. They're easy to find at almost every home and garden center and stay green even if you forget to water them—but you should water them when they need it.

Artwork and Photos

Like a desk at work, adding family photos helps people see you as caring and connected. In the virtual space, it works similarly, but you should use family photos sparingly. One thing you really don't want your audience doing is looking at your personal photos and analyzing them. Curate the photos you want people to see and think about *why* you want the audience to see them.

With artwork, it's a matter of personal taste. Everyone has a different taste in art and showing it off is part of the reason why even have framed objects. This is the most fun part of building a background as you get to choose what you think will make you happy and how much it will please the audience.

Balance the background if you can. Minimalism always works and a simple piece of artwork can do a lot to balance the room. If you use shelves, you can always space out the art on different levels, adding books, photos, small plants, and tchotchkes.

Adding Spice to the Production

Now that we have the background set up, we can talk a bit about how to be a unique and memorable presenter on screen. These are all optional and are somewhat difficult to do if you aren't use to these techniques, but they add some contrast to the same old sitting and talking shot that everyone uses.

Intentional Pauses

One method to keep attention is to break up your presentation and create spaces for interactivity. Instead of lecturing without a break, plan pauses and restatements in the middle of your talk. If you continue to talk uninterrupted, you may look like a YouTuber. YouTubers have the benefit of not speaking to an audience in real time and you most likely will be live, or at least present for a simulive event.

If the audience is watching you in the background or just listening, a pause in the presentation will cause the viewer to check on the screen or at least perk up. It's kind of like an air conditioner or background noise, sometimes we don't notice the sound until it stops. Not to say that you're just part of the ambient background, but audiences are fickle and get distracted. While you are presenting and you come across a keyword, stop for a moment to let it breathe, then reiterate and explain the keyword. Not only does this help the audience remember the point you were making, it tunes them into the sound.

If this is during a live event, you can use the pause to connect your presentation to the overall theme of the broadcast or livestream. The host will be very thankful for your connection and context and the audience will feel that your talk is part of something bigger.

As you near the ending of your talk, you should pose a rhetorical big picture question to the audience or to the host that may apply what you were saying. Be prepared to create a spontaneous or extemporaneous adjustment to your talk as you notice the questions coming in through the chat or the Q&A box on the application. It means doing your best to multi-task, but remember, being interactive reminds people that you too are paying attention and you're a real person. Taking pauses is a re-connection to yourself, the platform, and keeps the audience tuning in.

Audio and Care

Remember to breathe. As we went over last chapter, your involuntary mechanisms become very apparent when you start thinking about them. You don't think about breathing until you do, then you start to think about it. When we speak on our remote calls, we may feel like we are pressed for time, and we have to get in as much information as possible before it goes to the next panelist. We might run out of breath or feel the need for water or even a cough to clear the throat.

Some virtual software uses a "push to talk" microphone (Zoom for example uses the spacebar) and you can use it to make it seem like a walkie-talkie action. In our opinion, you should be aware of your mute settings and what that says to the other people on the screen.

In a professional setting, staying on mute unless you are speaking is the courteous method. If you need to clear your throat or drink water, people will not hear it. Of course, we may get too comfortable on mute and decide to start speaking while still in mute, taking away time from the show and having the inevitable "you're on mute!" notes from the host or fellow panelists.

One other thing to keep in mind is what the mute symbol signifies to other people. If you don't have something to say, keeping your mute on helps the host know who to go to next for an answer. If you feel you are about to contribute, listen closely to identify the end of a statement or when the host is concluding the question and then unmute. The pre-emptive unmuting tells others you are ready to speak. It's a really nice visual symbol that is extremely valuable in remote presenting that you can't really get in real life—aside from fidgeting in your chair.

Take care to think about audio as you present, it will help you remain professional and prepared for any experience. It takes some practice, but you'll get there.

Moving Around and Standing Desks

Public speakers usually stand when they are giving a talk. The recommendation for educators and speakers is to think of each audience member as though they are watching you through a screen. In real life, this translates to looking at one person for 3–5 seconds before moving your eyes to another audience member or student. (Some presenters look slightly above the eyes of the audience member as there is occasionally discomfort or nervousness when making eye contact.)

When you are virtually presenting through the screen, you can only really look at the green dot or camera lens; there's no switching between audience members. But that doesn't mean you can't create some variation. When it comes to eye contact, we've unfortunately become accustomed to the person on screen not looking us in the eyes. It's because we're looking slightly down to where the other person is on screen. It's tough to remember to keep looking directly at the lens even if there are other people sharing the screen with you.

Some presenters invest in a standing desk or place their computer in a place that allows them to have a bit more freedom of mobility while on camera. Moving around or shifting weight shows that you have a bit more control over the space you are presenting from. Standing while presenting feels more comfortable in the traditional sense of presenting and also shows the audience you are the authority. A quick warning: just as though you may fidget in a swivel chair, try not to fidget too much while standing.

Writing and Responding

One way of seeming interested in the production going on is to take notes but be visible about it. Using a notebook is a really nice way of showing the host or other guests that you are engaged with the topic and eager to learn. From the audience's perspective, you may look like you are randomly looking down at something off screen.

It's been helpful for many speakers to put their notebook closer to the camera, or at least partially visible. If the audience sees your pen moving across your notepad or notebook, they'll see that you are reacting to the material in real time. Investment in the remote production is both visible and mental.

Importantly, your notebook can be a good place to keep your presentation notes and actively using your notebook helps disguise your actions when looking down at the notebook to keep going. The audience will appreciate your preparedness in your presentation.

The Virtual Teleprompter

Finally, there are two pieces of advice on where to put your notes. One variation is to invest in the large post-it notes that can be peeled off and stuck to the wall. Educators and agencies use these quite often. You can write your notes at whatever size is readable from a distance and you can post the large post-it on the wall behind your laptop or web camera. Like actors on *Saturday Night Live*, you can read off your personal version of cue card to keep your notes in the right place.

Another good tip is to write your notes on your computer in Word or in your notepad program like Notes or Notepad. Reframe the Zoom or Virtual Event browser window to the side or lower on the screen at keeping the window of the text near the top of your screen. Make sure you add several blank lines below the lowest part of the text so that you have the ability to scroll further than the end of the text as you are reading it. This turns into your own personal teleprompter, and you can scroll as you are reading. Practice this a few times before going live as reading off the teleprompter takes skill and take steps to scroll smoothly so that it doesn't look like you are reading off the screen.

However you decide to use your notes is up to you, but whichever it works, think about how to be yourself. The audience came to see you, not the performance of you. You are in control of your personal authenticity.

Authenticity in Sum

You'll hear "Be Yourself" over and over during your life, but what that really means, is to home in on what you are to someone else. We should never live our life in fear of how we are judged but we should simultaneously understand the environment in which we are presenting. We all present differently, and we have different abilities. Learn to do the best with who you are and express the skills you have.

Learning the history of authentic presentation helps you identify where you are in the context of media history. Since we're all in the online space now, we can insist that we present ourselves more realistically than in the days where only a few people could be broadcast to the masses.

Watch successful influencers and their methods and practice repeating what they do. You'll likely have many opportunities to do so. Practice new techniques and keep notes on what you did differently and how the audience responded. Each and every time your authentic personality will shine through even brighter!

Notes

1 Goffman, Erving. *The Presentation of Self in Everyday Life*. 1. Anchor Books ed., rev. Ed, Anchor Books, 1990 (p. 72).
2 Wu, Tim. *The Master Switch: The Rise and Fall of Information Empires*. 1st ed, Alfred A. Knopf, 2010.
3 Joseph, Stephen. *Authentic: How to Be Yourself & Why It Matters*. Piatkus, 2019.
4 Zanten, Boris Veldhuijzen van. "There Were 17,000 YouTubes Before YouTube." *TNW | Boris*, 28 Oct. 2013, https://thenextweb.com/news/17000-youtubes-youtube.
5 Raindrops. Directed by Tyler Oakley, 2007. *YouTube*, https://www.youtube.com/watch?v=pIdT_tIPomw.
6 Frier, Sarah. *No Filter: The Inside Story of Instagram*. Simon & Schuster, 2020.
7 Frier, Sarah. *No Filter: The Inside Story of Instagram*. Simon & Schuster, 2020 (p. 83).
8 *Antibodyody Antibody Song - Raven the Science Maven*. Directed by Dr. Raven the Science Maven, 2020. *YouTube*, https://www.youtube.com/watch?v=KBpQg6JMxSc.
9 "Feel like a Fraud?" https://www.apa.org, https://www.apa.org/gradpsych/2013/11/fraud. Accessed 30 Aug. 2022.
10 Rushkoff, Douglas. "Act as If You're Really There." *OneZero*, 16 Mar. 2020, https://onezero.medium.com/act-as-if-youre-really-there-3e6e38dc4d1a.
11 Abadi, Mark. "The Classic Advice to Dress for the Job You Want Has a Major Flaw, and It Could Make a Job Interview That Much Harder." *Business Insider*, https://www.businessinsider.com/dress-for-job-you-want-advice-flaw-2018-11. Accessed 30 Aug. 2022.
12 Ford, Paul. "The American Room." *The Message*, 14 July 2016, https://medium.com/message/the-american-room-3fce9b2b98c5.

4

MULTI-PLATFORM PREPARATION AND PRE-PRODUCTION

Imagine this:

> You've been a cook for years and then out of nowhere one of your recipe videos went viral on Instagram and TikTok. Now you've been invited to be part of NBC's *The Today Show*. They've scheduled you for a 9:35 am live hit where you're supposed to rapidly—and energetically—recreate your recipe for a live audience. The producer tells you that you have to be in the studio at 7 am to go through security at 30 Rockefeller Center, get your guest badge, and make your way to the studios for make-up and prep. It seems like there's a lot of waiting time and you've been told that there's breaking news today so your bit may have to be pushed a little later, but they're glad you made it there early.

Around 8:50 am, the make-up artist asks you to sit down for a quick touch up. They clean up your hair and add foundation to your face. The pancake is to prevent any shininess reflecting off you while on set. There's going to be a lot of lights on you, and they want to make you look good. You go back to the greenroom where other guests are hanging out. The TV on screen shows you the live production, but you're also treated to the raw feed where you get to see behind the scenes during commercial breaks.

On screen between each act, a flurry of television crew reset the stage, slide pieces of the set away, and you see the stage manager joking with the on-screen talent. It's coming to the end of the second hour of the show and you can see them preparing for the lighter part of the program which includes your bit. Your heart starts racing a bit, but a nice associate producer walks and explains to everyone in the greenroom how the next hour will go. The associate producer (AP) has a rundown in their hands which meticulously breaks the show down into all its

DOI: 10.4324/9781003291718-4

elements—when parts begin and end, what camera will be used, what graphics will be displayed on screen, and a long list of names of guests.

You're told to remember that you are the expert, and the audience will be so glad to hear and see you. The schedule is pretty accurate, and you are asked to get ready. They have your recipe already made and ready to remove from the oven, but you're going to prep the first half live. One of the APs with a headset walks to get you and you're brought backstage. There, behind the flats, you can hear the show happening just beyond the plywood and plaster that makes up the set. You can hear how quiet it is and calm. The hosts throw to commercial and in a flurry, you're asked to follow one of the stage managers to the set. The crew is sliding the counter into position and all the cameras are moving. All the cameras are pointed at you.

The hosts walk over and shake your hand and go through some small talk, but your mind is racing and you're trying to keep up, but remembering that you only have a few moments to make this recipe. One of the stage managers tells you where your dish is, one is halfway made in this refrigerator and the finished version is in the oven behind you. Your ingredients are in front of you. Something is missing! You tell the stage manager as you hear "1 minute!" An AP quickly runs over with the missing piece. Relief.

You made this recipe for Instagram and the audience watched in less than a minute—millions of times. But in real life, it took you about an hour to make the dish. Time to make television magic. When people are watching at home, they'll have to be convinced you have it all under control, even under the pressure of the stage manager seemingly immediately telling you to wrap it up and the hosts explaining what you are doing along the way. You get halfway through the prep and from the side of your eye, you can see a stage manager cue you to move to the middle part of the recipe. The host does it for you, a bit awkwardly, but you recover right away, smiling. You can feel the sweat breaking through the pancake make-up.

With the flourish that made your video go viral, you quickly transition to the finished product, proudly pulling it out of the oven and presenting it dramatically to the cameras. The hosts are pleased and ask where they can find you on social media. You're thanked profusely and then, almost as if it never happened, you can see the camera point directly at the host and they throw to commercial. You did it! All the action took place in less than 5 minutes and you're thanked and an associate producer takes you back to the greenroom.

Television Magic

Television is a fairly thankless career. When television is done correctly, no one really notices. The audience only becomes aware of the magic if they notice an error. And in that case, the errors are rare when it comes to how much television is produced. Both the authors of this book are former television producers, and we did a lot of work in multiple forms of television before moving into our careers of education and multimedia production. We worked on everything from live news to reality television to music concerts to reporting in the field.

As you read back in Chapter 3, the history of television has a romantic backstory with people creating the field as it was evolving. When we joined the field of television in the 2000s, the landscape was shifting just like it had in the first years because television was facing new competition from the world of the Internet. New creators were getting as much attention as some of the most famous legacy television personalities. Storytellers had to adapt our methods to the way attention spans were shortening.

But in the end, as you've learned by now, storytelling is at the heart of producing any type of visual and auditory media. If you can compel the audience to stick to the story, you can make television magic.

In our example above, we give a first-person view of what you may encounter if you were invited on a live television show. To us, that experience is like a tunnel through television production. In that example, you'd likely only interact with 5–10% of the television production crew and staff that works shows of the magnitude of *The Today Show*. As we'll learn later in this chapter, behind the scenes on a show like that, there are writers, producers, associate producers, production assistants, set designers, set production assistants, audience coordinators, talent bookers, camera crew, stage managers, lighting designers, lighting crew, electricity technicians, sound technicians, audio engineers, audio assistants, make-up artists, editors, assistant editors, ingest operators, directors, assistant directors, technical directors, commercial directors, and master control operators.

Notice that those roles are plural. On a big show, there would be many people who do each role that go to work each to deliver a smooth production to your television screen in your house. On the other hand, we've both worked on television shows that have an extremely small crew. At home, you may never know how many professionals had a hand in making the show you watch. We've worked on productions where we are the camera operator, the writer, the reporter, the editor, and the audio person all at the same time. Sometimes, the crew is just a few people.

You've probably heard the phrase, "Speed, Quality, Price—Pick Two" at some point. This applies to most of the creative industries. You can have it fast, but it'll be expensive. You can have it high quality, but that will take some time. You can have it cheap, but something will be lost. In traditional media production, we take into consideration much more than what people think about when they are moving their idea to the screen. It takes years to learn, and much of that learning is done through learning from our mistakes.

THE IDEA TO TELEVISION PIPELINE

Likely at least once, you've been sitting with your friends and you thought to yourself: "this would make a great television show!"

Well, let's say that the idea is really great and it actually *could be a great show*. How would you do it?

First, you have to write your script. That's always the most important. But then you have to get it on a producer's desk. How do you do that?

Here's a scenario that includes an example of all the constitutive elements of going from script to air. Keep in mind that most all these parts will cost money and hopefully you find a producer willing to fund the work early.

Simply put, you need your idea to be produced into a pilot (a first episode) and be on a channel or a network to become a series.

It's highly recommended that you find an agent and manager to represent you and get your work in front of a producer or executive producer. What the agent will do is help you create a "package" to bring to the executive producer (EP). A package is a combination of your script with either a producer or a recognizable actor willing to work on your show. If the package is successful, you then need to create something called a "pitch document" to bring to the studios. The pitch document is made with you and your agent and manager to make your idea something someone would want to invest in.

The "studio" refers to what's known as a vertical, meaning the studio has everything from the crew to buildings to producers to the lawyers all employed by the same company. Studios can be different from distribution which is why some shows and films have multiple companies in the credits.

Once the studio is on-board, they're going to want to know how to invest in the project completely, so they'll need a plan which includes your pitch document to the package to your synopsis of your serialized plans and story arc to actors and casting information and locations.

Finally, after all this, you're ready to produce your pilot. The studio books the crew, the space, the locations, and the post-production crew. You watch as your idea is made into the beginning of a television series.

It has one more really important step though before it makes it to the audience—it needs advertisers to support it. (This is different in the new world of streaming networks like Netflix and Amazon, which can make decisions with other strategies than advertiser support. Many of the streaming companies are more interested in new subscribers than advertising support.) There's a yearly event called the Upfronts (https://variety.com/t/upfronts/), where advertisers get to preview the new series that could make it to air. Advertisers represent the legacy of television as a broadcast system. Television is extraordinarily expensive and advertisers support the cost of most of the productions.

Good news! The advertisers loved your pilot! Now you just need to keep the audience entertained for the next few years. No pressure.

Television Is Dead, Long Live Television

You probably don't know, but technically, television no longer exists. Television died in the United States in 2009 and died in the United Kingdom in 2012. But we still watch television, so how does that work? Television is both a technology and a form of media production. Television was invented and distinct from film by its technology and delivery mechanism. The invention of the cathode ray tube and phosphorous raster was called "television" and the technology could be built into a small box that could be placed in someone's living room. It was not a translation of film and theater; it was its own unique medium.

By being a unique medium, television developed its own grammar and codes (as we went over in Chapters 2 and 3). As history advanced, the technology pretty much stayed the same. If you wanted a television, you'd go to the store and buy a large boxy CRT television and put it in your house. This lasted well over 50 years even when new technologies like DLP, plasma, and LCD televisions were becoming available in the early 2000s.

The shift to new television sets and the end of television had two primary reasons. One, LCD technology was rapidly becoming more prevalent and lower cost and the access to these technologies were increasing. Second, the vast proliferation of mobile devices was causing a strain on our broadband spectrum. Mobile phones share their spectrum with radio, television, and transit (airplanes, trucks, trains) communication. There's literally only so much to go around. Television, because it carries such a wide signal that contains over-the-air audio and video, was hitting its limit.

While many people in the United States and United Kingdom were getting their television through cable connections, the majority of people globally still receive their television over the air. The bet was made that the future would be far more invested in mobile technologies and streaming media. In 2006, the United States Congress passed the Digital Television Transition Act to sunset the analog television signal and give the space to high definition television (which takes up much less space) and mobile signal. On the evening of June 11, 2009, the last analog signals were broadcast, and the invention of television was over. From that point forward, you'd need an HD antenna to get signal over the air or a cable box to watch television. Many would opt into the cable box because it also carried the Internet signal.

Television died, and yet, television continues to be a booming industry. In nearly a century, television's form and codes and grammar have enabled the content to outlive the technology in which it exists. Today, when we watch television, whether on Netflix or NBC, we watch on monitors. We may call our LCD screens televisions, but we are consuming media on monitors—computers, mobile phones, and large screens.

What was once an exclusive medium is now a participatory environment and the screen is the delivery mechanism. We now have the ability to produce our own content and have the same access points as many traditional media producers do. Because we recognize that skills, codes, and grammar outlive the technology medium, we want to focus on for the remainder of this chapter is to bring our skills up to the quality of television.

If we're using screens and the grammar is set, there's still room to be experimental within the constructs of media language and production. The important takeaway is that the language of television can be mastered in all your remote production methods and make your work not only successful in a digital environment, but translatable across platforms, screens, and a variety of audiences.

Remote Production: The Third "Location"

Just a few years ago, production occurred primarily in two locations: in the field or in the studio. Today, we have a third location and that is world of remote media production. But, there are still some forms of production that still hold true and the first thing to know is that there are two types of productions: live and pre-recorded.

Live production is when the content being captured on camera is being transmitted to the audience as it happens. Although there is sometimes a slight delay in transmission for safety or streaming, it's pretty much happening as you are watching it. Pre-recorded productions are when the content is being saved to digital media for later distribution to the audience. Pre-recorded content is often edited and can be produced non-linearly, over different times, and allows the producer to create a far more polished presentation.

Studios are facilities that are built solely to accommodate production, the presenters come to the space where equipment and crews are already ready to produce media. Some studios cater to a specific type of production like cooking shows, sports broadcasts, sitcoms, or newscasts. If there's a specific production, the studio is built around the content and every aspect of the space is designed for that type of production. A cooking studio would have an indoor kitchen that is functional yet aesthetically pleasing to the eye. It has proper ventilation, cameras pointed over the top of a counter, and cameras that can get very close to the subject (when filming food, close-up shots stimulate the senses and are the nearest thing the viewer can get to tasting the food).

A news studio might have multiple positions like a desk for anchors to sit and deliver an evening newscast, a couch for a more informal morning show, and a large screen with a map for weather or traffic reports. A sitcom studio is long, has seating for an audience, and a stage with all the sets next to each other. The magic of television makes us think things are different floors, but they're really laid out next to each other.

Field production almost acts like the opposite, flipping the idea of the studio around and the production is mobile and goes to a destination or presenter. Usually, this is done because the content is best served by filming at a specific location that isn't easily replicated in a studio, or because a presenter is unable to get to a studio for filming. Field production ranges from the incredibly streamlined and easy to terribly complex.

Remote production is a hybrid of field and studio production, in that it allows the production to be wherever the presenter is but gives control to the production team to work wherever they are. This saves time, cost, and has many forms. While there are no industry standard terms yet, many production companies break down their remote production setup in tiers. Each consists of the same core model, just with varying levels of complexity.

Breaking Down Production Flow

Any smartphone can live stream from almost anywhere in the world. It's amazing technology that is packed into such a tiny device. What we don't see is all the work that goes into that process.

Whether it's remote, field, or studio, the way we capture and deliver our message is actually pretty similar. A presenter delivers a message, a camera and microphone capture that message, the image and sound is encoded into a signal, the signal is transmitted to a destination, the signal is either received or amplified, and the viewer will receive that message.

For example, a flow could be: **Present > Capture > Encode > Amplify > Decode >Receive**

Present

The most important piece is the presenter, and that's why this book has so much detail on the traits of a great presenter. Your on-camera presenters might be referred to as "talent," "host," "anchor," or something unique depending on the production. No matter the subject matter or production method, without good on-camera delivery, the message will not make it to the audience.

Capture

Your primary camera and microphone might be housed in a smartphone. You may also be part of a multiple camera team with dedicated audio unit, lighting crew, hair and makeup artists, craft services, set designers, and so on. A camera can be any device that has a microchip that gets light and image through a lens, has a device that can record sound, and then convert all that data into millions of pieces of data and digital value that make up all the teeny tiny dots that make up an image. If you've seen a mammoth screen at a sports arena or concert venue or sat way too close to your television, you've probably been able to see the tiny dots that work together to make up the image. These dots are called pixels. A pixel is generally one of the three primary colors: red, yellow, or blue. Using advanced computer interpretation, these three colors can be combined to make up millions of colors.

Encoding

Imagine this:

> You've created a secret code language with your friend. 1 means A, 2 means B, and so on. You want to share your secret code with a friend, so you write

down on paper a diagram that explains 1 = A, 2 = B, 3 = C, and so on. This paper is your algorithm. An algorithm is a set of rules that determine the outcome of a planned computational process. So, when you translate your language into numbers, you are **encoding** and when you are using the algorithm to read the numbers and translate them back, you are **decoding**. This process can be computationalized and made into an efficient set of codes by adding short cuts and helping the machine read it and translate it far faster than a human can. If you have a format for this, it's called a "codec." Codec is a term that combines "code" and "decode."

Encoding is the process of taking the data from a camera and converting them into a streamlined file that can later be decoded. When we watch media on screens, you're actually viewing a codec's presentation of that media. You may not realize it at home because your computer or television is doing the decoding. Most, if not all video codecs, are proprietary depending on the manufacturer and the camera's use-case. Some codecs are designed to use less storage while others are designed for higher quality. Encoding can be done either in the camera or using an external piece of hardware.

The primary reason codecs are used is to help video take up less data space on a hard drive, memory card, or home video tool. The process is called compression and it's a very advanced method to keep file sizes small, but the video still watchable. Using artificial intelligence, codecs can compress video in a variety of ways. There are two primary types of video compression: lossy and lossless. All compression is done through removing redundancy.

Lossless is a method of compressing video or images so that it can fit on a hard drive, but reduced in size. When decoded, lossless video retains all the original data. Lossy means that when the video was compressed, it actually threw out some data to make the file size smaller (usually this is a "faster" codec), but when the decoded, that data is lost forever.

Let's break this down. Let's say you want to film a banana being peeled for the camera in high definition. An HD chip may capture all the light and convert into a full frame. If you are capturing in 1080p, that means the screen is 1,080 pixels by 1,920 pixels—a total of 2,073,600 pixels! That's a lot of data! But the good news is that the codec you are using is really smart. It recognizes that the yellow on the banana peel is repeated at the pixel level thousands of times. The AI "removes" the redundant information—in this case thousands of yellow pixels—and doesn't encode them. But leaves metadata (that's data that refers to data) about what color it *should be* when it decompresses in the decoding process.

Ready to get nerdy? Let's say, just for this purpose, that we want to shoot 1 minute of uncompressed video of the banana. The file would be huge is *every pixel* were accounted for. That minute would be about 3.6 gigabytes big. (We got to that number because one, full size photograph of a banana on an iPhone is about 2 Mb and multiplied that number by 30 for how many frames per second then by 60 for the duration of the minute.) There's no way we can store uncompressed video like that without huge drives and a lot of cooling.

This is where the codec happens. It removes the redundancy. If every, single frame of the footage is the same banana and the lighting doesn't really change, then the codec can remove most of the pixels and replace it with the metadata.

Here's the magic of the codec: when you see the footage on screen, the yellow is put back by the end point (if it's lossless) or told to duplicate the pixels from the uncompressed pixels (if it's lossy). In other words, the codec allows for the transit of the footage to be smaller as a file, but the look great at the destination.

When it comes to live streaming, there is no way that uncompressed video could be streamed through your home router. Most people connect to the Internet with speeds ranging from 5 megabits per second to 25 Mbps.[1] That's not even close to a gig, it's barely one-quarter of one-tenth of a gig per second. The video would stall almost immediately.

For it to work, the codec compresses all the necessary video and gives you the highest quality possible at the fastest speed possible at the lowest file size possible (for that codec). Codecs are the cornerstone of live streaming, and it would not be possible without this technology.

FILES VS. STREAMING

Along the path of production flow, you might encounter multiple codecs, sometimes working at the same time. You might have one codec for recording video to the storage device in the camera, while another codec is being used to convert your camera's live video feed into an Internet-based stream.

While a smartphone might have an encoder built into its software, it is common for professional broadcasters to use a standalone piece of hardware that has only one job and that is to encode the signal and send it to the right place.

When you watch a live stream, you are seeing a hardware encoder compress a file in real time. But it really isn't a file … yet.

All visual content, once converted from light in real life into digital media, exists as raw data. If it's going to a codec, it's just modified data. A stream is a flow of that codec from light to digital data to light once again on the viewer's screen.

Meanwhile, what you don't see is that the stream is being cached in a server, much the way a DVR would work. When the stream is finished, it goes through another codec that puts a container on it. Container files are like.mov,.mp4,.avi, etc. …

When it's a file, it depends how good the streaming codec is when it gets cached is dependent on how high quality the file will be. On most streaming platforms, you will know in advance what file will be produced from your stream and what quality to expect.

Amplify

When you live stream from your smartphone to a platform like TikTok or Instagram, it can take only a few seconds to reach millions of viewers. The work that it took to make that happen is incredibly complex; hundreds of software programmers designing a platform that is easy to use, an algorithm that makes your live stream discoverable, rows and rows of the most powerful computers sitting in an air-cooled warehouse ready to receive, decode, and broadcast your live stream. All of that happens without of having to think about it or do any work—it's amazing. This is amplification, the process of increasing your signal and transmitting it to the masses.

Cloud-based streaming platforms will continue to make this process even easier and reliable. It wasn't always this way. Not too long ago, when a reporter was live from a breaking news story, it wasn't just a smartphone or backpack streaming device. Live TV required a large truck that housed a convex-shaped dish on the roof that had to be pointed directly at a satellite in space, transmitted the video signal through clouds into space, where it would be decoded by a satellite and then beamed back down to earth, where another dish would receive it. This was only a tiny part of the journey of the video getting into a viewer's home.

Decoding

Just as encoding takes the bits of data from the camera and converts them into a compressed video format, a decoder uses the codec to unlock the digital code and turn it back into a video for the viewer. Decoders might be built into a smartphone, or they can be a standalone piece of hardware.

This production flow is amazing when you look at all the steps individually, but it has its downside. Every step along the journey from your presenter to the viewer creates the transmission loss that we explained in Chapter 2. This transmission loss can take away image quality, audio volume and quality, and add delay—ultimately, it can impact the product you want your viewers to see.

When you are sitting across from your friend at dinner, you can have a more intimate conversation where nuances in hand gestures, tone of voice, and projection are picked up easily. When you are FaceTiming with that same friend, your image is constrained to a box on their smartphone screen, limited to the volume they have set on the device, and might be competing with a delay or break-up in signal. Therefore it's important to understand the flow of data and account for it in your production planning.

Why Do We Say "Taped" or "Filmed"?

When discussing pre-recorded content, we sometimes use the term "taped." This is in reference to technology used to record video called videotape. While no longer produced, a videotape is a cartridge that is inserted into a camera and can hold anywhere from a few minutes to hours of content, and then is stored for later archiving and editing. Videotape is similar to a memory card or hard drive that is used in many broadcast cameras today, except that a video tape is linear, which means it cannot store clips but instead video must record in sequence and a user cannot delete portions of the footage—it's all or nothing. Videotapes can be as small as an inch or as large as one foot at its widest point. These tapes stored digital signals on ribbons of magnetic material that resembled adhesive tape—hence the term "tape."

At its peak, videotape was the primary method of recording and playing video content. Broadcasters would carry boxes of video tape in their equipment collection because if they ran out of tape, there was no way to store the footage on-site and re-use the tape immediately like we do with digital storage today.

Prior to videotape, a common method of recording video content was film. This is another linear video capture method that uses ribbons of material that has a chemical reaction from being exposed to light, capturing a series of still images in sequential order. Each still image is called a "frame." When played on a projection device at a high speed, the images appear to animate to the viewer.

Frame Rate

Until digital video capture methods came around, most movies and documentaries were recorded using film or tape. This was incredibly expensive, and directors had to carefully plot out each scene in order to efficiently use their allotted film budgets. Most feature films were, and continue to be, recorded at a rate of 24 frames per second. This is called "framerate," it is the measure of individual images, or "frames" as referenced above, taken within one second. Television and video, on the other hand, is traditionally recorded at a rate of 30 frames per second in the United States and 25 frames per second in the United Kingdom. Now more commonly, 60 frames per second is being used in prosumer cameras.

Due to limitations in broadcast video technology, a lot of broadcasts are presented in 23.98 frames per second instead of an even 24 frames per second, or 29.97 frames per second rather than the even number 30. See the next section for more detail on that, but the important thing to know is that this is an important difference that should be noted when live streaming to some platforms. Most technology is able to work with any and all framerates, but a broadcaster should know what framerate the content will be distributed and then work backwards to ensure that the content is captured and edited in that same framerate, otherwise this could create major technical issues like having audio and video out of sync.

DROPFRAME VS. PROGRESSIVE

Throughout the history of film and video, there have been some technical artifacts that we can never shake. As we learned earlier, television technology is dead, but we still watch television. One of the most interesting artifacts of the past appears when you come across a strange number choice in your video camera. There are these numbers that are close in quantity, but some have decimal points. We know film is 24 frames per second on film and we know television is 30 frames per second on a broadcast, but there's these pesky numbers like 23.98 or 29.97 that are there too. What is that?

Those rates are for whether you want to capture video in drop frame or non-drop frame. Shooting video in the United States is still complicated by the audience's technology to view television. While the CRT television itself no longer exists, many US citizens still have their old boxy television in their house. That television receives (or converts) all video to 29.97.

Here's why: Way back in the day before cable television, television was captured in black and white. As you can imagine by now, black and white video was much easier to transmit across the airwaves. It was a light signal and could be seen on original cathode ray tube that only had one electron gun. The electrons would shoot the phosphors on the raster (the screen) and light up the screen with different values of grey. It happened fast.

What many earlier broadcasters learned the hard way is that sound doesn't behave like video. There are no *frames* in audio. Audio is made of waves. They work in sync, and only if, the video is broadcast (streamed) at the same speed as the sound. With black and white footage, it was! Then color was invented and televisions were sold with three electron guns: red, blue, green. Color was technically slightly slower because it carried a bigger signal. By about 10 minutes in, the audio would be significantly out of sync with the video.

Then came the invention of drop frame. Some brilliant set of engineers out there figured out that if every 106th frame was dropped (every fourth second), no one would notice, and the audio would stay in sync.

With the invention of flatscreen monitors came an end to drop frame rates and the introduction of shutter speeds. Flatscreen monitors (which, as we said earlier are not televisions), display progressive frame rates. Thirty frames per second are 30 frames per second. It's like film where photo after photo is displayed on screen. (It's still compressed, but it's 30 frames per second.) Many cameras now acquire video in 30, 60, 120, and 240 frames per second to create more natural slow motion effects and to match shutter speeds on my high end HD TVs.

If you are faced with the choice still, go with the progressive (whole number) frame rates for Internet video.

Positions within a Live Production Flow

Live video productions can go from the really simple (one person pointing a smartphone at a speaker, streaming it to Instagram) to the incredibly complex (several hundred people on a single location, production trucks, multiple locations with a central control room on the other side of the planet, etc.). No matter the size, the breakdown of the crew putting it together is nearly the same. Producing staff is generally responsible for the editorial content and logistic planning. Directing staff is a general term that we'll use here to categorize the creative team, responsible for executing on the creative vision. Finally, the engineering group is responsible for making sure that the equipment used to capture the presentation is working as needed. In some conditions, all these jobs can fall onto a single person!

Here are some summarized examples of just a handful of positions within a production team:

Producers

Producers are responsible for editorial content and logistics planning. They are the generalists, much the way the general is in a military service. Depending on the production, the producer and the director may have similar power roles in the production process. Producers on larger productions help oversee the story content and the technical logistics like locations, permissions, casting, and travel. Producers on smaller productions can also be the cameraperson, the director, and the editor all in one.

Executive Producer

The executive producer (EP) is often in charge of the money and financial support of the programming. This person will work with the team to create and manage the budget and oversee costs. An EP is also often responsible to make sure that the producing team is staying on track to hit deadlines. The EP might also oversee scripting and have final say on the editorial content. On many productions, the EP is the liaison to the client or distribution company.

Senior Producer/Producer/Associate Producer/Production Assistant

Producers have infinite roles and responsibilities. When someone is a producer, they are managing a specific piece of the production. A producer might oversee coordinating on-camera talent, another might be responsible for the event's music, while another producer might be tasked with ensuring the crew has lunch breaks and that food is available. Believe it or not, some productions can become so complex that people might forget to stop and eat.

Production Manager/Production Coordinator

The production manager (PM) is usually the person that works with the EP to create a budget. A PM will have a contact list of production crews and will make the calls to individual freelance crews to hire them for a project. Production managers will make sure the crew is prepared with the right equipment (rentals, if needed) and that they are paid.

The Creative Team

Directors

There are many types of directors on a production and they are in charge of operating the equipment and actually *directing* the crew to follow through on the vision for a production.

A **creative director** will oversee graphics, visual aesthetic, mood, music, and so on to set the tone for a production.

A **director** for a live production might be someone that instructs the technical crew to push the right buttons and make sure that the right thing is on the screen.

A **cinematographer** and a **director of photography** are people that are responsible for making sure the camera is pointing at the right place, that the lighting matches the vision of the project, and that the presenters are being captured in the intended manner.

A **lighting director** oversees making sure the production lighting is operating as intended by the projects vision, working with the team to set the tone of the project.

A **technical director** on a live production is usually the person that sits at a panel of buttons, called a video "switcher," and will physically control the production by turning on and off the appropriate graphics and camera angles.

The Technical Team

Engineering

Engineering for a live event is crucial. You might have the best camera angle and lighting, but it is worthless if that camera shot isn't making it to the viewer.

A **technical manager** is responsible for overseeing all of the technical aspects of the production flow. It is common for a production to have a technical manager in a control room, where they are communicating with camera operators and engineers in the field or studio to ensure that the signal makes it from the beginning to the end of the production flow. On a production where the presenter is at home on their own laptop, the technical manager will often work with them to make sure the shot looks and sounds good before going live.

IT stands for information technology. The IT team is responsible for computer hardware and software that would work in conjunction with the typical production equipment. IT does not deal with cameras, audio equipment, or lights.

They will ensure that the computers used in a remote production environment are functioning and that Internet access is fully operational.

The above are only a few generalized examples of positions within a live production, there can be hundreds more or, if it's a small crew, just one person to handle it all.

Platforms

A platform is the place where your video will be amplified and distributed to the viewer. There are countless platforms and each has a different use-case. As smartphones and computers become the primary device where consumers receive video content, the core principles remain.

Broadcasting

Broadcasting refers to a one-to-many method of transmitting video content. This refers to a one-way delivery of video from the broadcaster to the viewers at home. The viewer cannot talk back, chat with, or communicate in reverse to the presenter. Television has been the traditional platform where people can consume content until recently. There are four methods for a television to receive programming: over the air, cable, satellite, and "over the top" (OTT).

Over the air broadcasting is the earliest method of distributing a television signal. A broadcast station in a local TV market has an antenna. An antenna is a metal device that is connected to an encoder. The antenna takes the encoded data and amplifies it using radio waves. Radio waves are pulses of electronic signals that can carry for dozens of miles. The radio waves are received by an antenna within a TV set or on the roof of a home or tower, they are decoded back into a video signal and shown on the television. Over the air video is free and in most countries are regulated by a government agency.

Cable television is encoded by a private company and uses wires run underground or through power lines directly to the viewer's home or office. The viewer plugs a decoder box into the cable wire to display the programming on their TV set.

Satellite television is encoded by a private company that uses directional radio waves pointed at a satellite in space from a large convex dish on the ground. The viewer at home then points a smaller convex dish (usually roof-mounted) at the satellite and can watch TV using a decoder provided by the satellite company to watch the programming on their TV set.

Over the top (OTT) television programming comes in many forms. It is programming that can be viewed over the Internet and displayed on a TV set. Smart TVs allow for apps to be installed directly for many OTT networks. Alternatively, a viewer can use an external device, such as a Roku or Apple TV, to view OTT programming. Some viewers will stream OTT programming on their smartphone or tablet and then beam it to their TV set using screen casting, which uses WiFi to share the video from the handheld device to the TV set.

Multidirectional (Cloud-Based Video)

Cloud-based video streaming is quickly replacing traditional video broadcasting methods. This is due to the advancement in encoding technology and the availability of reliable high-speed Internet access.

The term "cloud" refers to any computing that is done outside of the individual users device or away from the broadcaster's facility. Cloud computing is generally a "farm" of computers that are located in one or multiple locations and are maintained by a cloud provider who's sole job is to make sure that system is running efficiently and around-the-clock. Some examples of cloud providers are Google, Apple, Microsoft, and IBM. These companies store your photos, documents, and videos in multiple locations with backup copies on servers that are monitored 24/7 by engineers. Not long ago, individuals had to store their own media on storage devices within their home, making them susceptible to fire, water damage, or theft—that is no longer an issue thanks to cloud computing. With cloud computing, video can be streamed to viewers at little or no cost, with minimal equipment. What is more exciting is the addition of multidirectional communication that the cloud makes available, such as text commenting, video talkback, and clip-sharing.

Video Conferencing—Bidirectional

Video conferencing platforms are integrated into every smartphone or tablet today. FaceTime and Google Meet are two examples of this. More robust platforms such as Zoom, Webex, or Skype are often used in business or educational settings. These platforms require little encoding to be done on the local device, with all the "heavy-lifting" done in the cloud. As we've learned, this allows for more people to connect and has really democratized communication in the post-COVID world. Video conferencing platforms are bidirectional, meaning that all parties can participate equally in a conversation.

Video Content Networks—One-Way or One-to-Some

Video content networks are an easy and inexpensive way for producers to host recorded content and stream live video. Some examples of this are YouTube, Vimeo, and TikTok. These platforms allow content producers to choose the level of interactivity they want to have with the viewer by enabling comments, reaction videos, or clip sharing. This gives the creator the option to have a more traditional broadcast model (one-to-many), to limit visibility to a private group of company (one-to-some), or to open conversation with the viewer (bidirectional).

Webinar—One-Way with Bidirectional Functionality

A webinar platform is very similar to the above but adds more control for the content producer. Video conferencing platforms such as Zoom Webinars or

On24 allow a producer to control exactly how much the viewer can participate in the broadcast. For example, a platform might allow the option for live polls, open chat, and for viewers to turn their camera on and ask a question of the presenter.

Some producers prefer to keep their content more scripted and controlled, due to timing or sometimes legal purposes. To encourage a bidirectional communication with the viewer, these producers might use a moderated chat rather than open. Moderated chat is a chat window that only the producer can see and will select which questions/comments are visible to the rest of the audience. Another option for more control might be to offer a "hand raise" option for questions from the audience. This allows the producer to talk to the audience member prior to joining the live broadcast (perhaps in a private chat) and make sure that their question is relevant and contributes to the broadcast.

Producing Quality Media

Components of a Good Video Shot

Whether you're recording a feature film or streaming a live TikTok, the basics are the same: audio, lighting, and framing.

Audio is the sound captured by a camera or external microphone. Depending on the number of speakers and distance from the camera, your audio setup will vary. Audio also varies depending on the type or production—music, for example, requires specific microphones that are designed for instruments. There are several options for microphones as well. A lavalier, or lapel, microphone is clipped onto the speaker's clothes and is ideal for interviews or presentations. A boom or shotgun microphone is placed out of the camera's view and can capture multiple speakers at once. There is a wide variety of mics out there to suit the needs of your production and choosing the right one is important.

Lighting is dependent on the vision of the production. If a simple speaker in on camera delivering a message to camera, you'll likely want even lighting on the subject using three points of light; a "key" light that is positioned to highlight the subject, a "fill" light that is positioned to fill in any shadows created by the key light, and a "backlight" to separate the subject from the background. If the production requires mood lighting to emphasize a tone or will be used to enhance a performance, the lighting will certainly be more complex.

Framing is the positioning of the subject within the cameras view. "Frame" describes the cameras view as if it were a picture within a frame. Depending on the subject matter and vision for production, the framing may be simple or complex. Simple framing will have your subject centered on the camera's "frame" looking into the camera's lens, while some interviews might have a subject looking slightly off-camera and be positioned just off-center.

THREE-POINT LIGHTING

Lighting is what separates basic production from high-end production. A simple set of lights, strategically placed, can completely change how an image looks on screen and enhance the video quality. The classic lighting style is known as three-point lighting.

Three-point lighting is two lights in front of the subject on camera, and one in the back. The reason we do this is to create depth on screen. Not only is there transmission loss with media that appears on your screen, but the depth is almost completely removed by the way cameras and lenses capture video. (On higher-end cameras, you can adjust the iris [f-stop] to open the lens more creating a blurry background [called a "bokeh"] to create faux depth without too much lighting.)

The two lights in the front should be on either side of the subject—45 degrees away from center. One should be brighter than the other, so the subject's face looks three-dimensional. The back light should be behind the subject and at 45 degrees pointed to their shoulders. The shoulders will light up and there will be depth and separation of the subject from the background. Note that 45 degrees (90 degrees is directly ahead, 45 is halfway there) is used for all three—that kind of makes this easy to do.

The best lighting you can do is in front of a window though to create a nice, soft light for your face. Beyond that, a simple ring-light will do the trick as well. If you have the room, you should add a backlight. You'll see a huge difference.

Remote Production Scenarios

We have now explained the various components to live production flow, the personnel that make it happen, and the components to a good camera shot. Now, we're going to look at some examples of a remote production setup, from the basic one-person-operation to a more complex production. Remote production may be a broad term, but for the most part it can be defined as a method of capturing content, live or recorded, where the presenter is in a different location than the producer.

Basic Remote Production

Basic remote production is the most common tier of capturing content remotely. This requires no equipment other than a consumer-grade smartphone or computer. A producer will use a cloud platform, such as Zoom, to connect with the presenter and record the content. Platforms such as Zoom offer internal recording features that might be limited, so many producers will use an external recording device to capture higher-quality video and audio. This is because platforms like Zoom, Google Meet, and WebEx use heavy compression in their recording encoders since the majority of users of these platforms don't care as much about recording in top quality.

The advantage of this basic remote production method is that it is simple. In video production, keeping things simple can be priceless, especially when working with a presenter that might not know anything about production. Sometimes your talent is a CEO or a thought leader on a subject. You cannot rely on them to know as much as you do as the producer. You also don't want to put added pressure on them to install fancy software that requires many steps to set up. This takes them away from what's important—getting the message across. When evaluating your options for production, don't forget the mission—use the method that best serves your audience.

Supplemented Remote Production

This method adds a few extra touches to the basic approach to make the production team happy, but also doesn't overwhelm your subject with a lot of equipment to set up. In this scenario, the subject is sent a USB webcam and lavalier microphone along with a single light to place on their computer or desk. You'll still connect with them using a traditional method (Zoom, Google Meet, FaceTime, for example), but supplement their computer's limitations with higher-quality picture and sound.

When you have the time to plan the logistics for this type of production, it's well worth the cost. In fact, the cost of a webcam, light, and microphone might be cheaper than the return shipping. In many cases, it's worth sending these items directly to them from an online retailer that offers free shipping and letting your presenter keep them after the presentation as a "thank you" gift.

Store and Forward Remote Production

When a production does not need to be live, Store and Forward it a great option to ensure higher quality than basic remote production while still maintaining a simple user experience for your presenter.

The term "store and forward" refers to a method that involves the smartphone, tablet, or computer to both record the video locally on the device at top quality while simultaneously streaming a lower-quality video for live interactivity with other presenters and the producing team. The video file begins uploading while it is still being recorded, it is *storing* the file on the device while simultaneously *forwarding* it onto the cloud. In the event of a signal drop, the file is still stored on the device for later uploading. This method can also be supplemented with a webcam, light, and mic to increase quality. There are a number of platforms that use this method such as Riverside.fm, Zencastr, LiveU, and AviWest.

Remote Production Kits

Prior to the 2020 pandemic era, there were few options for kits that were sent to presenters for remote production. Most of these options were geared toward high-end broadcasters or corporate video, with a price tag around $10,000. Once the pandemic hit the world, innovation kicked in and production companies around the globe began to develop solutions for all budgets.

Here are just a few samples of remote production kids that solve a specific need.

Quicklink

Geared toward broadcasters that will be on camera many times and need an at-home or portable setup that will be controlled remotely by a professional crew. The Quicklink kit has a teleprompter screen, lavalier microphone, light, and a PTZ camera. A PTZ camera is a camera that can remotely be controlled and can "pan, tilt, and zoom," hence the letters PTZ. This unit can be deployed relatively easily for "talking head" content (when a presenter is sitting on camera and does not need to move around).

Sorrentino Media Remote Production Kit

This kit is designed to be sent to a presenter that will do only one or two on-camera projects. The idea is that the kit is easy to use with a familiar interface and is small enough to ship to the presenter and then packed up and returned. Using a technology called "cellular bonding," this setup can be remotely operated and acquire high-quality video that doesn't rely solely on the presenter's home Internet. Cellular bonding is a technology that will combine multiple Internet connections into one super-fast pipeline. A presenter will connect one of the included smartphones to their home WiFi, the software will combine that with the devices cellular broadband to create a reliable connection. The kit is also ideal for talking-head content and includes two smartphones, a flexible LED light panel, lavalier mic, and stand.

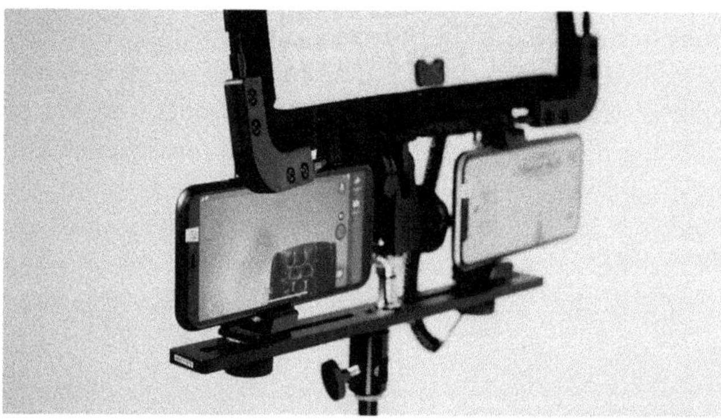

FIGURE 4.1 Sorrentino Media Remote Production Kit

FIGURE 4.2 Sorrentino Remote Production Kit

Hayden5 Drop Kit

Hayden5 is a production agency that responded quickly to their clients needs in the early days of the 2020 pandemic. This kit is designed for high-end commercial productions that require a cinematic look and camera movement. The drop kit is delivered to a presenter's home or office, is assembled by a local crew member just outside the door, and the presenter just needs to wheel the cart into the building. It is remotely controlled and features a 4K cinema camera with PTZ movement, and cinema lighting along with wireless audio.

These are just a few examples of kits that are available on the market today for sale or rent. The best part is that the technology is out there and the options are endless—if you can't find a solution that fits your needs, build it!

Hybrid Remote Production

As things opened up following the initial shock of the pandemic, presenters began to feel more comfortable allowing a small crew into their homes, such as a camera operator and audio technician. While it has become commonplace following the pandemic, hybrid remote production is not entirely new. In fact, news organizations were using a scaled down approach back in the late 1990s, early 2000s. For example, a news producer would send a trusted camera crew to the home of an interview subject. Using a device made popular by a company called Gentner, the audio technican could connect the on-camera subject's microphone to a telephone line, allowing the producer to conduct the interview remotely.

Today, we are able to use cloud-based video platforms like Zoom or Google Meet along with the on-site camera crew to see and hear the subject (and vice versa) using an encoder that takes a video feed directly from the professional camera. The advantage of this method is that you get a professional camera team on location to ensure top-quality and taking the production pressure off the presenter, while the producer can remotely have visibility into the cameras framing, lighting, and audio quality.

Some Things to Consider When Choosing the Right Remote Approach

There are countless options for remote production, each having its own benefits and limitations. The key is not to remove the complexity of production, but to *move* the complexity from the presenter (who should be focusing on the message delivery) to the production team, so the more of the "heavy lifting" you can do remotely, the better. Here are some things to consider when weighting your options:

Content

What is the vision of the production? Does it have a more informal feel or a more cinematic approach? Who will be watching this and how will they watch? Does high-quality matter when most people will be watching on a low-bandwidth connection? Try to think about what's important: the message. Don't let production get in the way of telling the story.

Connectivity

Spend some time, if possible, with your presenter in advance of the recording or live stream. Get to know the locations pros and cons. If their Internet connectivity is limited, you might want to go with an approach that includes pre-recording their content using store and forward, or with a cellular bonding method. Try to think about the time of day when you'll be working with them—Internet connectivity can vary depending on who is online at home and the time of day.

Lighting

In your preparations, consider what lighting is available in the presenter's home. What time of day will you be filming with them? Can you use natural light from a window? Do you need to consider supplementing with more lighting?

The Presenter

Not everyone is a tech guru. Even the CEO of a tech company might not be the most knowledgeable in camera angles and webcams. Think about that presenter and try to get a read from them on what their expectations and limitations are from a production standpoint. If they are on board to spend an hour playing with lights and moving the camera around—great! Or will you only have them for 10 minutes before your live stream? In that case, you'll want to play it safe and keep it incredibly simple. Remember, they are the presenter, not the production crew. They should focus on the message, not the delivery platform.

Remote Education and Unique Approaches

Possibly the people most impacted by the rapid shift to online production and virtual presenting were students. Nearing their Spring Break in 2020, many students all over the world were told they'd be taking two weeks off to "flatten the curve." As it became obvious, a pandemic doesn't play by easy to manage rules in a globally connected world.

Without warning, teachers were expected to "figure it out." To their credit—most did!

There's been guide upon guide to help educators modify their lesson plans to accommodate successful online learning and we won't repeat those here, but we will provide some tips for making the virtual classroom unique.

Interactive Courses

Many courses translated fairly easily to remote production like humanities courses or science courses without labs. But what if you taught television or film production? What about ceramics or pottery? How did art classes work?

When it comes to making remote production work in these settings, the challenge was to make the education as rigorous as in-person classes, but remotely. This was the time for many teachers to experiment with the modes of production we've considered throughout this text. Media classes could switch to remote media production and pseudo virtual events—there's an entire pedagogy to be explored in which we hope this book can be useful to those educators.

If you were teaching courses that required a bit more space and display, some investments should be made in wide angle web cameras and modified camera equipment.

During the pandemic, GoPro, the action camera company, released new software that allowed users to turn their GoPro into a webcamera. GoPros have pretty decent audio and an ability to offer ultra-wide camera angles and narrow angles. If you are teaching practical education, like arts and film, you may need more than just your upper body seen on screen, and GoPro afforded this.

Prioritize Audio First

As you are preparing your virtual course, think about audio before you begin anything else. As we've learned as producers: *Ears don't blink.*

Students and participants will always be listening, but they may get visually distracted. If your audio is muddy or distorted, people may tune out. Practice with intonation and pauses and timing in your audio to keep attendees interested. Invest in a podcast mic or a directional "shotgun" mic for the top of your camera. Perhaps a lavalier kit is best for you. Regardless of what you choose, make sure to test the audio on the stream or on the recording before you start.

Camera on a Rolling Tripod

In the film industry, we call them dollies, but you can make your own by taking your tripod and taping it or using a bungee cord to attach it to a rolling chair. If you have the room to teach, you can roll the camera away and closer. You can even tie a string to the chair to pull the camera closer when you need to speak to the class.

Optimizing Zoom to Layer Up the Experience

Zoom allows you to use your slides as a virtual background (more on that next chapter) and if you set up your space with a green screen, you can make your deck the background. It will look a lot like weather reporters on television and allow you to move around your deck and point out things with your actual body rather than with the mouse.

If you want to get even more creative, you can use a document camera to share using the second camera sharing feature in Zoom. You can than show the contents of a book or do close ups of artwork or machinery or crafts without changing or moving your primary camera.

The Mobile Laptop Stand

Entire industries for remote work appeared during the pandemic, and one of which was really impressive: the flat top laptop holder for a tripod. This allowed people to use their laptop anywhere a tripod could be set up. You can make your own.

Tripods occasionally come with additional plates (or shoes) that connect the camera to the tripod. You take a small piece of wood the size of your laptop and attach it to the plate with a power drill or you can use wood glue or super strong Gorilla Glue (be careful) to attach the plate to the wood or platform you choose.

This allows you to move the tripod with the laptop around when you teach. You can easily change angles and height depending on what you need to do with it.

Selfie Stick Teaching

If you need to have more angles at the touch of a button, using a selfie stick with a camera mount could be useful. Attach your web camera to the end of the selfie stick and use it to extend or shorten the angles you may need to show things close-up or far away. Just be careful with how shaky you may be because you don't want to make the students dizzy.

POV Arts

Back to the GoPro. You can attach your GoPro or web camera to a head-mounted strap to show students your point of view. This is extremely useful if you are teaching a practical course like art, fashion design, machining, or pottery. While students may not have the access to making their own work in a remote setting, they can still learn technique from your POV angle.

In several machining and engineering courses, faculty used this method to show how their hands operated certain machinery. Thanks to the ability to record the class sessions, often this became as useful as in person class as they can see how to operate their equipment or learn specific techniques from the angle that they would be able to see it from.

Multicamera Switching

If you are up to it, you can add additional camera inputs using more camera devices and switch between angles by choosing different cameras in the Zoom controls. These angles can be pre-set up to show close-ups, certain details, important angles, or just a different view of the instructor.

If you want, you can invest in small HDMI switcher like Blackmagic's ATEM switcher. You can add several HDMI inputs which outputs as a single input and switch manually. This can also be used in a shared screen setting, enabling you to share multiple screens from one monitor input.

Virtual White Boards

Zoom has an interesting feature that has proven helpful to some faculty: the White Board. It's exactly how it sounds, but somewhat hard to use. Zoom lets you launch a white board drawing space to "draw on the board" so to speak. We suggest you invest in a stylus pen in addition to your mouse so you can write smoothly on the board.

You can also get a portable white board or use large post it notes with an erasable marker part to put in the background.

Accessibility

Real time captioning is getting better every day. You should enable this option as much as possible. Speak clearly and enunciate and the artificial intelligence will caption far better than you may imagine. Remember for those who may be sight impaired, you should remember to keep the text on the screen large and readable for at least 3–5 seconds. If you are on-camera, make sure your lips are visible to the audience so people may be able to read your lips.

If you are adding graphics or using a physical white board, be sure to write clearly and post images with high contrast (meaning sharper than they should be) so users with different video resolutions can still read or see what is on screen. Access isn't just about ability, it's about care.

Watch Parties

If you are teaching a film studies course or showing films in your course, you can use streaming software like OBS to stream a film into your course. By using the

OBS software (which is fairly hard to learn), you can create split screens to point certain scenes out or add educational criticism.

On the other hand, many apps support their own watch parties. Many are text only, but the option is better than nothing. Netflix, Hulu, and Amazon all have features to have simultaneous viewers on one stream.[2] On the downside, you'll need a subscription for most of this content.

Be Creative

We are in the nascent days of learning how to make education work in virtual settings. You can't really get it wrong at this point. Focus on outcomes assessments and be transparent with your students about your experimentation. Ask for their feedback often and listen carefully to their ideas.

From an educational perspective, we can say that finding the core of your education and focusing on that is more important than throwing everything into a virtual class. Students will learn more and remember what they learned longer if you focus the education on specific core concepts rather than just convert the in-person course to a virtual setting. The world online is different and unique—treat it that way.

A GUIDE FOR CLIENTS AND PRESENTERS ON THE HOME SETUP

To better prepare you for your recording date, please closely review the following information. Most of these guidelines will help you get the best image for production and get you looking your best!

Choosing a Location

When deciding on a spot to film it is always our goal to try to convey depth (video is flat but it doesn't have to feel flat). Here are some tips to achieve that:

- **Avoid** shooting in front of a blank/plain wall
- **Avoid** physically putting yourself up against a wall if possible
- **Avoid** having a very bright window in the background
- **Be cognizant** of how loud you/your surroundings are! We need to be able to hear you clearly! Find a relatively quiet place to film
- **Mute** notifications on your devices!

An ideal setup would be a location where you are facing in front of a large window (window behind the camera, not behind you). In a quiet room (or semi-private space). With a good amount of distance behind you and your background. It is important to take a look at what is behind you and make sure it fits the project you are filming. Try to make sure there are no distracting elements or things you would like to keep private. Some examples: bright objects, water bottles, family pictures, important documents, identifiable landmarks. Obviously if the background makes sense for the mood/tone the project is going for, items like family pictures or identifiable landmarks may be fine/desirable.

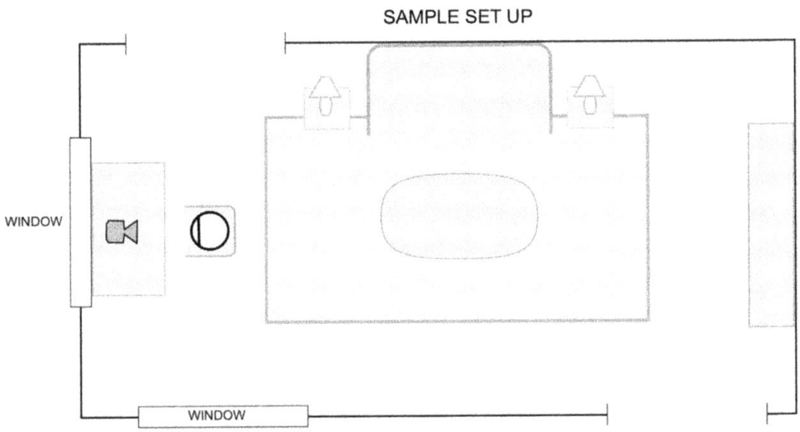

FIGURE 4.3 Correct setup for indoor presentation—courtesy Omar Lopez

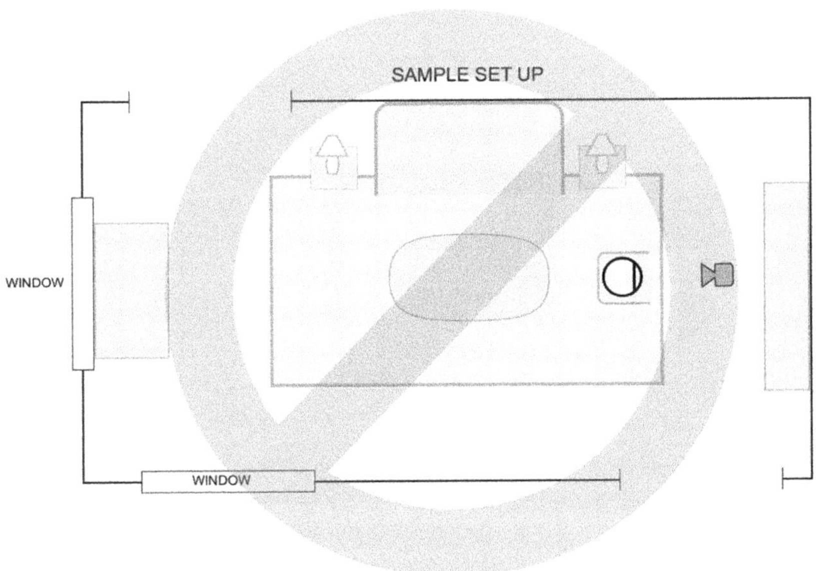

FIGURE 4.4 Example of an incorrect setup for indoor presentation—courtesy Omar Lopez

Shooting Tips

If using a phone:

Do not turn or change the position of the phone during filming.

Camera should be eye-level or slightly above, so that it is even with your face. You are aiming to have the camera slightly above your natural eyeline. **Please use a tripod to hold your phone or place your phone on a stable surface.**

Lighting (natural, indoor, or video) should be facing you, have the light shining into your face, not your back. Try to keep the light even so you don't have a dark shadow on either side of your face.

Avoid having bright light in your background or facing your back. Shooting with the sun, a window, or bright lighting source behind you can cause you to look like a silhouette.

Avoid wearing extreme shades like all white or all black. Phones and laptops make numerous auto adjustments to make us look good. When we wear all white or all black, it becomes more difficult for the phone to make those adjustments. **Try to avoid** wearing a color similar to your background, if you have a grey wall in your home and wear a grey outfit it may cause issues. Try to aim for contrasting colors!

Remember everyone's homes are different and these are just tips to make the best decisions possible. Hopefully all these guidelines are clear and concise so you can have a successful shoot!

FIGURE 4.5 Example of correct setup with a cellphone—courtesy Omar Lopez

FIGURE 4.6 Example of an incorrect setup with a cellphone—courtesy Omar Lopez

FIGURE 4.7 Example of correct setup with a laptop—courtesy Omar Lopez

FIGURE 4.8 Example of an incorrect setup with a laptop—courtesy Omar Lopez

Notes

1 Antonelli, William. "What's a Good Internet Speed? How to Upgrade Your Internet Setup to Fit Your Needs." *Business Insider.* https://www.businessinsider.com/guides/tech/what-is-a-good-internet-speed. Accessed 30 Aug. 2022.

2 Ashworth, Boone. "How to Host a Virtual Watch Party." *Wired.* www.wired.com, https://www.wired.com/story/how-to-host-a-virtual-watch-party/. Accessed 30 Aug. 2022.

5

VIRTUAL EVENTS, WEBINARS, LIVESTREAMS, AND CALLS

The Production of Remote Media and Virtual Presenting

This chapter will focus on the different ways we can produce media remotely and excel and virtual presenting. The following is a guide to the many modalities of producing media in our virtual world. This chapter will start from the small and manageable and scale to a guide on how to produce a virtual event that can host thousands of attendees and provide your keynotes and key opinion leaders with the trust in your project or organization.

You made it through the book learning basics on presenting, how to be authentic in the world of media, and how to excel at preproduction. Now, it's time to put all these points together and create a memorable production that will have people telling their friends about it for years to come. Producing online media or remote production is unique as we're still in the early stages of defining what qualifies as a successful virtual event or remote production.

This type of production is distinct from traditional media production and should be celebrated for that fact. We don't want to recreate television; we want to make something that people can attend and feel like they are part of the project and have a say in its outcome.

It's a double-edged sword when you create a remote media production: you have to use the grammar of traditional media to keep the audience engaged, but you need to enforce online personality authenticity throughout. It's a hybrid media environment that is exciting, new, and open to interpretation. What we set out to explain here is the structural basics that absolutely work and note some experimental projects that we've produced and encourage you to try. You do not have to incorporate everything in one production, and you shouldn't (that would be crazy), but think different when you make your production.

DOI: 10.4324/9781003291718-5

Finally, remember that nearly every production we talk about for the rest of this chapter is a collaboration where you may need to take a leadership role. If you're reading this book, you've already taken an interest in making your productions better and more engaging.

We'll start with some universal pieces of technical and production advice before we get into each part of virtual presentation tools in the remote media production landscape. These are as comprehensive as we can imagine, but the software does consistently update and introduces new ways to think about our projects. This is just the beginning!

Registration, Attendance, and Leads

Before we get into the details of how many of these productions are built, we need to go over some of the boilerplate parts of remote media production and virtual presenting. Some topics of forethought include registration, audience attendance, and marketing leads.

Why start here? Well, one key difference between traditional media and remote media production is your ability to have access to data, metrics, and key information almost immediately. If you want to know your success metrics in traditional media production, you have to wait for the distribution companies to aggregate data or Nielsen to inform you of the ratings. Another key point is that remote media production often works hand in hand with the sponsor or advertising agency who helps to subsidize the project.

Registration and Data

What data do you want to collect from your attendees and why? What good does the data do? What do you want to give to the client? Should the data be an additional cost? Are you creating a future mailing list?

Consider these questions before you begin your registration page. Most virtual and remote media production software comes with its own proprietary registration page, but we also have used Eventbrite or third-party registration products. The upside to using the registration page that is supplied by the software is that it automatically creates the link path for the attendee to register and keeps the attendance limited to the number of registrations that you have designated. As we'll read later, some platforms limit the number of attendees based on price tiers and you don't want to go over the limit.

If you are charging for your event, sometimes the platform may take a cut of your earnings when the attendee registers. This is the case with many third-party registration tools as well as they need to support their own system. You may use a company-specific registration form, but you need to know how to export your list and import it into the platform properly.

When it comes to data, you need to be very clear about what data needs to be collected for you and the client and how the data will be used. We live in a time where you must be aware of the limitations of your data and the international laws that regulate people's private information. For example, you should become familiar with the European Union's (EU) General Data Protection Regulation (GDPR) (https://gdpr-info.eu/) and their compliance requirements. This will help you protect yourself and the client. For the sake of safety, all registration forms should consider adding a radio button that allows the registrant to opt-out of data re-use.

Importantly, you, your company, or your client may be very interested in collecting a lot of information from the registrant, but with longer registration forms, you risk some attendees opting out. Every click and piece of questionable data collection may be considered a "barrier to entry" for some and reduce your registration rate. Make the following part of your discussion.

- Minimum Data Requirements
    - At the very least, you'll want to collect first name and last name and email address. Usually, these are built into the system, so you don't have to worry about it, but double check.
    - Many companies are very interested in geographic data especially because virtual productions are accessible nearly anywhere the Internet is (barring regulatory exceptions). A zip code or postal code is the most valuable piece of information, but you should also include state and city.
    - You only need to collect home addresses if you plan on adding their data to a physical mailing list or want to send the audience a gift for attendance. Collecting home address data may be considered intrusive and personal and may be a barrier to entry.
- Company, Education, and Title data
    - Typically, a registration form will have the space for "Organization" rather than company as its a more agnostic question and allows the registrant to put down their school if they are a student.
    - Depending on the level of your speaker, keynote or key opinion leader and your subject matter, you may be interested in where the registrant works as well as their job title. In many cases this data will help you understand *who* is interested in your project and at what level.
        - If you have an abundance of students attending, you can tell that your project is good for those learning in the field.
        - If the data shows the registration of high-level and C-Suite executives, you can tell that your production is being shared in spaces and networked and generating high-level interest
    - This data helps inform the level of approach for your production and what access point may be necessary for the host or MC of the show to take.

- This data is good for marketers to see where their audience is generally coming from.
- Some producers work with teams that require more distinct information and most registration forms allow for customization and drop-down choices. You may want to create subsections of data for the registrant to choose from rather than input their own information.

- Photos and avatars
  - Photos are extremely helpful for the networking portion of the event and are genuinely recommended for the registration process.
  - The benefit of a photo is to also weed out any trolls or attendees that may be acting in bad faith.
    - This is rare (and we'll go over this issue in the "Warnings to the Wise" section) but in practice, adding a photo to the registration page encourages a thoughtful process in registration.
  - Avatars have been used more frequently in virtual event software that have an immersive or virtual networking component. Avatars are sometimes customizable and add a fun interactive element to the registration process. Like building a character for a video game or customizing a Bitmoji, registrants feel some ownership over their virtual appearance.
    - An added component of using an avatar in registration is for a registrant to feel more comfortable as their virtual avatar may feel more authentic than their actual appearance.
- Custom Questions
  - Most registration forms will not be super specific. If you are using the registration form to generate sales leads with your team, you may be seeking additional data. Be aware of barriers to entry and compliance issues.
- Disclaimers
  - On livestreams and small-scale productions, most people are just interested in being there. If you are **ever** going to reuse the data or use the data for sales leads, you **must** put a disclaimer on the registration form. This will save you many headaches later. It can be a simple disclaimer acknowledging that the data will be kept (or even acknowledging it will be removed) and used for research purposes or it can be a note that says it helps you improve future productions.
  - Your company likely has a legal team or human resource official who may be able to navigate this murky water and you should incorporate this into your production discussion.

- In the EU, this is mandatory with all data collection because of GDPR. If you are broadcasting and including a global audience, a disclaimer is highly recommended.

- Opting out
  - On any registration form where you are collecting data, you should include a radio button with language that provides the registrant to request their data be destroyed after the production.
    - Many companies have software that enables them to safely (see: encrypted) store and destroy data. Be sure to discuss this with your team.
    - Destroying data must be certain and your IT department is typically aware of this.
    - If you are a small business without software and IT, consider investing in a secure data tool.

GDPR

In 2018, a long-term project regarding user privacy and data was completed in the European Union, the political union of 27 countries on the European continent. Along with the shared currency, the union enables citizens to travel freely between countries and access the Internet through a source that connects the collective population.

Many of our laws and regulations that control rights, copyright, and privacy in the United States were written in the 1990s. The same was for many European countries. In a years-long project, the EU developed an update to these regulations with their General Data Protection Regulation (GDPR). The GDPR comprises 99 articles and, in the EU's terms, "harmonizes" data privacy laws across the continent.

For the most part, GDPR is a protection around personal data. Personal data may include everything from your IP address to your personal information. As Matt Burgess writes in a Wired magazine article, personal data can be, "information about racial or ethnic origin, political opinions, religious beliefs, membership of trade unions, genetic and biometric data, health information and data around a person's sex life or orientation."[1] Burgess clarifies that "the crucial thing about what constitutes personal data is that it allows a person to be identified—pseudonymized data can still fall under the definition of personal data."

Many people often take their personal data for granted, not often thinking about what their privacy means and how their data is used. Most of us are aware that websites contain cookies that are downloaded on our computer, but don't have the slightest idea what those cookies do. Usually, the cookies are designed to help websites remember you next time you visit, but they also may glean data from the other cookies in the folder—including data of your browsing history, what you clicked on, where you went, and how long you stayed on the site.

This data is sold over and over as you use social media to customize the ads you see on the platform. It learns what you *may want to purchase* by seeing your history and comparing it to everyone who has a similar history like yours. Does this sound invasive? Well, that's why regulators are interested in making sure you are not exploited.

Beside technical data like cookies, GDPR is also concerned with data transparency, accuracy, and long-term storage and your right to have your data deleted.

Here is Article 5 of the GDPR "Principles relating to processing of personal data":

1. Personal data shall be:
    1. processed lawfully, fairly, and in a transparent manner in relation to the data subject ('lawfulness, fairness and transparency');
    2. collected for specified, explicit and legitimate purposes and not further processed in a manner that is incompatible with those purposes; further processing for archiving purposes in the public interest, scientific or historical research purposes or statistical purposes shall, in accordance with Article 89,[2] not be considered to be incompatible with the initial purposes ('purpose limitation');
    3. adequate, relevant and limited to what is necessary in relation to the purposes for which they are processed ('data minimisation');
    4. accurate and, where necessary, kept up to date; every reasonable step must be taken to ensure that personal data that are inaccurate, having regard to the purposes for which they are processed, are erased or rectified without delay ('accuracy');
    5. kept in a form which permits identification of data subjects for no longer than is necessary for the purposes for which the personal data are processed; personal data may be stored for longer periods insofar as the personal data will be processed solely for archiving purposes in the public interest, scientific or historical research purposes or statistical purposes in accordance with Article 89[3] subject to implementation of the appropriate technical and organisational measures required by this Regulation in order to safeguard the rights and freedoms of the data subject ('storage limitation');
    6. processed in a manner that ensures appropriate security of the personal data, including protection against unauthorised or unlawful processing and against accidental loss, destruction or damage, using appropriate technical or organisational measures ('integrity and confidentiality').

As a remote media producer who may be required to build and maintain registration forms and handle user data, you need to know more about GDPR than you may think. It isn't just about the ubiquitous "Allow Cookies" button on websites, it's about care.

Exporting and Importing Your Registration Data

If you are using a third-party registration system, you will need to export that data and import into your virtual presenting software. It can get tricky, depending on how your system works. Most often, the registration software has a very specific syntax for data import. If you are working with Excel as your data collection, you may want to resave as a .CSV (comma separated value) file. It's basically the data stored in line with commas acting as the delineation between cells.

We cannot offer a one-size fits all solution for you in this book because there are so many variables in the way data is collected and imported, but we can suggest you practice this operation quite often.

When it comes to exporting your own data after a production, whether for marketing leads or for follow-up questionnaires, you should sort by compliance first before organizing the data. Separate the data that opted out of the GDPR compliance or the disclaimer and then save the main file separately before sending to another department.

Key Opinion Leaders and Keynote Speakers

Like television, an increase in viewership is sometimes a direct result of hosting and casting a recognizable guest or key opinion leader (KOL). Recognition and expertise are field specific, so this can mean a top doctor in a medical field or an author of a recent book or a professor at a local college. The right speaker is in the context of the event as well as the expectations of the audience. If you are selling tickets or looking for a high number of registrations, you may be interested in having the right personality on screen. In the case of a workshop, the content is likely the draw. Regardless, a good, authentic speaker is someone who will draw a crowd even from behind the screen.

EXPERTISE IN A FIELD DOESN'T MEAN EXPERTISE ON THE SCREEN

A few years ago, a 1950s video of author Vladimir Nabokov went viral on YouTube.[4] It wasn't because Nabokov, who has written some of the best prose in the 20th century, had said something profound, but rather the manner in which he was speaking to an interviewer. Nabokov was being interviewed and he brought along index cards to the interview. This shocked many people online as they were witnessing someone who is truly gifted at words struggle to say them out loud on television. We were reminded at that moment that expertise in your field does not translate to on-screen expertise. Vladimir Nabokov is a writer, not a speaker.

As we've covered in previous chapters, media training is very often now part of an author's toolbox. But this isn't the case for every expert in their field. Media training for authors is usually necessary because authors rely on publicity to increase sales of their books. But that's not the same for scientists, doctors, engineers, mathematicians, or any number of fields where their work should be shared. When you are bringing on an expert, you should ask if they have had any previous media experience from being interviewed about their work in front of an audience to sharing their work in a lecture hall. You may ask them their comfort level with presenting to a camera or being recorded.

Make sure to prepare time to a pre-interview or a rehearsal at least a day before your production. It will help the process come together and put the speaker at ease when they have to do their presentation. If they need index cards or a teleprompter, you now have the knowledge of how to help them present comfortably.

Comfort for a KOL is key (no pun intended). Since your KOL or keynote are the experts, their confidence in their own content is likely spectacular, and you need to be able to tap into their passion as you may recognize the border between comfort and their nerves. Even if you don't understand their subject, you should do a nominal amount of research of who they are and what their subject is. As a producer, you have the main responsibility of getting them to seem natural on camera or on audio. A brief meeting with your KOL is highly recommended and should be scheduled for at least a day before the production. This will put them at ease and ensure them that their content will be handled professionally and with quality delivery.

There's also a distinction between the terms keynote speaker and key opinion leader that is important to mention. A keynote speaker is usually your headliner for a production with multiple speakers. The keynote will likely deliver the opening speech or closing remarks on a given production. Keynotes are meant to either summarize the overall theme of the production or to set the tone for all the speakers going forward. The keynote does not have to frame out the event as very often, keynotes are specifically part of the production to increase attendance and registration as well as raise the level of prestige that your audience is expecting.

An additional reason for working in advance with your KOL or speakers is because in many cases there are technical issues that neither party is aware of until it's too late. For example, scientists or researchers working in some institutions may have a limit of what browser they may be able to use and some software is browser specific. Most of the webinar and virtual event platforms run well on the Chrome browser, but some institutions are skeptical of the security that Google may provide and limit their employees to Microsoft Edge or their specific company-wide browser.

Speakers who work internationally may also be limited by their ability to share their screen with people outside of their organization. In this case, sometimes they hit a wall with the VPN (virtual private network) that their company provides. Many of these issues are only identified when the production begins which is far too late. When you send out your email to schedule your rehearsal, you need to ask whether the location of the rehearsal will be the same as when they present. Sometimes, people practice their appearance while they are home but intend on using their work office on the day of the production.

If you are doing a panel or have multiple speakers, you need to be aware of how the platform works when your speakers turn off their cameras and microphones and be very clear with the speakers about what you expect them to do when they are cued. Most platforms contain a backchannel to "backstage" of the platform—basically a private chat for anyone given host or speaker privileges—and you should make the guests be very aware of how to use the chat. Though many of your speakers should be well aware of how to connect and use remote platforms, some tools are very specific and difficult to see.

Troubleshooting with your KOLs and speakers

- Executive Level or High-Level KOLs and their Executive Assistants
  - Many times, your KOL or Keynote Speaker will be a high-level speaker and have a very busy daily schedule. Their calendar is likely managed by their Executive Assistant or administrative team.
  - It's best to consider that all KOLs may be busy, so work well in advance to prioritize their rehearsal. If possible, try to get the Keynote to do the rehearsal, but if this is not possible, identify the main executive assistant (EA) who may properly handle the training.
  - If both the KOL and the EA are working remotely and separately, have the EA create a working training for the KOL written in their communication style. It will help the translation process—especially if your platform is more technical or proprietary than Zoom.
- Headshots and Bios
  - In the earliest part of confirming your speakers, you should prioritize requesting a headshot and bio. You'll need this numerous times in your promotions, productions, and marketing campaigns.
  - You should create a standard email that requests these assets from your speakers. Headshots should be high-resolution and larger than 600 × 600 pixels. (Resolution and images size are not the same.)

  - There are two types of biographies to request, a short biography, which is also known as a sketch, and should be about 3–5 sentences long. A longer biography could be a paragraph or two with more details. Regardless of which you request, having this information is invaluable to later parts of the production process.

- WiFi and Ethernet

  - It is ALWAYS recommended to use computers that are plugged in via ethernet cable rather than using WiFi. WiFi is often unstable and has limited bandwidth. If many people are using WiFi at the same time, it reduces the speed.
  - If the speaker cannot plug in, ask them to move their wireless router to be closer to their computer or vice versa. The closer the signal, the better.

    - Tech note: Some routers come with a choice of 2.4 or 5 GHz signals 2.4 GHz signals are lighter and go further into the distance, but sacrifice Internet speed. 5 GHz signals are denser and faster, but that means they don't reach as far.

- Wires, power, and movement

  - All the signal from remote media production is reliant on the computer being on and stable during the production process.
  - Please be sure to ask to your speaker if their wires are clear of them in case their feet kick either the power supply or the Internet connection out of the computer while broadcasting live.

- Audio Levels

  - Most webinar and virtual software will not include audio meters. In the past, we've used external hardware to see levels and a mixing board, but for the average producer, these tools are unavailable.
  - When you plan your rehearsal, you should invite the host or a colleague as well. It gives you a good way to compare audio levels. Use your best judgment when it comes to clarity and whether the sound is muffled. Some headsets will sound dull or distant.
  - You can also send your talent a microphone beforehand, so they have access to good quality audio.
  - Most computers have an option to raise or lower the input volume of a microphone. Be sure to practice where these settings are before you rehearse.

- Talking over one another

  - Patience is ultimately the most important skill to have when producing a virtual program. Remind your hosts and your guests to let each other complete their sentences or points before responding.

    - If you are using live captioning or plan on captioning or transcribing after the production, guests talking over each other will damage the text quality.
    - Practice your "silent laugh" or mute function or respectful nods.
- Practice on both a PC and a Mac computer as if you are the guest speaker. Each machine has different tools to access microphones and web cameras.
    - Good software will automatically detect the error and highlight it, but often, it's unintelligible to the guest speaker. In the upper right of the browser at the right of the web address are the extra features for interactivity from cameras and audio. A small settings window will open to permit access to certain devices. Practice knowing where these are.
- On a Mac computer, often software and browsers need to be given permission to access the cameras and the microphones.
    - To use the web camera in Chrome or some other browser, you may have to give permission in the Security and Privacy settings in the System Preferences. You'll need to allow Chrome or the software to have access to the camera in the Privacy tab.
- Camera issues may appear if the speaker has their native communication software open.
    - Some KOLs leave their Microsoft Teams or their WebEx open all day and when they are trying to use the VE or webinar platform, the camera will not work.
    - Have them close all their other programs to free up camera access.
- Some newer computers given to employees will bar users from changing settings.
    - If this happens, you need to see if the speaker has access to another computer or may access the event from a different machine or location. Make sure to put them at ease with an unfamiliar machine.
- Bluetooth is an exceptionally difficult technology to use during live events that are streaming. Whether the guest is using AirPods or the newest Sony over-the-ear headphones, Bluetooth is a radio signal that can be interrupted by any number of interferences.
    - The best bet is to always use wired headphones, but many speakers have become accustomed to their own devices.
    - Be certain where the Bluetooth settings are on both a PC and a Mac to help work through difficult situations.
- Screen share is also permission based. In technical terms, any user sharing their screen is technically joining the call twice. Once as their camera and once as their screen.

- On many computers, sharing a screen will cause the display to be altered.
- For example, on PowerPoint, presenting often means the presentation will be made into a full screen broadcast and the KOL will not be able to see the controls or the host.
- It is recommended that PowerPoint presentations are presented in their own window so they can be shared as a program rather than as an entire screen presentation.
- To do this, you can use the Slide Show tab and click Set Up Slide Show. Under the Show Type, have the guest choose "Browsed by an individual (window)" mode. It will create its own mini-presentation. When the guest chooses what input to share, they may be able to pick that specific window.

- Sounds, Videos, and Gifs may have translation issues during playback across a webinar stream.
    - Many presentation products either require some time to load multimedia resources or require the file path to point to a folder with larger files like videos. Remind the speaker not to change their setup after a successful rehearsal.
    - Lag is common with multimedia and while it may not have lag at the beginning of a presentation, computers may fill their cache and RAM (the temporary storage memory) and slow down as the project goes on.
    - Aside from warning the guests of this situation (if it is noticeable), be calm and ready to use the backchannel to guide the presenter through the lag on screen.
- Freeze ups and nerves are common. Sometimes when a guest feels they have slipped up or skipped something, they may freeze or pause.
    - Rehearsal should remind the speaker not to look at the attendee number or the questions even though they may be distracting on screen.
    - As we went over numerous times, remind the speaker that this is not only natural, but acceptable in remote media production. Imperfections remind the audience that the speaker is a real, authentic person.
- Clearing the Room and Warning Family Members
    - Most KOLs are taking time away from their fairly normal day to present on camera. For the time they're needed to be the "star" of the show, they'll require a quiet setting.
    - In advance, double check that they've informed their family that they'll be on camera for their allotted time. Often the keynote video is shared after the production, so their preparation will be very important.
    - Since many remote workers split their time among family duties, parenting, and pet-sitting, your production may not fit into their normal

routine. Most speakers are aware of this, but they'll appreciate the check-up.

- It's your job to get the best performance from the speaker, KOL, or keynote speaker, but remember not to sweat the small stuff.
    - Maintain positivity and professionalism no matter what happens.

PERSONAL STORY

Jamie here.

Nearly everyone has seen the adorable viral video from the BBC where Professor Robert Kelly was accidentally interrupted by his children while streaming on live television.[5] First, his daughter walked in followed by a scooting little sibling in a child walker. Professor Kelly did his best to remain composed a few squeaky seconds later, his wife frantically entered the room and grabbed the children. It was a nice little moment on live tv to show how remote production really means home production and how to handle surprises like this.

One time, during a large breakout room session, one of the panelists was greeted by their toddler looking for the spoons so she could have her snack. It was that moment that the speaker realized she had forgotten to leave the spoon out *and* forgot to temporarily turn off her mic. What ensued over the next 45 seconds was an empty seat with noises of chaos and silverware falling all over the floor. The other speakers were polite and kind and some winced. As the producer, I typed into the chat "That's live TV!" and it broke the ice a bit.

Life is part of virtual presenting, and we can't just turn off our family responsibilities during our productions. If things happen, roll with it. It's authentic to its core. Remain positive and run as much damage control and provide as much kindness as possible and all will come back together.

Moderating Q&A and Content Moderation

When the production is live, or simulive, you will hopefully be receiving questions or responding to interactive features. Someone has to moderate the questions and filter them to the host and the guests. If it isn't you, a designated host or even guest can field this portion of the livestream, webinar, virtual event session. Make sure all parties are familiar with the way the Q&A feature works and where the questions appear.

In the best-case scenario, every single attendee will be on their best behavior and participating in good faith and productively. However, some questions may be off-topic, too personal, or be a troll-like question (see "Warnings" section later in this chapter). As either the host or the MC, you are responsible for the trust and safety of the production and the successful conversation that is implied in remote media production.

Typically, there are several ways to interact with a question when it appears in the queue. Before the show, have a discussion with your team on who reads the questions and how they should be answered. On some platforms, all the panelists or guests can see the stream of questions coming in and this can be distracting. Some platforms highlight notifications, like you are receiving a text message, others have an entire column where the questions exist. Panelists and guests often see the administrative side of the Q&A section.

Many pieces of software contain easy interactive features for the questions allowing you to remove the questions from the queue. You can answer the questions live on air by having the host or you ask, but make sure to hit the "answered live."

You can answer the question in the Q&A feature as well, but sometimes, those questions would benefit from being answered by multiple guests instead of just one person. Questions about technical issues are easily answered by text responses, whereas ambiguous questions should be answered live.

Finally, there's usually a feature to dismiss or delete a question in the queue. These are questions that are harmful to the production, designed to troll, or are completely meaningless. A simple delete is helpful.

As the producer, you are the final line of defense for content moderation. Your goal is to keep the show going, but also prevent any derailments. In virtual events and webinars, there are failsafe measures in place (like not allowing the audience to use the camera or microphone) or methods of moderating the live event. But in meetings and livestreams, there have been horror stories of "Zoom bombing" and audience interruptions.

TRUST AND SAFETY

Trust and safety is a growing field of content moderation that is especially important in the world of remote media production. It's often an afterthought, but we recommend making it part of your production process from the beginning. Trust and safety is beneficial for several reasons, but most importantly, it helps keep a healthy environment for your digital counterparts, from your colleagues to your guests to your clients.

According to Spectrum Labs, Trust and safety is "the set of business practices whereby an online platform reduces the risk that users will be exposed to harm, fraud, or other behaviors that are outside community guidelines. This is becoming an increasingly important function at online platforms as they look to protect their users while improving customer acquisition, engagement, and retention."[6]

You are the front lines between the production and the public. Everyone should feel safe in your environment and in your production. Many of the virtual presentation software projects are feeling more and more immersive, and you want to make the audience feel as though they are part of the show and would like to return to your next production.

The Importance of Time

When should you plan your event and how do you greet your audience? The timelessness of the Internet is a conundrum when you are planning events that can be accessed from anywhere on the planet. The Earth has 24 time zones, almost all separated by an hour. The international dateline is in the middle of the Pacific Ocean (exactly opposite the prime meridian—0 degrees—which is in Greenwich, England). If you are running a live event, you need to take your audience locations into account before you begin.

Because the United States has four time zones, producers should plan around audiences on each coast as well as international attendees. In addition, producers might consider conversion rates and having registrants attend live, rather than watching on demand. (If the production is more valuable as on-demand, this doesn't matter as much.)

Questions to ask:

- When are the typical working hours for your audience?
- When is lunchtime or a possible break to attend?
- What are evenings like where your audience resides?
- Do you want international input from diverse locales and distant countries?
- What time may your KOLs be available?

While several studies have been performed to find the "perfect time," there is no exact science to figuring it out.

A livestream or webinar does well when it means the timing needs of your major markets. If you are producing for a US/Europe/South America audience, an 8 or 9 am Pacific Time (PT) is good because it will be 12 or 1 pm Eastern Time (ET) and 6 (18:00) or 7 pm (19:00) Greenwich Mean Time (GMT). This satisfies the time zones of nearly half the Earth.

However, if you are interested in streaming to far more populous regions like India or Eastern countries like Australia, Japan, or South Korea, you need to consider the international dateline and when the production will be best. An 8 pm (20:00) Eastern Time (ET) production would satisfy a 4 pm (16:00) Pacific Time (PT) and an Eastern audience (the next morning) at 9 am in South Korea or Japan and 10 am in Sydney Australia.

Note as well that international times are usually based on the 24-hour clock, so double check your times. If you say 8 pm, that may accidentally translate to 8 am, because 8 pm is 20:00. Also note that we use ET/PT/GMT, not EST or EDT, etc. This is because Daylight Savings Time is inconsistent globally and Standard Time and Daylight Time may not align correctly. Dropping the "S" or the "D" is more acceptable.

Time is fairly difficult but working well in advance to figure it out saves you much confusion and questions later on.

PERSONAL STORY

Jamie here!

When I worked at CNBC at the New York Stock Exchange on Wall Street, the markets would close at 4:00 pm ET and our shows would end at 5 pm before switching over to one of the many studio shows on the channel. Often, I was tasked with staying on the floor of the NYSE until 5:35 pm ET. This was because at 5:30 pm ET, South Korea would start their next morning's stock broadcast from the floor—albeit empty—at 6:30 am. There was a bit of a rush knowing that the anchor was speaking to an audience the next morning while I was standing there ready to go home for the evening.

Time and access are important, and we have to work globally in matters of markets and livestreams!

Production on the Medium Scale

Before we get into the large-scale projects like Webinars and Virtual Events, we're going to cover some of the medium size productions that are most common. These are usually budget-friendly and suit the needs for the client without investing in new software or licensing additional features.

Recorded Interviews

In the early days of video production, there was one way to record an interview and that was using a broadcast-grade camera and microphone along with expensive and bulky lighting. Having to record even a simple interview would take an hour or more to set up the lighting, sometimes an hour or more for the interview itself, and then an hour or so to break down and pack away all that equipment. Today, we don't have that problem.

While it is still common practice to use high-end video, audio, and lighting equipment to capture interviews, it's becoming just as common to capture interviews remotely. This certainly became popular in the early COVID-19 days, with many of the methods outlined in Chapter 4 being used to remotely record. There is a variety of advantages and disadvantages to remote recording.

Pros

- **Scheduling:** remote recording allows for much more flexibility. Without having to travel to a remote location or set up in a studio, the guest and producer both can schedule their interviews easier.
- **Time:** recording from a presenter's laptop, phone, or via remote kit takes significantly less time because we are removing the time-consuming set-up and break down of complicated production equipment in a studio or location.
- **Cost:** Clients love this one. Remote capturing is very cost-effective. Depending on the method and equipment used, it's possible to record remotely for free.
- **Authenticity:** Usually, a remote record is done from the presenter's home or office. This adds a level of authenticity to the content, visually showing the viewer that this is not over-produced.

Cons

- **Production value:** Most remote records are done using the subject's home computer or smartphone. In these cases, the quality of video and lighting usually aren't going to look as good as a professionally produced camera shot.
- **Inconsistent needs:** Every person has a different computer or smartphone setup. There are a host of things that we must work out before even recording. Do they have the right equipment? Will their home setup provide a decent camera shot?
- **Problem Solving:** When you can't be in the same room as the interview subject, it becomes much more difficult to diagnose any technical issues. In some cases, it might become more time consuming to fix a remote problem than if you were sitting in the room across from your subject.
- **"Talent" now has to be a producer, too:** When you remove the camera crew and fancy equipment, you're relying solely on your interview subject to set up the camera shot. Not everyone is a tech expert. Adding this layer of complexity to an interview can really frustrate your subject or throw them off from focusing on what is important – delivering the message.

Methods of Remote Recording

When recording a subject remotely, there are four methods to record and transfer the files of your footage. These options are local (at the location of the recording), store and forward (defined in Chapter 4), cloud recording, and off-site recording (a non-cloud location that is not at the location where the video is being captured).

Local Record

When you record a video onto your smartphone, you are recording locally to that device. The file is saved in the devices microchip storage. Smartphones make local recording very easy and the quality is great, but the downside is that the remote producers have little or no control. Desktop and laptop computers have decent webcams and can store footage locally, but are not as intuitive as a smartphone. Apps and software are available that allow a device to record locally while allowing the remote producer to view the shot and sometimes have minimal control over the camera's settings.

The advantage of local recording is usually quality. Because the file is recorded directly on the device, less compression is required. However, that might result in a really big file and getting that footage from the interview subject's computer or phone to your editor could prove problematic. File transfers and lack of control are the biggest downside to local records.

Store and Forward

We discussed store and forward in Chapter 4. This is a great hybrid approach to recording since it involves recording video locally, for higher quality, but has the advantage of uploading the material either while recording or immediately after. Store and forward can have some downside, as you will need high bandwidth on the part of your interview subject, and since you are recording and uploading together, you will need to ensure they have a relatively new device. This is because store and forward uses more system resources on the device. Trying to use an old smartphone with a store and forward app could cause it to overheat in some circumstances.

Cloud Record

Cloud recording takes a lot off the plate of your interview subject. They basically need to point the camera in the right spot and the producer can view and record the video in the cloud. This method is very bandwidth dependent. If your interview subject has a weak Internet connection, it's likely that the video will be heavily compressed, resulting in a lower-quality video recording. If your subject has great bandwidth, you could have a simple and decent-quality video with no uploading required.

Off-Site Record

Similar to cloud recording, off-site recording takes the upload responsibility off the hands of the interviewee. The difference with off-site and cloud recording is that this method records in a physical location (maybe the producer's control room or office). The downside here is that you are relying on both the producer and the interviewee to have solid Internet connectivity. If the connection is great, off-site recording allows for the highest level of control and instant access to their video files for editing.

Cellular Bonding

Cellular bonding is a technology that helps combat low bandwidth on an interview location. This involves using multiple Internet connections (cellular, wifi, ethernet) and combining them into one solid Internet connection. You effectively can take four mediocre connections and combine them into one super connection. Cellular bonding allows for even more control using off-site or cloud recording.

COMMON REMOTE RECORDING ISSUES

In your time as a remote producer, you're going to have some great days and some days that really put your patience to the test. You'll see it all when it comes to remote interviews because remote recording methods vary widely, from Zoom to a browser-based cloud platform to remote camera kits that ship to the interviewee. Here are a handful of some worst-case scenarios that might come up in your projects.

Permissions

The Problem:

> You are producing an interview series for a Fortune 500 tech client. You've elected to use Cisco WebEx to record, because this was the platform of choice for this client's IT department. The client has landed an interview with one of their top financial partners and wants to record it as soon as possible to avoid scheduling issues. The last-minute request means that you didn't have a lot of time to prep.

When the interviewee tries to click the link to join your meeting, he is unable to do so. Frustration is mounting. The client is waiting, and you are troubleshooting while trying to maintain your composure.

The Fix:

> The reason is that in his particular company, the only video conferencing platform allowed is Skype for Business. This is due to compliance issues in his financial sector and region. Very quickly, your team launches a separate Skype for Business call, and then using a complicated system of audio and video cabling, patch the two calls together. This allows you to record the call with external devices and work with the two traditionally not-compatible platforms. You've also learned that the interviewee's company does not allow for calls without a headset, so you have to make-do with his bulky headset in the shot.

The Lesson:

> When using a browser-based platform or even a Zoom-like video conferencing app, take into consideration any privacy settings or limitations on your interviewee's computer or phone. A lot of corporate guests, especially those in finance or healthcare, cannot load software onto their computer or install a USB device without the permission of their IT department.

Pick the Platform Around the Person

The Problem:

> You have a corporate client that hires you to do monthly records with their top executives. The first time you are recording you are planning to use a browser-based store and forward platform that records in the cloud. The idea is that the quality is better and since it is browser-based, there should be less tech issues. When you sign on for the recording session, the CEO insists that he have a virtual background in the shot, rather than show his luxurious Hamptons home. Your platform of choice did not offer this feature.

The Fix:

> Luckily, the client knows this is a last-minute request and you shift to a more simple Zoom approach.

The lesson:

> You now ask a list of specific questions before booking remote interviews to ensure you're on the right platform.

Clear the Room

The Problem:

> You'll see a fair share of background action when recording in an interviewee's home. When the whole family is home and the speaker is on their computer, it's common that others in the home won't know about the recording. They might even think the camera isn't even on. Recently, a popular Fortune 500 tech company was recording a panel discussion with three speakers, each from their own home. In the middle of the chat, one of the panelists husbands walked right across the room in his underwear and proceeded to cross the shot about thre times before any of the panelists realized what was happening!

The Fix:

Luckily, this was a prerecorded conversation and the production team was able to edit around it.

The Lesson:

It's important to have a protocol in place for remote records, making sure to instruct all panelists to tell everyone in the household that they are being recorded on camera.

Tying it All Together: Check the Shot Before the Shoot

In the end, it's good practice to encourage clients to participate in a brief "remote site survey" before a recording session. This is usually a few days prior to recording, and you'll want to schedule it around the same time as the interview so that you know what the ambient lighting will be. Remember, the sun moves (well, the Earth moves, but that's a different textbook), so you need to plan on what the lighting will be like in that room at the time of day you are recording.

Just 15 minutes with the interview subject (or someone on their team) using the exact same setup and location will yield a better interview. This is because you're able to test the connectivity, test the platform permissions, adjust the camera angle, move anything distracting from the background, and generally be more prepared to hit the ground running on the actual interview recording session.

We remember some advice from a friend and mentor to the authors, Barry Katz. Barry is the Senior Vice President and General Manager of the global production company, NEP Group. Barry has a million great phrases, one of them is that "cheap is expensive." In other words, do your due diligence and pick a platform and method that works around the project needs and budget, but also know the limitations. If you're going into an interview "blind" and need to be prepared for the unexpected, give yourself the options to pivot if needed. Otherwise, you could run into a situation where you're re-recording or having to pay an editor to fix mistakes from the recording session—cheap can be very expensive. Test, ask questions, and test again.

Livestreams

In the early 2000s, serial entrepreneurs and tinkerers Justin Kan, Emmett Shear, Michael Seibel, and Kyle Vogt pitched the idea to an investor to stream every minute of Justin's life online. At that time, there were a handful of upstart livestreaming platforms but the bandwidth wasn't what it is today so the quality was not high definition. With some seed money, the group launched Justin.tv and Justin strapped a webcam to himself with a cellular modem (smartphones were not capable of streaming video yet) and shared every detail of his life.

The launch of Justin.tv was really a marketing gimmick to show others that livestreaming was here and available to anyone. The site began to grow as one of the first successful platforms for anyone to livestream and build an audience. After the initial excitement wore off and finances were waning, Emmett pitched the idea of pivoting to focus on game streaming. He had seen a handful of Justin.tv users streaming screen shares of their video game play, with their video in the corner discussing the game and replying to comments. Most people told Emmet that this idea would never work. Laughing all the way to the bank, Emmett and the Justin.tv team had created Twitch, the go-to streaming platform for gamers that has since been acquired by Amazon.

Twitch is just one of many streaming platforms available today, just about any social media platform allows for live video streaming. There are so many options that, like remote recording, you need to dial into the needs of your audience and talent to decide the best platform based on the needs of the production.

As you learned in Chapter 4, there are many steps in the production flow from the presenter to the audience. Let's dive in a little deeper into these components and look at some of the tools that enhance a livestream beyond one-way video.

In any livestream, you have at least one incoming signal from a camera. In more complex livestreams, you might have multiple cameras from a studio, a remote guest, video playback from a hardware or software device that stores and plays video, graphics (such as lower third name and titles, animations, title screen, slides), and off of this needs to be mixed together to be streamed out. The key locations here are the remote location (where the video is originating) and the control room (where the video is being compiled and produced.

In the Control Room

The term control room usually refers to the room where all the magic happens in a production facility. This is where your audio, video, and graphics are mixed together under the direction of Producers, Directors, and technicians. In modern livestreaming, a "control room" might just be one person sitting at their computer at home or at an event. No matter the size of production, the same thing is happening.

Input: Feeds

Incoming video from a camera, remote guest, or any device that is sending a video signal is referred to as a "feed". This is because the video is being "fed" to the receiver from another source. Most control rooms will use a combination of the below options. In an ideal situation, each feed has its own isolated audio and video. This is referred to as an ISO, it's when you can have a clean video feed of a remote guest without the audio or video of another mixed in.

Wired Local Feeds

Within a single location, video is traditionally fed over one of four methods: SDI, HDMI, Fiber, and NDI. To help explain these formats, we'll use the example of a studio with three cameras and a control room next door that will receive and broadcast the livestream. All of these formats can work with HD video as well as 4K.

SDI stands for Serial Digital Interface and was standardized by SMPTE (The Society of Motion Picture and Television Engineers). SDI has been the broadcast-grade standard for transmitting video over long distances within a single location. SDI generally uses a coaxial cable (round, heavy-duty braided wire) with a BNC connection, and a round metal socket that can be locked in place.

HDMI stands for High Definition Multimedia Interface. It was introduced in 2002 when High Definition television took over as the primary standard. HDMI is traditionally a consumer or "prosumer" format in that offers much of the same properties as SDI, but the connector is not a locking mechanism and can dislodge if pulled by mistake. Some HDMI cables and devices can have a separate ethernet channel, allowing to it to carry Internet communications.

NDI was invented as an open-source standard by the NewTek company. NDI stands for Network Device Interface and is quickly becoming commonplace in small productions as well as large production facilities. NDI uses existing computer networks (your Internet router or at a larger facility, the wired ethernet network) to send and receive audio/video.

Cloud-Based Remote Feeds

Remote video can get to you in a wide variety of ways. Here are a handful of common methods:

- **Video Conferencing**
  - This one is pretty simple. Call up your guest on Zoom, FaceTime, WebEx, whatever video calling platform of choice. To integrate that video into a stream, there are lot of options. Most common is to "pin" the speaker within the software, make the video full screen, and connect your device to your control room via HDMI or NDI. The downside to this method is that you likely will not have an ISO feed of each guest because Zoom and other platforms tend to mix the audio together. There are, however, a variety of hardware and software solutions to give you more control and isolate the audio and video of each speaker into a separate NDI feed.

- **RTMP**
  - RTMP stands for Real-Time Messaging Protocol and has been for some time the industry standard livestreaming format. A remote camera or production site will transmit a video to a cloud-based server (such as Wowza, Brightcove, Amazon Web Services). The control room will then "pull" down that feed from the same server. This method usually creates a significant delay from point to point and is really only ideal when the delay is not an issue.
- **Point To Point Remote Feeds**
  - Point-to-point methods use either Internet, fiber optic cables, or satellites to transmit video from a remote location to the control room.
- **Internet Transmission Protocols**
  - Much like RTMP above, these methods use the open Internet to transmit video. The difference is that it doesn't rely on a cloud-based server as a midway point, but broadcasts directly to the receiver in the control room. Some popular protocols are SRT (Secure Reliable Transport), WebRTC (Web Real-Time Communication), RTMP, and FTL (Faster than Light).
- **Fiber**
  - Large fiber optic networks have been installed throughout the globe dedicated to the transmission of video. In the United States, some examples are The Switch and VYVX. These companies own the fiber optic lines and rent time on their network to clients. This is ideal is latency is important and by using this technology, you are ensuring a more stable signal since you're not relying on the open Internet.
- **Satellite**
  - The remote location will have a satellite dish or a satellite truck (a vehicle designed to park at a location and operate as a mobile production unit with a large satellite dish on the roof). A coordinator will arrange for time on a satellite floating in space, and the remote location satellite dish will point to that satellite in space and beam the video up to it. At the control room end, they will need another satellite dish to point to that same satellite up in space and pull down the video. Quality here is top notch and you're not reliant on wires, especially if you're in a very remote area. However, bad weather can ruin a satellite signal and it's expensive. As Internet bandwidth increases, the need for satellites in this use case continues to decrease.
- **Compositing the Program With a Switcher**
  - With all these video feeds you're getting, we need to dress them up and turn them into a real show. This is where you're using some type of

video switcher. A switcher allows you to take all your incoming video, combine it with graphics, and mix your audio. A switcher can be a free app or a huge multi-million dollar production unit, and surprisingly some of the free software is just as good as the expensive options. This is where you are going to add any dissolves or transitions between camera shots, as well. It is simply real-time video editing.

- **Hardware Switcher**
    - A hardware switcher is a dedicated device that has a variety of physical inputs to collect the various feeds. Small hardware switchers might have two inputs with the option to switch between one or the other (called an A/B switch). More complex switchers will have more inputs, heavy graphics and animation capabilities, "green screen" chroma keying ability (which replaces the green of a green screen with another video or image), and more.
- **Software Switcher**
    - Software switchers have the same functionality as a hardware device, they just require a computer to operate. Most software switchers require a high-powered computer with special input cards to take in SDI or HDMI feeds. Examples of these are OBS (a free open-source switching program), Wirecast, and VMix. There are even smartphone apps that allow basic switching functionality.
- **Cloud-Based Switcher**
    - Cloud-based switchers offer much of the same functionality above, but with less control and flexibility. These options are very cost-effective because you don't need any hardware other than a device with Internet access. The downside is that you're limited to bandwidth and at the mercy of the Internet.

Adding Layers to Your Livestream

Once your switcher combines all the videos to make a beautiful broadcast, your livestream can become even more dynamic. Most livestream platforms offer a variety of add-ons to enhance the audience experience and do things traditional TV cannot.

Live Chat

Live chat is not to be confused with comments. This is a live feed of unedited text, which appears as viewers hit "enter".

Q&A

Usually used for events where there will be some level of interactivity, question and answer panels add the ability to take questions directed to the on-screen talent. This is usually separate of the live chat box.

Moderated Chat and Q&A

If you're looking for more control over your chat or Q&A, moderation is a feature that allows the producer to screen each chat or question and approve only those relevant to the broadcast.

Real-Time Polls

This is a great add-on to encourage audience participation with minimal effort on behalf of the viewer. By using a real-time poll option on your livestream, you can host trivia games, take the pulse of your audience on a hot topic, or adapt the conversation around what they want to hear.

The Call in and Live Hit

When you're the expert but they don't want you traveling to the city and you have to make do at home.

The Big Stuff—Webinars and Virtual Events

What justifies investing in a large production? There are many reasons to go beyond the standard production levels and accessible software or freeware for small and medium productions. The larger productions will not only resemble traditional media production, but they will also combine all the interactive elements we've covered so far in this book. Large productions are complicated and require time and patience and a lot of preproduction. They can be built with small teams, but we highly recommend working with a larger team on Webinars and VEs.

In most use cases of Webinars and VEs, there is a cost associated with the software or hardware and this should be justified by its return on investment. Most of these projects are typically subsidized by company budgets and/or sponsorships and advertising. Larger productions are important when you have high-level KOLs or keynotes or require a production that is a bit more one-sided or one-to-many.

On the upside, webinars and VEs are used because they offer far more interactivity than small and medium streaming projects. Many webinars allow for breakout sessions and polls, chats, and Q&A and VEs offer networking, gamification, lounges, and lobbies for hosting data and downloads.

In the following, we're going to go through some of the most commonly used styles of productions and some experiments we've done and encourage you to do as well. There's a lot that can go into these productions and they can become unwieldy very quickly. Remember, an audience appreciates simple, easy to use, interactions and they are there to learn, communicate, and participate. It's about the audience and it's about authenticity. Keep it simple but build your project to impress.

Your Setup

When you're ready to start producing media to larger-size remote productions, your computer setup may change a bit. While we've gone over the technical and much of the production, it's also important to build yourself a space where you can produce with clear access to the platforms, spaces for viewing the output, clear audio inputs, and low clutter or distractions. Live remote production is just like live TV and you must keep your attention active the entire time.

Checklist

- Primary computer
    - With Ethernet connection
- Second monitor
- Web camera and lighting
    - Even if you are not on camera, you can use your lighting set-up to show panelists and KOLs an example of what lighting can be used
- Headset and microphone
    - We recommend a professional, external microphone rather than the computer's microphone receivers—the audio difference will be noticeable
    - You can also invest in a nice gaming headset with a microphone boom and external muting controls. This will free up your hands from fumbling with a microphone
- Secondary computer or tablet to watch the livestream
    - Using your "sock puppet" account (explained later in this chapter), you should sign in as an attendee and view the output of the program
- Third-party communication apps on the second monitor with prebuilt groups for stakeholders
    - Slack, Teams, Discord, Apple Messages, etc ... Having this prepared in advance is super helpful when the live show begins
- A notepad and a few pens or pencils

FIGURE 5.1 Jamie's set-up for a 6-hour, 3-keynote, 24-guest virtual event

You should give yourself enough landscape on your desk to easily move around and not get tangled in wires. Your notepad or notebook should be available near your writing arm next to the mouse. You may need to take notes more than you imagine. This helps you improve next projects or write down any glitches that may occur during the production.

Investing in the right setup makes all the difference. The more you feel you can see all the parts of the production, the better you'll feel. While you cannot really make too many updates during the live show, the second (or third monitors) can be good to monitor other rooms on the event or make quick changes with spelling or details (Figure 5.1).

The output monitor or tablet is a good way to know what the audience is seeing—just don't let it distract you!

Webinars and Workshops

Webinars are technically web seminars, but their versatile modality makes this style of production one of the most accessible and producible of all the formats of remote media production we've covered. There are a lot of ways to make a webinar and with a few upgrades, you can create an incredible project for your audience. A virtual workshop is similar to a webinar but is usually built as a meeting or enables the audience to take part in the event. Workshops are typically live events whereas a webinar could be live, simulive, or on-demand.

From the production standpoint, there are many things to consider before building your webinar.

- What is the outcome you'd like the audience to take away from the webinar?
- Who is your expert or KOL that will deliver your information?
- How many guests will be speaking?
- What is the length of the content?
- Is there interactivity?
- Does the audience expect to be educated?
- Is there an expectation of a certificate or proof of completion?
- What type of data should be collected from the audience during registration?
- What is the data for? Is it to prep the speaker or for sales leads?
- What type of feedback are you interested in after the end of the webinar?

These questions are mainly designed for you to consider when a client is interested in hosting a webinar. Any good producer will have this in their head before they begin the preproduction phase that we covered in the previous chapter. Now that we're ready to produce the webinar, let's go over the basics.

The Story of Webinars

Webinars have an interesting history in the world of technology. In the late 1980s, before the World Wide Web was launched, users would connect to one another using Internet relay chat or IRC. It was basically just typing on a screen and waiting for someone to respond. Typically, IRC was directed at a specific other user and you had to have their IP address to speak with them. The idea of time sharing became integrated into IRC and enabled multiple users to communicate with each other simultaneously. It was always the dream of computation to share images as well as text in a live setting. Since the 1970s, a company named PictureTel had been experimenting with video conferencing and when the World Wide Web launched in 1989, AT&T chose to use PictureTel's technology to establish a live video session between the United States and Paris.[7]

It wasn't that spectacular and had a lot of technology glitches, but it gave way to the idea that video conferencing can be combined with time sharing and audience interaction. AT&T acquired PictureTel and it pushed to develop a video hardware system. In 1993, it worked out and companies were buying "videophones" (a far cry from our iPhones using FaceTime) where computers could broadcast live images. Due to bandwidth limitations, it was only possible for high-end companies to utilize the technology. There was a realization that software, not hardware, would be the future of video conferencing and PictureTel developed a software called LiveShare which incorporated LiveTalk, "the first software-only product to enable the simultaneous transmission of speech and data over one analogue telephone line using standard modems and sound boards."[8]

In 1996, companies competed to dominate the webinar space. The term was coined in the late 1980s as a portmanteau of web and seminar, but it had yet to be used commercially. Both Microsoft and Xerox created a webinar software market. Microsoft created NetMeeting and Xerox Parc created PlaceWare. These softwares did something new and unique from the previous software that existed: multiple presenters, chats, and most importantly, audiences from all over the world could attend live.[9] The late 1990s saw the development of WebEx by Cisco and the early 2000s, along with the higher broadband speeds, introduced familiar names like GoToMeeting and ClickWebinar.

Used primarily in industry markets, webinars turned out to be a phenomenal resource for companies wishing to inform a lot of people of a subject or new information in real time and all at once. Webinars differ from virtual meetings in that they usually focus on a speaker or panelists that may share their screen and the audience is separated and lack the controls to turn on their camera or microphones or share their screen. The audience still may be able to ask questions and participate in interactive features like polls or surveys.

Educators used webinar technology to highlight speakers that fit into a particular subject. Webinars filled an important gap when academic budgets did not provide enough funding to support flying a speaker to the institution or if the speaker would draw an audience bigger than any auditorium the institution may provide. Having an audience be able to participate in digital webinars was also a great way of collecting data that may be beyond the registration page such as questions and poll data.

Unfortunately, for the most part, webinars were seen as a colder or duller version of any type of in-person event and were attended by necessary parties or those interested in the niche subject. When the pandemic completely shifted the world, webinars rapidly became a very popular medium, providing the public with new opportunities for learning and engaging with people in a live setting. Webinars saw a vast increase in attendance and new markets were created in companies that did not traditionally provide media or multimedia production. For a brief moment, everyone wanted to host a webinar or a workshop.

In the hybrid world that follows the lockdown period, webinars are still extremely popular tools. With the right amount of creativity and the right speaker, speakers or panelists, a webinar can fulfill the needs of information sharing in small communities to models for Internet television shows using accessible tools like Zoom. Their ability to be recorded and with many tools offering advanced solutions for recording remote cameras separately and audio through mixers make modern webinars nearly as high quality as traditional television, but far more accessible.

There are three main styles of webinars and hundreds of variations of production techniques that can be used depending on the goal of the project. For the most part, webinars can be live streamed with a live audience, recorded and hosted online for on-demand viewing, or simulive, meaning the webinar is broadcast at a specific time and incorporates live interactive elements.

We'll cover the three main flavors of webinars and give several examples of how to incorporate interactive elements into the productions. This breakdown is intended to help you make the best use of webinars from their format to their toolset and inspire you to create unique projects.

Live Webinars

Imagine this:

> You're an academic publishing company that specializes in peer reviewed and editorial articles and journal entries about genetic engineering. The business model is print, but occasionally, due to the demands of social media and new media marketing, you create videos and author interviews. Many of your journalists and paper writers also happen to use Zoom as their primarily tool for conducting interviews. They record the session and get them transcribed; the footage is often stored or deleted, never to be used again.

The pandemic hits and everyone begins to work remotely. The news desk now meets over Zoom and Microsoft Teams. The interviews haven't changed at all. But then an idea appears—what if the interviews became part of the product that the company can use to promote the journals?

A new division is created and multimedia producers are hired to develop "programming" for the publishing company. This means thinking about how the formerly private interviews could be converted into video productions with a live audience. Soon after, it's decided that Zoom would be the delivery platform for many of the productions. There would be a host and an interview and the producer would roll an intro and outro just like a real television show. In a few months, an entirely new market for video production opens up in an industry that was pretty successful with just print.

This story actually happened at one of the companies we worked at, but it's most likely a scenario at dozens of companies that decided to think of new video products during the pandemic lockdown period. New departments were introduced and media producers were hired to create webinars and video productions.

The live webinar is useful for its content, but especially as a promotional tool. The interviews would only show up in one product in the past and now can be used twice. Once live for a limited audience and again for the print subscribers. We are very aware that Zoom is not the only tool so we will break down webinars more generally, but also how a webinar is produced in the Zoom tool. Most webinar tools engage with similar technical abilities, including how the host operates the cameras, how the guest see each other, and how the audience interacts with those on screen and with one another.

The Live Production

After you've settled on your platform and rehearsed with the speakers who will be on screen, you need to consider how long your webinar should be, what the project will look like, how the audience will interact, and identify the goals of the production.

For live webinars, you must treat the production as though you were producing a live television show. This means that all marketing material is clear on when the production airs (and in what time zone), the hosts and speakers are ready 10–15 minutes early and signed in, your polls or interactive media are prepared in advance, and settings for interactivity (Q&A, chat, polls, etc.) have been set in advance.

In most webinar platforms, the ability to have a "practice session" is built into the software. Meaning the production team, the hosts, and the speakers can be online before going live to the home audience. Typically, though not always, when someone's camera and microphone are disabled, the person is not visible to the audience on the livestream—this should always be confirmed in a practice session days before the live broadcast.

The producer and production team play many roles, from director to technical director to stage manager and graphics producer. The host, no matter what background they come from, should be fully trained by the producers to be aware of what goes on behind the scenes. This often takes patience and efficacy, especially with people who believe themselves to be technically challenged. (Note: in our experience, everyone can learn these tools.)

When the show goes live, the producer should monitor the entire project, from screening questions to "switching cameras" (we'll explain how to do that in Zoom shortly). Either through the backchannel text ("Panelists only") or through a separate chat, timing cues must be shared (15 minutes, 10 minutes, 5 minutes, 2 minutes, and "wrap up", 1 minute and 30 seconds). If there is a "hard out," the producer must end the webinar as close as possible to that time. While in the world of digital media time is not as structured as in broadcast television, audiences expect, and schedule, the time to be accurate.

AVOID SURPRISES—PREPARE YOUR AUDIENCE

You've likely seen a TED Talk before, and you probably noticed that they have a formula. The TED Talk is a format of presentation. With webinars or workshops, you have to think like a TED Talk mixed with teaching a class. It's a good idea to start with a catchy hook, something that will get the audience's attention, and perhaps lead them to the point of presentation. After you put your hook out there, make sure to give the audience a table of contents of what you'll be covering. It sounds weird because you may feel you are spoiling the ending, but it's not. It helps the audience with their time investment and ensures them that you are going to cover everything they are showing up for.

By offering a table of contents, it also mitigates any questions some of the audience may have. Many times, just like in class, you spent time thinking about your question rather than listening to the teacher or presenter. The content is a good way to let the audience know you'll probably cover what they may be thinking.

In order:

- Come out with a memorable hook. This should be a few minutes, but don't let this go on too long.
- Present either a slide or explain what you will be covering during the presentation.
- Let the audience know whether you will be taking questions during the presentation or at the end.
- Make sure to sum up your talk in time for interaction. Keep an eye on the clock.

A very simple format, but very effective!

Zoom Webinars—Some Techniques

Zoom has several production methods within their Meetings, Webinar, and Event features. The Zoom Webinar is an upgrade feature on the Zoom software and requires a license, meaning you need to upgrade a standard account to access the feature. Since Zoom is a stand-alone software, it's fairly easy to use and is quite adoptable by many industries. Zoom Webinar features are also very popular and affordable and the main difference between Zoom Meetings and Webinars is the camera and audio functionality for the audience. In the Webinar, the audience sees a completely different view than the producers, speakers, and hosts: they only see what the producer enables them to see.

The same Zoom software you use for meetings is the identical software for Webinars. The price tiers are based on the number of audience members you'd like to have attend your webinar. As we went over earlier in this chapter, the registration and attendee list are both important. In most cases, webinars utilize a registration page to gain access to the streaming content. With Zoom, you can use the registration page that Zoom provides. Before we get to that, we'll go over some of the backstage details that are important to remember.

WHY DOES HAVING AN AUDIENCE COST MONEY?

You'll notice on nearly every streaming platform that there is a significant cost difference when it comes to the number of attendees you'd like to have as part of your production. There's a good reason for this, though it's not often explained.

Unlike television where the media is streamed through the cable box or streaming receiver, Internet video must use your personal device's memory to cache data in real time in order to buffer the video. This means that when you watch livestreaming video, some of it is locally stored temporarily to keep up with the stream. The platform streaming the content is also responsible for making sure that every viewer gets the stream smoothly and without any lag. This means that the overall bandwidth from the origin server must be big enough to stream to as many users as possible.

If you were to rent space on the Internet to host your website, you're also allocated two types of storage. One, static storage for the content of your website—let's say 5 gigabytes for this example. You are also allocated a bandwidth limitation—let's say 5 gigabytes for this too. If you were to make a mostly-text website with only a few photos, your site might have 100 megabytes of static content stored on the server.

When someone *visits your site,* they actually download the site to their computer locally in the computer's cache directory. (Which is why you often hear technicians ask whether you cleared your cache.) Every time someone visits your site, it uses your server's bandwidth limitation. If one person visits your site, you used 100 megabytes to send your site to their computer leaving you with 4 gigabytes and 9,900 megabytes remaining for the month.

If, for some reason, your site becomes wildly popular, you may get hundreds of visitors simultaneously who each use up that bandwidth. Rather than only allowing one person in at once, time sharing enables all the users to access your site at the same time. That is, until you've used up the bandwidth and your site gives an error that the server is overloaded. (Hackers can weaponize this tactic with something called a Distributed Denial of Service (DDoS) attack.)

Regardless, when it comes to video, the bandwidth is much larger than images and text on a website, and servers must be robust enough to handle the throughput of streaming the content and connecting it to each user simultaneously. This costs money to the service provider who must allocate bandwidth to your project. Likely, the platform is limited by their server as well and if they have many projects running during the same allocation period, they may have to purchase more server bandwidth. In turn, they will charge you fees per attendee or limit your number of maximum participants.

On Zoom, the free tier limits the number of attendees to 100 simultaneous viewers for a meeting, but each tier jumps in both number of attendees and cost. For the Zoom Webinar, 500 attendees cost less than $100 for a month, but when you need to increase your capacity to 1,000, the cost skyrockets to nearly $400 (https://zoom.us/pricing/events).

Another vital reason for the cost increase is data. Each registrant to an event may use the Zoom registration form and that data must be stored somewhere and that storage costs money. In addition, Zoom has incredible metrics including how long the attendee stayed online, timing data, interactivity data, and access data. The more attendees, the more the data needs to be cared for.

It's extremely important to have a discussion with your client or colleagues about how many attendees you hope to have attended your webinar or event. It happens to be a "good problem" if you have too many attendees, but it could be embarrassing when you reach your attendee limit and some hopeful attendees are left out. They can always watch it on demand, but it's not the same as a livestream.

Hosts

When you are building your Webinar, you are the host of the stream. In the Webinar setting for Zoom, it's a bit different than that of Meetings where you can transfer Hosting to any other meeting attendee. In Webinars, only Panelists can be made Alternate Hosts, but must be registered Zoom users. This makes the role of a Webinar administrator a little more complicated and sometimes stressful. The stakes are slightly higher, so you'll be safer using the Webinar feature with the computer plugged into power and the Internet connected through an Ethernet connection. If your Internet connection fails, the webinar will not end, but you'll lose control of the features and the panelists may not know what to do.

Hosts have an incredible amount of control over a Webinar, including directing features. The Host is the role that can add Panelists, create polls, control panelists' cameras and microphones (though you cannot turn a microphone on), and put the Webinar "on air."

When you are building the Webinar, the first steps are similar to that of setting up a Meeting, but importantly, Webinar links may be shared, so your Description is important as it will populate the field in a social media post. If you are working with a marketing team, you should set up a Webinar well in advance, even before you may have some of your Panelists locked so you can begin to advertise the show and get people to register. (Make sure you tick the box for Registration Required.)

You may edit the features of the Webinar after it's been published, but we'll go through it as though we are setting it up for an actual webinar. There are some unique features for Zoom we really enjoy so we'll go through them.

Screen Sharing

Zoom's screen sharing is interesting because it does different things depending on how you've set up the screen share. If you share your screen, it will provide you a window with every available open program on your computer. You can choose to share an entire desktop or just an application.

If you have a two-screen setup, you can share your second screen in a manner that's set up for presentation. (This is recommended for most presentations.) You have the option to share just the browser as well and it will show the entire browser, not just the tab you are working on. If you feel some of your tabs are too personal, open a new browser window to share. You can also share the Whiteboard or devices attached directly to the computer.

In the Advanced feature, you can adjust the screen sharing capabilities to **only** share a portion of the screen. This is helpful in second-screen setups where you have laid out the desktop to have multiple different items you'd like to share during the presentation. You can also just share audio or video. If you want to put the slides behind you when presenting, sort of like a television presenter, use the "Slides as a Virtual Background" feature. If you are an educator or you are doing a seminar, you can use the "Content from a 2nd Camera" input to share content from another input.

Finally, make sure to click "Share sound" if you are sharing a video. If you do not click this button, Zoom will only share the sound coming out of your speakers and it will contain an echo. If you are showing a video, you can also click "Optimize for video clip" which minimizes Zoom's features altogether to prioritize the screen for showing the video you are sharing. However, while it may look clear to you, users may see a different video quality if their bandwidth is slow.

Zoom Webinar Options

There are a series of options for the Webinar: Q&A, Enable Practice Session, Enable Host control of panelist appearance, Make the webinar on-demand, Automatically record the webinar, and Approve or block entry for users from specific countries/regions. Note that there is no "chat" feature here. That is a toggle switch in the Settings button. You should have a discussion with your team whether or not you'd like the chat feature to be available as well as the Q&A.

As the Host, you can make yourself "invisible" during the live show by simply turning off your camera and microphone. The audience will not be able to see anyone with their camera and microphone off, but you still may be able to share your screen or sound with them. Our advice is to change your on-screen name to the name of the production or the company name before you start so that if you do happen to share your screen, whether to roll an introductory video or share sound, it shows it coming from the production and not a name.

Q&A simply enables the audience members to use the section to ask questions to the panelists. It's a basic feature but is important to explain its use to the audience at the beginning of the broadcast. Many panelists will use the chat feature if it's enabled to ask questions. While the chat is archived after the broadcast, the Q&A serves an important role for clients who are interested in collecting the questions to either respond to later or for additional marketing lead data for those who asked questions that are more focused.

Enable Practice Session is by far the most important feature in our opinion. This allows the Host to start the webinar "backstage" before going live to an audience. The practice session is similar to a Zoom meeting, but just for panelists. As a host, you'll see an omnipresent button at the top of the screen that enables you to pull back the curtain and broadcast live to the audience. This feature is now part of many webinar software systems and it is really helpful to the panelists.

If you have your webinar set for 1 pm, you as the host can start the webinar at 12:30 pm and check all the settings. It's important that you ask your panelists to join the session through their specific link at least 10 minutes before the live production. This gives time to go over the KOL tips we added earlier and bring comfort to all the speakers. When everyone is ready, you can hit the Start button and you'll notice that the audience appears immediately and are now able to see your stream.

Important note: When you hit the start button, it takes anywhere from 3 to 10 seconds for the audience to see the stream begin since the stream has to buffer to their computer. If you are rolling an introductory video, you should edit in a few seconds of black video before it starts so the audience will see the beginning. We recommend five seconds whether it is a shared video or if the speaker begins. You should tell the Panelists to wait before beginning to make sure the audience catches the start of the presentation.

Once live, the show will run until you stop the broadcast. When you do so, it ends the Webinar similar to a meeting and everyone is disconnected. You can change these settings, but this is the default and it's nice to prep the panelists before the broadcast that the ending will mean the session is over. Thankfully, to end the webinar, you will be asked twice so you cannot accidentally turn off the production.

Enable Host control of panelist appearance is a new feature that enables the host to control the "look" of the show. This is a powerful feature that helps with overall branding. The host can assign an "event wallpaper" which is the look of the webinar (this can be a logo or branding style). In addition, the host can assign virtual backgrounds for the panelists, enabling the host to access their settings from the host end. You may also change their name tag in case they didn't enter their information correctly or you'd like to input additional information.

This feature should be a discussion with the team, the panelists, and the client as this is part of the preproduction aspect of remote media production. A lot of decisions should be made in regard to look, esthetics, and consistency and communication is extremely important to the success of your project.

Make the webinar on-demand and **Automatically record the webinar** are both related. If you click the Make the webinar on-demand, the Automatically record feature lights up with the "In the cloud" toggle preselected and unchangeable. To make your webinar on-demand, it must record into the cloud. Each license comes with a specific amount of storage, so be sure to check your storage levels consistently. A one-hour Zoom webinar could be as big as 2.5 gigabytes if the streaming quality is high and several people shared video or high-resolution materials. A good rule of thumb is to remember that Zoom is typically 1 gigabyte per hour.

When you record into the cloud, it will take time to process the video for sharing and will automatically keep the recorded stream password protected. (This is a good safety feature.) You'll need to go to the "Share" settings to turn off the password so that registrants can access the on-demand video.

If you decide not to make the webinar on-demand, but rather host it yourself, you can record the webinar on your computer. You will need a fast computer for this and the computer will use much of the processor to record and stream at the same time. The upside to this feature is that the quality of the recording will be significantly higher because you are not recording the highly compressed version, but rather the mainstream as it is broadcast. The downside is that you'll have to host the video yourself either off your own server or on a video site like YouTube. Again, use a robust computer if you want to use this feature and we highly recommend using the automatically record feature even if you are not going to share the video.

Approve or block entry for users from specific countries/regions is a security feature that filters out IP addresses for either automatic entry or automatic rejection. When you use this feature, a pop-up will appear that is a setting for automatically allow or block from designated regions. In case you are hosting a webinar with sensitive information that is specific to a country or region, this feature is incredibly helpful and allows Zoom to be used by state departments and corporations with intellectual property that is country-specific.

Panelists and Attendees

Panelists and attendees of a Zoom Webinar are on different sides of the digital stage. Panelists require a special link to access the backstage and should not register for the webinar. There are really two ways to get a panelist to be part of the production and it's up to you which is more effective. The first requires you to add the panelist's email address and it will generate a special email directly to the recipient. The downside is that you really have no idea if they received it. In our experience, sometimes this email ends up in their spam folder. If you choose this option, make sure to immediately send a follow-up email asking them (or their EA) to confirm receipt.

The second is to generate all the links yourself by adding their names and your own email address. This will send you the "magic link" and you can customize your own email to your panelist. Some appreciate this method, but it does an additional level of production to the producer and host.

Attendees will use the Registration Link to access the webinar. When they register, it will generate a confirmation email with calendar links. They must use the link to attend the Webinar. Keep in mind, the email settings tell the webinar attendees who to email if something goes wrong. This email is defaulted to the licensee of the Webinar account—which could be your address! This means you will be fielding questions from the benign ("Thank you for hosting this!") to the downright annoying ("I can't make the webinar work, can you help me?"). Since it's Zoom, you have little control over the attendee's experience, so just be polite.

Registration

Aside from the information we discussed earlier in this chapter about registration, you should know that Zoom enables you to create up to 50 Source Tracking Links. Your marketing team may be interested in data from their marketing plan and this link is customizable to each outlet. The unique links can be generated for email messaging, social media, newsletters, banner ads, etc.

Branding

Zoom enables you to use some customization features to brand your production with visual upgrades consistent with your company or show theme. In the newest iteration, you can use the branding to put a "wallpaper" behind the video tiles. This offers the audience a consistent view of backgrounds if someone has their camera off or the participant has an odd aspect ratio.

The features also allow you to customize the virtual background for every on-screen participant and panelist. In the past, you'd have to send your panelists a virtual background for them to use, now you can add it for them. As we discussed earlier, the audience appreciates an authentic background, but if there are quality or privacy issues, consider added consistent backgrounds instead. In many cases with webinars, the company will want a consistent look across the board and this feature simplifies the process.

You can also customize the banners for the panelists' names. This is a nice feature for look and feel of the project.

One of the best features of Zoom's customization feature is the ability to create a custom registration email that automatically sends to the recipients when they register. The banner feature is for the title or the larger show image for the production. The logo section is set for something much smaller than the banner but can be very useful. In some cases, you may want to use the banner as your space to show the show title and the logo space for the sponsor of the project.

If someone shares the registration link on social media, it uses these images to populate the social media post. Later, in the promotions and marketing part, we'll go over how to effectively promote your project in the social media world.

The speakers feature is important to add to your branding section because the auto-generated email will include speaker information in the body of the email. You'll need to request from your KOLs, keynotes, and speakers a headshot and short bio to make this work.

Polls, Q&A, and Surveys

Polls and surveys should be created in advance of the production and should be part of your preproduction process.

Also, check your Q&A settings and your chat settings well in advance of the production (make this part of your preproduction checklist).

More

Zoom has built-in features that enable you to livestream your broadcast to other platforms. Further in this chapter, we'll go over some of the more technical features in regard to *how to* livestream using RTMP. If you happen to have a YouTube channel that enables you to do livestreams, you can grant Zoom permission to broadcast to your channel. The only downside is that the Zoom logo will appear on the livestream output.

On the upside, if your webinar license is limited by how many audience members you may have, there is a feature that allows you to remind your viewers that they can attend the livestream of your broadcast if you went over capacity.

Audience Information

When it comes to the audience, you really don't have to do too much work with Zoom. When someone registers, they'll receive a confirmation email that includes all the information that you added from the title, description, banner, logo, and speakers. The email contains links for the recipient to add the event to their calendar—in some cases, the email client will automatically add it anyway.

Your team may be very interested in the conversion rate of registrants to live attendees. According to a study done by On24 and a variety of other sources, a successful conversion rate is around 40%.[10,11] This means that if 500 people register, approximately 200 people will be attending the event live. This is crucial to keep in mind when marketing your event. Of the 40% of registered attendees that attend live, usually only 40–50% of the live attendees will attend for the entirety of the production.

These conversion rates are not a static number, it's just the average, so you can always increase the number of people attending your event by incorporating more interactivity and more exclusive speakers. However, don't feel bad if the conversion rate is lower, according to the same studies, 25% of registrants intend to watch the recorded broadcast. Most attendees are aware that by registering, they will have access to the on-demand version of the production.

Directing the Show

As the host, you have control over what the audience sees on their stream. During your practice session, you should keep everyone on the panelists' side of the production well informed of anything that may distract them, such as Q&A or the chat. The goal is for everything to look both professional and authentic.

Here are some tips for directing a Zoom using just the Zoom software: (more advanced techniques can be found in the following section using external hardware tools):

- You can roll an opening video like a television show. First, prepare a short video or promotional opening sequence for your production. There are many sites that sell editing templates that can be used in Adobe Premiere or Illustrator and the site Canva has a multitude of editing tools to create templates for video promotions.
    - Edit the video so there is "pad" at the beginning of the video - approximately 5–10 seconds is good. This should be a black video that fades up to your opening sequence.
    - The video should also fade out of sound **before** the video fades out. At the end of the sound, you can stop sharing and this should "cue" the host to begin.
    - Export the video using any settings that prioritize livestreaming or video streaming.
        - The file should be .mp4 and as previously noted, the best compression codec for this is H.264.
    - As the host, you should change your name to the production's name or the company name because you'll be sharing the video with the audience and it will show your screen name being shared.
    - Prepare the source of the video and practice "rolling" the video during the rehearsal period before you go live.
        - Hit Share Screen and check both boxes for sharing - the one for optimizing for video and the one for sharing sound.
    - We recommend you ask all participants to mute their microphones so their audio doesn't override your shared video.
        - Keep in mind that you **cannot** turn a panelist's microphone on, you can only remind them to do it themselves.
    - Before hitting "Start Broadcast," start sharing the video.
    - Hit "Start Broadcast" and wait several seconds (even though you do have a pad) and then press play.
        - Remember, the audience will see your mouse hit the play button before you play the video, so to prevent this, create an even longer preroll, press play, then press "Start Broadcast." This is a lot to juggle, so don't stress about it. If the audience sees your mouse hit the play button, it doesn't really matter to the overall production.
        - Hint: You can always edit your production after you are finished and host it on YouTube.
    - Finally, make sure you stop sharing at the end of the audio.

- You have "cameras" on zoom which can be "switched" live. Zoom has two viewing options: Grid and Full Screen. You may not have known, but as the host, you can show the audience what they should see.
    - Webinars are unlike meetings because the audience has less ability to control their screen or turn on their camera, but that also means that you can control the view.
    - Depending on the type of production, the Grid or the Full Screen could be the best for the show if you just want to leave it, but if you want to keep the audience entertained, you should switch the views during the show.
    - When someone is talking for some time answering a longer question or doing a keynote speech, switch to Full Screen. When panelists should interact with each other or there is a conversation, the Grid view is far better.
    - Like television, you can anticipate the switch when you **hear** an answer coming to a conclusion or **see** a panelist getting ready to interject or respond.
    - You should lead the edit with the Grid view and let the speaker lead the edit for Full Screen.
        - If it is Full Screen, switch to Grid **before** the other panelist speaks.
        - If it is a Grid view, switch to Full Screen **after** the speaker is already speaking.
- You can mute panelists and turn their cameras off. Only do this if you warn that them you may do this for the show.
    - As you likely know, a small sound can automatically switch the camera while in Full-Screen view. If there are small children, pets, or background noise, occasionally you may need to mute the panelist.
    - As mentioned, you cannot turn the microphone back on, you can only remind them to do so with features to the right of their name.
    - Remember, when both the camera and microphone are turned off, that panelist is invisible to the audience watching when it is in Grid View. You can see them, but the audience cannot.
- Know when to wrap up the Q&A. Be in contact with your host as much as possible using the chat feature.
    - If you are running the production on a "hard out," use the chat to all panelist feature to communicate on the backchannel.
- Optional: Put up a final slide with information about the show, the company, contact information, or where to learn more before ending the stream.
- Remember, when you end the broadcast, it hangs up the call for everyone.

StreamYard

There are many livestream options for people who are interested in directing their productions more like a television show. StreamYard, owned by the virtual events company Hopin, is a simple-to-use, web-based tool that provides high-quality streams, virtual background and green screen functionality, camera switching with transitions, lower-thirds, a backstage, and RTMP and multi-stream capabilities.

What StreamYard offers the guest is even more important—ease of use and knowledge that a producer has the controls. StreamYard is web-based platform, rather than an application like Zoom, and therefore allows more access than other streaming solutions may have.

Most of the virtual presenting web-based solutions work best in Chrome, Firefox, or Opera and some work with Safari or Edge. Some have limitations based on the software. StreamYard only works with Chrome, Firefox, and Opera because it requires 64 bits to operate.

StreamYard is an elegant solution for a small group (up to 10 people) live-streams and smaller productions like small panels, salons, and social media live-streams, all the way up to inserts into the Hopin virtual event software.

On-screen participants receive a special link that puts them backstage during the broadcast. They are given a note that they should be ready, as the host can bring them "on stage" at any moment. Some StreamYard producers opt to have a director that never appears on screen, but rather just controls the switching, lower thirds, and comment moderation. This is actually an intensive job for this type of production.

What's nice about StreamYard is that it works really well in a salon or small webinar setting. People can ask questions or add comments and the director can bring the comments or questions directly on the screen for the hosts, panelists, and audience to see. With upgrades, there are many branding customizations you can add, including your logo and colors.

StreamYard also allows you to roll clips and insert images live on air. Just be careful with the buttons.

StreamYard's major benefit is its ability to simultaneously stream to multiple social media at the same time. The company developed an API (application programming interface) that connects with Facebook, YouTube, LinkedIn, Twitch, and Twitter. You can stream all at once, or just a few. The next section will talk about why and when you'd want to use social media platforms for your streaming destination.

The recording functionality of StreamYard is very high quality and they use nice codecs to compress a high-resolution version of your stream for you to download and post after the production is complete.

Vimeo Pro

Vimeo remains an industry-standard platform for video collaboration. Think of it as a more enterprise-friendly version of YouTube. The platform prioritizes video quality and is client-friendly in that it has an intuitive interface that allows stakeholders to share notes and versions of a video during the editing process.

Vimeo integrates livestreaming into its higher-tier accounts. Much like other platforms, Vimeo allows streaming directly from a device's camera via an app or web browser. Additionally, the platform allows for external encoders to send video via an RTMP connection. Once the signal is received by Vimeo, it can be simulcast to a handful of other locations and platforms.

Outside of broadcasting video, Vimeo's livestreaming platform has a handful of useful tools to make a livestream more dynamic. Live polling, chat, moderated Q&A, and on-screen graphics are all built directly into the cloud-based streaming platform.

Vimeo is a great tool for working with enterprise or corporate clients. In addition to allowing account holders to "turn off" the Vimeo logo, the video player can be embedded. This means that the video player (and any relevant "widgets", such as chat, polling, Q&A, etc. can be inserted into an external website simply by copying a few lines of code. This allows producers to create a branded video experience where the audience doesn't need to navigate to a Vimeo link but instead to the website of the client or production company.

Social Media Livestreams—Facebook and LinkedIn

Over the last decade, social media platforms have toyed with "pivoting to video" on multiple occasions. Aside from YouTube and Twitch, the text native platforms have never really successfully built a go-to model for video producers. Fortunately, platforms like StreamYard and Zoom and some others enable producers to stream to the social media platforms.

There are benefits and drawbacks when you plan on streaming to social media sites. In this section, we'll go over streaming to Facebook and LinkedIn and what benefits these sites provide video producers.

Facebook

Facebook Live has been a fairly standard video outlet for many years and people have used it as their destination and streaming provider for a variety of reasons. First, the biggest reason is audience. Nearly 2 billion people use Facebook daily (which is almost a quarter of the world's population). While, at the writing of this book, users may have plateaued, Facebook still remains the global center for social media use.

Facebook Live is the input software for its streaming capabilities.[12] It allows you to stream live to a page, a post, a group, or an event. You can use Facebook's onboard tools to produce high-quality streams or use a product called "Live Producer" which requires you to have your own encoding software and camera input ready.

If you are using StreamYard or Zoom, you can connect to Facebook through its API, which is basically a handshake between the programs, and it will allow you to use your streaming software to stream to the site. These settings should be built well in advance so you are not fumbling with settings the day of your stream.

When you stream to Facebook, you will be using their platform and be able to personally be the content moderator for comments. You can even add comment moderators to moderate on your behalf. Like Twitch, they can like parts of the show in real-time and comment along with the stream.

A nice feature is that you may make highlights of top fans, promoting their comment to the top. This encourages other users to see how to interact with the stream. Facebook enables some sort of gamification (explained later in the chapter) and allows you to "award badges" to some of the viewers.

The bottom line is that you may choose Facebook as your destination for Vimeo, StreamYard, Restream, or Zoom because you know the audience is already there and likely already has access to Facebook. It takes out a large barrier to entry for some audiences that may be uncomfortable with new software or URLs they are not used to.

LinkedIn Live

LinkedIn Live, much like Facebook's system, allows you to broadcast from the platform or directly from a third-party product like StreamYard. Also, like Facebook, the benefit of streaming with LinkedIn is your built-in audience. LinkedIn seems to be interested in conversion rates and automatically sends out reminders when your stream will be airing as well as when you go live.

The only drawback to a LinkedIn Live presentation is the format the stream resides in. When you make a LinkedIn live event, it creates it as a post. That post may be liked and commented on by some of your connections. Those who sign up don't have to go to another destination, that post is the space where viewers will interact with your stream. The drawback is that the comments left before the live broadcast remains during the livestream and other users may interact with comments that are not timely.

But as a streaming destination, LinkedIn live is a valuable streaming platform for professionals and your network.

Simulive

Not all live events are actually *live*. Some events are completely prerecorded and only played out as if they were live. This is called "simulive," as in a simulated live event. These events are designed to be attended life but are actually being streamed to the audience. Sometimes, simulive broadcasts include live Q&A at the end, but most simulive events are designed to *look like live* but were preproduced well in advance.

With always a flair for the dramatic, Apple used to hold live product announcements from the Steve Jobs theater in Cupertino. The iPhone and Mac makers would invite hundreds of tech journalists to come and watch the event in person, while anyone not there could watch online. When COVID-19 virtually shut down the world in 2020, Apple had to shift the method of producing these events. What resulted was a heavily produced product video that rivaled the production value of some Hollywood films. Apple records the content for these events weeks or months in advance, allowing for editing and polishing. On the day of the "live" announcement, all they need to do is push "play."

Why wouldn't they just post the video so that people can watch on demand? Because there is an energy that comes with a live event that you cannot compare to an on-demand video. Apple knows that everyone in the tech community is waiting for that event to start and the excitement builds on social platforms as tech journalists and fans speculate on what the news will be. Even though the audience knows the content is entirely prerecorded, they are watching together, and that energy is irreplaceable.

There are a handful of ways to play back simulive content. Either a video playback device in your control room can hit "play" at the right time, or you can use a cloud-based software option to upload your video days before, program the start time and destination, and relax.

There are some things to think about if you decide you want to broadcast your webinar as simulive. First, you will need to watch your finished video before compressing it so you can identify any spelling mistakes or visible errors. Then, you'll need to export your video.

When you build a simulive event on a platform that handles simulive production, you usually must follow the technical specifications necessary for the software to run the video properly and smoothly to the audience. Glitches, lag, and sync issues are a bummer that takes the audience out of the moment and could possibly ruin the magic.

Most platforms have very specific requirements for long videos, especially in terms of file size. This is where a good knowledge of codecs is really important. Also, remember that compressing a 30-minute or 1-hour video will take time—sometimes **a lot** of time. Build this into your production schedule because after the video is uploaded, you'll need to also likely wait for the software to convert the video into its specific format designed for streaming. First, it's your codec then it's their codec. None of this is done quickly unless you have an extremely powerful computer.

Simulive Using PowerPoint

PowerPoint is a powerful tool. It does far more than displaying your deck and providing some great infographic templates—and far more than we'll explain here! If you want, you can use it as a rudimentary video storytelling tool that incorporates video, audio, and graphics.

There is a form of simulive where you can use PowerPoint to create the feeling that there is a live slideshow, but the presentation is preproduced. Many webinars and presentations are just PowerPoint presentations anyway, so the need to make a live presentation is unnecessary if you use these tips. Preproducing a PowerPoint takes out the possibility of error by the presenter, like loss of Internet, glitches, stumbles, and misspoken words.

To preproduce a PowerPoint Simulive, you should invite the presenter to do a recording of their deck and you can record them using Zoom. The presenter should pretend to present to you while you record the presentation on something like Zoom. (Be sure to check that the audio settings are high quality.) While they present, advise the presenter to take a short break between each slide—thereby allowing you to create better edits—before they move on. This takes a bit of practice, but nearly all presenters can manage this.

The presenter should go through their entire deck, and you should take notes if there are flubs or any need to repeat a slide for clarity. If they make a mistake on any slide, you can interject and ask them to repeat, but make sure you add an audio marker for yourself to know where to edit. Say something like, "Slide 7, take 2."

You may also notice that the presenter becomes more comfortable and changes tone as they progress through the deck. If this is very noticeable, you can ask them to go over their first few slides again to bring up the energy. It's always nice to start with energy, but be careful, as you want to remain authentic and real. Many viewers will believe this is happening live and you don't want to ruin the magic.

After you've recorded all the audio, now you can edit a "show" for the simulive. If you want it to look like a PowerPoint, you should actually *use* PowerPoint to edit the program.

Using an audio editing tool like Audacity or Adobe Audition, break each slide audio into its own file. Then, on each slide, insert the audio onto the respective slide.

When you add the audio, you'll notice a small audio icon now appears on the slide. There are a few steps necessary to make the magic happen.

- Click on the audio icon to get the status bar so you may see the length of the audio file.
- A new set of menu items will appear after you click the audio file including Playback.
    - In the Playback feature, click Hide During Show.
    - This is the most important part because it hides the fact that the audio is not live.
    - Next, select "Automatically" in the Start feature drop-down.
- If you are using transitions between slides, remember that this affects the timing of the audio.

  - Transitions take time, and PowerPoint refers to the time in milliseconds
  - When audio is going to play on a slide, it will wait for the transition to complete, so make sure your transition isn't too long or creates an in-authenticity for the audience.

- If you have animations you'd like to use on each slide, you may need to time these to the speaker. Each animation can be fully controlled on the Animation pane.

  - Select timing to start With Previous and use the timings to keep each animation working as cued.
  - If you feel uncomfortable with timing your animations, you can duplicate the slides and add the cues on different slides.
  - However, if audio needs to go across slides, you'll need to use the feature "Play across slides" for the audio to continue.

One of the benefits of preproducing a simulive with PowerPoint is that you can control the show and make some corrections on the deck that make it more visually appealing. Most presenters are not thinking of entertainment when they've been asked to present a deck, they're interested in being the informer. Your job is to make it look nice.

You can add more animations or highlight certain words or images on the deck as the speaker is presenting it. This works to help the audience see the particular thing the presenter is mentioning. This is not really possible in a live presentation setting because the timings wouldn't work.

Going a step further, you can really increase the quality of your simulive event by using PowerPoint's video recording feature. This requires you to ask the presenter to rehearse the deck before recording because they can record themselves presenting the deck. Their recording is cued to each slide and PowerPoint adds the timings.

Remember, you will need to make time to export the project. Set your deadline at least 24 hours ahead of your simulive event to make sure you complete this task.

Go to File, Export, and choose MP4 as the file format. You should use the H.264 Codec set to "Internet Quality" (HD 1280×720) and **make sure** the "Use Recorded Timings and Narrations" button is selected.

You may have to recompress again depending on the platform, but at least you'll have a movie file.

Programming Your Simulive

Most platforms allow you to program when your simulive will "air." As we discussed earlier, time is extremely important in this business, so you should double and triple check that the time is right and set it to the correct time zone.

This may sound obvious, but we wouldn't have that advice in this book if that mistake didn't happen every so often.

If you want to get advanced, you can time different clips into the simulive to switch between video and static features. Practice this well in advance with several teammates before scheduling the simulive event.

PERSONAL STORY

Jamie Here.

During the COVID era, many huge organizations relied on their pivot to online meetings, workshops, and webinars to keep their communities involved. Several times over the stay-at-home period, I was tasked with helping out local municipal organizations replace their in-person meetings with online versions. Some were easy translations, others were expecting a simulation of real life but online. Many of these organizations didn't have the funding to produce a full-scale virtual event, so we made do with the tools we had.

Using one of the browser-based webinar platforms, I learned how to create cues and timings for a robust simulive for a New York City-based organization. They wanted polls to be interacted with in real time and several stops for community voting. The production was 1-hour and required four or five interactive features to automatically appear on cue. In order to do this, I knew that I could technically air multiple simulive events literally one second after another.

I broke the simulive into five clips, timed them to the second, and scheduled the broadcast like it was five webinars in consecutive order. For example, the first act went 24 minutes and 11 seconds, and the second act was 13 minutes and 45 seconds. I scheduled part one to air at 3:00:00 pm, part two to air at 3:24:12 pm, and part three at 3:37:57 pm (building in the previous extra second)—and so on until the production was complete.

This manipulation of the software is likely not what they designed it for, but made me realize that more often than not, you can assist the client with their needs even when it may seem impossible. You just have to be creative—and patient!

Creative Uses of Existing Technology

Every live event is different. When a client approaches with a unique request, we often try to bend over backward to accommodate. Sometimes you have to innovate the solution. Here are a few unique requests that required us to use a few different pieces of technology in a way that they were not originally intended but did the job perfectly.

Remote Kits

When COVID shut down the world in 2020, several clients had already booked services to film live events. Because of social distancing measures and safety precautions, most of these events quickly became virtual or were canceled. This offered a unique challenge: get a professional-looking camera to an executive's house without sending a person to operate it on-site. The requirement was that the shot looks better than a webcam, be versatile in use, and be easy for the on-camera presenter to set up on their own.

Michael toiled around in his home and iterated several versions of a remote camera kit that fit the bill. The first version was very bulky with a large camera, laptop computer, and while quality was high and the remote director had a lot of control, it was not easy for the presenter to set up. The end result was to keep it simple: two iPhones on a tripod, a broadcast-grade lightweight video light, and a quality microphone. Because we used the iPhone, it was a familiar device for the speaker making for an easy setup.

Back in the New York control room lives a server from a company called AviWest. One phone uses an app that connects to our server using cellular bonding, creating a reliable point-to-point video feed. The second phone uses a video conferencing app of the client's choosing in order to communicate with all parties. The end result is a kit that was easy to set up, a server that allowed for high-quality video and for the Director of Photography to operate and control the camera from anywhere using a web browser.

Hybrid Remote Using RTMP

One of Sorrentino Media's agency partners, Likeable Media, approached the team to help on a livestream for the waterpark, Great Wolf Lodge. The stream was to be a cooking demo, taking place in Arizona. The video crew needed to be minimal, we'd need to switch it from our New York control room, and then send it out to Facebook and YouTube.

For this case, an RTMP feed was chosen from the Arizona set location. The camera out in Arizona was connected to a cellular bonding encoder called a LiveU Solo. The LiveU box sent video to a cloud-based server hosted by a company called Wowza, via RTMP. In New York, our Technical Director was able to pull down that RTMP feed and incorporate it into the video switcher. The end result was an HD video feed with graphics and animated text. We had about a 45-second delay from the location to the control room, but because we were not requiring any two-way communication with a studio or remote guests, the increased quality was worth it.

Mixing Multiple Video Conferencing Platforms and Recording ISOs

During COVID, a client required a multi-day virtual event that was to be prerecorded and would play out as a simulive cast. Using the in-house studio, an emcee would communicate with up to seven remote guests. The challenge here was twofold: One, some guests could only use Zoom to connect, while others were limited to using a browser-based connection called VMix Guest (which is built into the VMix switcher program) and two, record an ISO of each guest.

The first challenge is audio: getting Zoom callers to communicate with the VMix guest callers, and have all remote callers be able to talk to the studio host. The biggest issue here is getting audio crossed over to each platform so that everyone could hear one another but *not* hear themselves back. You've probably had this happen if you call someone that puts you on speakerphone and you hear your own voice echoing back to you—it can be very distracting. To prevent this, we create something called a "mix-minus" feed to send back to each speaker. Mix-minus is essential for all the audio of the program MINUS the sound coming from an individual speaker's mic. With a total of 7 remote guests, that means that we needed an audio mixer that allowed for a high-level of control—luckily, VMix has a relatively robust audio mixer built into the software.

Second, we needed to get an ISO feed from each caller routed into the switcher and also to an external recorder. For the VMix Guest callers, we were able to utilize a function on the software that outputs an NDI feed for each remote guest. For the Zoom callers, we use Zoom's enterprise-grade software called Zoom Rooms. In short, the Zoom Rooms has a function to output a clean isolated NDI feed of each caller.

Finally, how do we easily record eight individual NDI feeds? The best and most expensive option would be to use eight NDI receivers and eight recording decks. We were limited in time and space, so we improvised. What I learned was that the Apple TV 4K model makes for an amazing NDI receiver, using a third-party app called NDI Monitor. We scooped up eight Apple TVs and plugged them into a prosumer video switcher called an ATEM Mini Extreme ISO. This switcher has eight HDMI inputs and has the ability to record each input separately onto an external drive. This allowed us to get clean feeds of each speaker recorded as an ISO.

Simultaneous Streams

Box.com is a cloud-based collaboration and storage firm aimed for enterprise, or corporate, usage. They requested an ambitious project; a live event hosted live by two emcees in Silicon Valley. During the stream, the emcees would give the viewers a choice of which panel or keynote they wanted to attend (akin to an in-person conference, where you can walk into one of several rooms) based on their interests. This event was 90% live, so that meant we would have to run up to three simultaneous livestreams at the same time from three separate switchers.

We used a combination of Zoom Rooms (to get ISO feeds of each guest) and VMix Guest. Our crew set up three control stations at our offices in New York. Each station was to manage a particular session that would consist of up to three remote guests. At each station was a Coordinator, this person would welcome the remote guest prior to going live, set up their shot, confirm that the tech was working, and give directions. Next to the coordinator was a Technical Director that ran a video switcher.

Each station fed their program feed (a program feed is the final composited video that is coming from the switcher) to an external encoder via NDI. We used a special encoder called an AviWest StreamHub that could receive NDI feeds and send up to eight simultaneous streams at the same time. That encoder was then operated by a livestream technician who would route each program feed to the correct RTMP destination when the time was right.

Remote media production empowers you to be creative, connect traditional and new technologies, and put on a good show in a new environment. Everything is possible, you just have to think of unique ways to make it happen!

Virtual Events and Summits

In September of 1988, Autodesk's co-founder and former president introduced a new initiative to the computer-aided design company: Cyberspace. Named after the fictional space for virtual worlds in William Gibson's *Neuromancer,* Walker was interested in making science fiction a reality. Autodesk was, and is still known for their computer-aided design software (CAD) and realizing the value of digital three-dimensional objects, he figured they could leap to immersive architectures beyond the screen. In a manifesto titled "Through the Looking Glass,"[13] Walker explained the history of immersive computing from plug-boards to graphical controls and made the bold prediction that goggle-based computing was next. People wanted to not only *use* computers but be *in* computers. The initiative would become what we know today as virtual reality.

People had been tinkering with the technology of virtual reality since the 1960s. Ivan Sutherland invented a huge headset-based computing system in 1967; NASA used headsets at the Jet Propulsion Laboratory in California; Morton Heilig created an immersive technology called the "Sensorama" in 1961—but the technology was not yet commercially available. John Walker intended on changing that and assembled a team in Autodesk's Sausalito, California office and called it Cyberia.

Cyberia was made up of researchers, engineers, and artists who would consider how people wanted to use the computer with gloves and masks. The biggest downside up until that point was the cost of the technology. There was a good reason VR wasn't commercially available yet, it cost around 250 thousand dollars for a functioning rig. Cyberia's goal was to figure out how to introduce the world to affordable (around 15 thousand dollars) virtual reality.

Over the next several years, the first virtual reality boom occurred. By 1990, it was a huge fad and people started to believe VR would usher in the next generation of computer user experience. But it didn't get off the ground.

Two things stunted the growth of virtual reality: it was still too costly and cumbersome to maintain and keep for its low amount of uses and a version of immersive computing was invented at the same time called the World Wide Web. As it turns out, people weren't interested in putting goggles on their faces to become immersed in the virtual worlds, they wanted learning, community, sharing, and hyperlinks.

By 1992, the VR phenomenon was starting to dry up, with only a few companies continuing the initiative. Most recognized that the true virtual worlds were going to be built-in software. In the background, entrepreneurs, event hosts, performers, and artists still were interested in the ability to broadcast their projects to audiences all over the globe and the virtual bug was making everyone anxious to create the next immersive space and experience. That's when former video director Alan Saperstein and his partner Randy Selman decided to create a new type of event that used physical space along with the web and video for a "virtual trade show." In 1992, Saperstein and Selman founded Visual Data Corporation (now called Onstream Media) and pitched the idea of virtual shows.

In April 1993, Saperstein and Selman created the first virtual event at the Waldorf Astoria in New York City. The event was a presentation to investors and the duo videotaped exhibition booths, digitized the footage, and then mapped the floor map to a rudimentary HTML webpage. When a user moved across the online virtual map, they could see the short videos from each booth. The event was a success and by June of that year, Visual Data had developed a new video codec and virtual software called "HotelView" which showed off the properties of thousands of hotels. The new video codec enabled videos to stream across the Internet rather than being downloaded. The virtual event was born.

In a recent report, the virtual event market will reach 367 billion dollars by 2027 (https://www.linkedin.com/pulse/virtual-events-market-size-hit-usd-3665-billion-2027-owing-khatode/). From its exciting beginnings as an offshoot of virtual reality, the virtual event is a space to host conferences, exhibitions, summits, conventions, and trade shows in cyberspace. Events can mix physical and virtual together, provide additional data, collect data, and provide networking experiences impossible without the technology.

Virtual events experienced two leaps forward in technology and user needs. The first, in the late 2000s during the recession, showed people that travel expenses were unnecessary when the virtual event could satisfy the conference goals. The second, during the pandemic when meeting in physical space was ill-advised. As with all the previous technologies, the market was introduced to companies that traditionally didn't serve video production or remote media production departments. The virtual event satisfied marketing departments globally because the amount of data that could be collected from users from the time they registered to the time they spent on the virtual "floor" would be immense. Leads were more accurate, marketing improved, and the prestige of a virtual event became equivalent to their physical counterparts.

The future is hybrid. Right now, the virtual event market was valued at 114 billion in 2021, in the height of the pandemic and investors believe that as more people use online services grow, as will the market. In addition, virtual events are better for the environment and for public health.

This section of the chapter is going to bring us through all the parts of the virtual event. We'll cover production basics as we have before, but this time tuned specifically for the VE. In addition, we'll cover the features that virtual events offer that can and should be considered when you are in the preproduction stage of VE planning. We encourage you to think about how an in-person event would translate into the virtual world, but implore you to think differently. As the market grows, you'll want to find your niche in the development of the next generation of VE production.

There's a lot to cover, from compliance to networking to data collection to gamification. If done right, your VE, whether it's a few hours or a few days, will be memorable for your attendees and your speakers and guests.

The Virtual Event Basics—Planning

- What's different about your VE from a Webinar or Livestream?
- How many speakers are you planning on inviting?
- Will you be accepting speaker submissions or doing a call for proposals?
- Are you going to run concurrent sessions?
- Do you want to offer networking opportunities? Why?
- What should the networking look like?
- Should you incorporate breakout sessions? Who will run them?
- How does the software work when it comes to presenting?
- What does the backstage look like?
- Will you be offering badges or certificates?
- Is your platform designed for accessibility?
- Do you want to gamify the attendee experience?
- What data do you want to collect and why?
- How are you going to market the VE? In parts or in whole? Both?
- Are you offering a safe environment for the speakers, guests, and attendees?
- Is this going to cost money? How will you collect it?
- Are you going to have your event sponsored? By who and how many? What do they want in return?

A lot of forethought goes into planning a virtual event and you and your team need to consider as many of the details as possible before you go into production.

The Show

A virtual event is a show. It can be big or small, it could be similar to a conference, it could look like a convention, it may be partially hosted in a real location, it could be made into a game, but it's a show.

Why are you interested in creating a virtual event? In most cases, it's because you have an idea or a theme and know just the people to talk about the subject. In the best-case scenario, you have a plotline to follow as well.

First, start with the theme. Virtual events work best with a narrow focus and a point. This helps attendees recognize their return on investment. Attendees are interested in learning more about something specific that they cannot get elsewhere, and likely your network provides you the opportunity to host the experts and KOLs as a collection that likely isn't available elsewhere.

Think about all the conferences you've heard about or been to, there's always a theme. The theme speaks for itself and helps speakers plan what they'll be talking about. The theme should be pertinent to the time and be important to discuss. The theme should be inclusive and be relevant to your community, but accessible to audience members on the fringe of your subject. Finally, the theme should help the marketing team promote the event.

What Makes Virtual Events Unique?

Imagine This:

> You've flown across the country to a familiar city, and you check into your hotel. It's a modest room as you really can't splurge because you're using your institution's budget for travel and conferences. But it's a nice room. You set your alarm for early so you can get up and get breakfast before a full day of panels.

The conference is usually in a hotel or convention center and each panel or paper presentation is booked in a room with a few dozen chairs set up. This time, it's in the hotel's conference rooms on the second floor. You get to the room and the podium and dais in the front is outfitted with microphones and there's a podium for the main laptop and a slew of unruly cables running down the length of the table.

The first few minutes of the panel is filled with the fumbling of USB sticks, signing into Google Drive, setting up a PowerPoint, microphone issues, and chatter from the audience who are awkwardly watching the minute chaos. Occasionally, a veteran of the conference steps up after recognizing the issue and helps out. The session is only 75 minutes long and 7 minutes are already gone when the panel moderator steps up to the microphone and introduces the guests.

As the presentations begin, the moderator jumps to the first row to watch the panelists present their work. After each presenter finishes, there's a shuffling of machines. Is it HDMI? Is it RBG? Where's the audio plug? More minutes pass. You can tell the last panelist is already getting somewhat irritated that the time may run low by the time they speak. Anxiety is building among some crowd members who know the feeling.

The last speaker starts with 15 minutes remaining, but the moderator seemed to really be interested is summing up the talks, so the final presenter talked, well, quite a bit faster than the previous guests. Some slides are dropped (and you kind of wish some of the other panelists dropped some slides too) and the talk goes on. They were all good presentations, but you can't help being distracted by all the fuss. And deep down, you know it's not the last time either.

You go get a quick coffee and a snack and head to a room a few doors down for the next panel. This one should be exciting, but you're pretty sure you're going to see a repeat of the last panel's issues.

By the time you're done with the day, you have pages of notes in your notebook with new trailheads for your research. When you get home, you receive a survey about the event, but it ends up in spam. The conference hosts don't actually really know what panels you attended nor do they know how you felt.

Now, imagine this:

> You noticed that an organization that you love is hosting a virtual event in a few months. You mark it on your calendar. There's a fee to join the conference, and you see it's the same as the in-person event would be. But this time, you don't need to factor in travel, hotel, food, and erroneous costs like high-speed WiFi or forgotten batteries.

The time of the conference comes up and your calendar sends you an alert to remind you to set up your user profile and join the "lobby" to connect with other attendees. You sign in, upload your photo and short bio, you add some categorial hashtags to help people find you. And you "enter" the event.

You're still sitting in your office chair in your own space, but your mind is transported to the magical world of the virtual event. A banner appears on the top of the browser window: "Keynote will begin in 10 minutes in the Main Showcase Room."

While in the lobby, you get a ping from an old friend. A small chat window opens and you're happy to hear from them. This will be a good day. You click on the Main Room link and there's a huge window where the stream will be and on the right is a chat and Q&A column. At exactly 11:00, you see a graphic appear on the screen, and a few seconds later, you see the host of the event appear, happily introducing the keynote speaker. The screen splits in two, they're both visible. Then the host pops away and you listen to an incredible and uplifting keynote speech.

On the side bar to your left, there's a button that tells you the program and where each talk will be. This conference has concurrent panels and multiple stream rooms. You plan your day by seeing what you want to learn the most, but you know you can switch rooms if you'd like.

For each panel you attend, you notice that there's a small number that keeps increasing. You're being rewarded for your attendance! Since you're online, you notice it's somewhat like a game. By going to the Poster session, you got extra points too. You hope to see what else gives extra points.

While you're on the platform, the hosts know what room you are in and how long you were watching. If the platform is robust, they may even know if you switched browsers and just listened. Before you sign off for the day, the VE platform pops up a survey and you take it. It's only a few questions.

There was no fumbling with wires. There were good talks. You spent the day listening to great talks and panels free to get up from your seat and get food or go to the restroom without distracting anyone on stage. Deep down, you feel good about saving some money, but also helping the environment. The virtual event may become your favorite thing to attend.

The Virtual Event—In Parts

The virtual event is a combination of all our previously discussed technologies. It's part webinar, part livestream, part digital interview, part video game, part networking event, and sometimes, a certificate-giving project.

Most platforms contain all the elements to create a unique interactive and multimedia experience, but in many cases, not all features are turned on or even necessary. The following are the features and the reasons for implementing them. Some may seem like a given and others may be advanced features. Each is important, but for different reasons and you and your team (which includes marketing, the clients, the sponsors, and the institution or company) should discuss. A virtual event game plan is important.

The Platform

Scoping out a platform is not an easy task. There are dozens of different services and companies that cater to this project and we recommend you dedicate time to a demonstration by a product representative. However, keep in mind, their goal is to sell the license, so they may take advantage of your idea if they feel they can accommodate many of your requests and requirements.

Obviously, the first thing to take into consideration is your budget. Some of these platforms are exorbitant in price—but you get what you pay for. These expensive products are usually from companies that have been around for a while and have a vast amount of employees and engineers.

Most, if not all, VE platforms structurally do similar things: they livestream from a mainstage, they offer some sort of networking and profile pages, allow you to host content, and enable you to offer on-demand hosting. Where they differ is in their interactive technologies, the number of simultaneous streams you can offer, and how much customization of your branding you may be entitled to.

In many cases, there are two versions of a license that offer customization: co-hosted and white labeled. Co-hosted means that in many places around the platform, audiences will see the logo of the platform company. White labeled means you'll have access to some of the CSS and source code to add your own logo in place of their branding. This is especially helpful for a high-level sponsorship that may stipulate their logo on the project as well as the logo of the event and the host.

Choosing a platform also includes how the audience will use the space. Some platforms are two-dimensional, offering interactivity like a Zoom webinar at a larger scale. Icons/avatars and names will represent each user, and everyone will have a similar access point to interact on the platform. There are more robust platforms that enable three-dimensional avatars and movement around a virtual space.

Also, consider your modality, many platforms specialize in hybrid events and user experience, others specialize in high-quality streaming technologies, and others, networking. Do your homework and plan ahead.

Also, seek out whether there is a mobile version of the platform and what operating systems and browsers work best—make sure to ask why! When helping attendees or guests, you should be prepared to answer questions about a platform that you are licensing rather than owning.

When it comes to cost per attendee, there are usually tiers and limits, make sure to ask which works best for your event. Attendee costs may range from low cost and less than a dollar to several dollars per attendee. Ask about their registration page and whether you can import data from an external source. If you are hosting an event that requires attendees to pay for entry, ask about the security of the payment system and whether it offsets the cost per attendee and whether there are transaction fees.

Finally, some platforms come with assistance the day of your show, be sure to ask if that is included in the package or an additional cost. Assistance is nice, but sometimes completely unnecessary.

DAY OF SHOW SUPPORT

Live assistance is helpful. Having a company representative along with you during your event is nice for several reasons. One, is that you always have someone to immediately troubleshoot from the platform side. Two, is that they have been trained to speak to guests and it offers you, as the host or producer, an opportunity to relax while they step in and cover some presentation basics.

On the other hand, you may have a good grasp on talking to your guests and are not interested in someone getting in the way. You should negotiate with the representative on what type of support is necessary and how you may work together.

While rare, you need to remember that these platforms run on servers and servers can be faulty. Platforms that use larger server systems (say Amazon

Web Services) may have more guaranteed up-time, but smaller servers may overload with too many concurrent attendees on the same server or multiple events on the same day. A real-time assistant can simply talk to their colleagues in their chat to get an immediate response rather than you chatting with the support through a portal.

Some platforms we've used and recommend:

- Bizzabo
    - https://www.bizzabo.com/
    - Considered one of the best VE platforms and uses a service called Event Experience OS
    - Great interface, but costly. They specialize in hybrid events
    - Employees love working at Bizzabo, meaning customer service is good
- On24
    - https://www.on24.com/virtual-conference
    - Good for webinars and VEs
- Hoppier
    - https://www.hoppier.com/
    - Specializes in virtual networking and virtual guest catering
- Hopin
    - https://hopin.to/
    - Extremely robust and scales to 100,000 attendees
    - Good for trade shows and large conventions
    - Owns StreamYard
- Accelevents
    - https://www.accelevents.com/
    - Allows for nice customization and has a good starter price and allows for pay-per-attendee
- Remo
    - https://remo.co/
    - Like the origin of VEs, you can map a floor plan in the virtual space
    - Lots of networking features
- Weve
    - https://try.weve.co/

  - Smaller group virtual events platform with excellent networking features
- Tame
  - https://tame.events/
  - Great for customizability and making the space your own
- Filo
  - https://www.filo.co/
  - Great platform with a lot of robust features and Zoom integration
- Communiqué Conferencing
  - https://www.communiqueconferencing.com/
  - High-end VE software with immersive stages, avatars, and rooms

The next sections will help you decide on what type of platform you would like to license.

Preparation

Aside from rehearsals with your talent, speakers, and keynotes, you should request that each presenter with a deck provide you with a version of their slides two days before the live event. In the case of a malfunction, you should be prepared to share the deck from your computer. Save all the decks in order in a folder that is shared with your team. We like to use the grim phrase "in case I get hit by a bus folder." All extra-show materials should be accessible by everyone. If anything needs to be explained further, use the notes feature on the computer or the text editor to add small Read Me files with explanations.

While an event may only be a few hours long, you need to prepare to be active the entire time. Do not forget to add in breaks to your event for what we call "bio breaks" for the audience. You can add 5–10 minutes between some of the event streams for this break. You need to have a break too, so make sure you plan ahead when you can take those breaks. Usually, the best time is during a long talk when there is only one stage playing a stream. This is also why it's crucial to have multiple team members ready to take command if something happens.

Virtual Event Site Set Up

When you license your virtual event platform, you will be given a dashboard to build your productions. From this end, you'll have the opportunity to create templates (in case you'd like to build multiple productions with the same look and feel) and have the ability to see a snapshot of your statistics at a glance. These stats include information like registration numbers or alerts on what parts of your setup remain.

Most good platforms will provide a checklist for launching your VE site. There will be a draft mode and a publish mode when you are ready to make a URL that is static and a registration page that works. The first thing you need to set up is the registration page (for obvious reasons), but you should customize the Lobby right away. On several platforms, when the attendee registers, they are usually taken to the profile page for them to customize or directly to the lobby where they can see initial information about the event.

The description is usually scalable and enables you to write strong details about the event. This description should also be keyword and SEO friendly. This means that the first paragraph (approximately 250 characters) is all that will appear on a search or in the text box when posted on social media. Keywords and SEO mean to write strong sentences where every word counts. The first description is not the place to wax poetic.

The front page/description should definitely include the keynote and any high-level KOLs. Search engines will detect these names and help you with organic registrations outside of the work your marketing team is doing.

After adding your logo and blurb, the set up should include some entry details—reminders to set up a profile, networking details, and reminders to put the event in their calendar.

You do not need to build out your breakout rooms or populate your poster sessions with the initial setup. Most, if not all VE platforms, only show minimal features to a new registrant until the day of the show. On the day of the main show, the "doors" will open (sometimes an hour or half-hour before the show begins) and the attendees will see the full navigation bar available.

Navigation

Remember, users like easy controls and navigation to each room. Many users are primarily trained to use the web through their use of the browser, which means the more similar the navigation to a webpage, the better. Many users enjoy using the back button on their browser, but some VE platforms do not react well to that type of engagement and would prefer that the attendee clicks around rather than use the browser controls.

Typically, most VEs use a left-side navigation vertical bar, but this is customizable on most of them. Traditionally, that's where navigation was on older websites and older attendees may be more comfortable with that set up. The other option, of course, is top navigation like modern websites. If you are running concurrent sessions, be sure to demo whether the links change while the sessions are live. As in, do the links add an icon of a screen, or do they become bold as the streams are live?

Another part of navigation is the alert system built into many platforms. When a session is about to go live, the platform posts a site-wide alert letting attendees know the session is about to begin and how to navigate to the session. This alert should contain a link, but if it doesn't it should offer you the ability to tell people how to easily get to the session using the navigation features.

"BIO-BREAKS"

Do not forget to schedule in time for presenters **and** the audience to take a short break to use the bathroom, check on their kids, feed their dogs, or get a drink of water. These are very important to schedule into your production, especially if it is scheduled for a long period of time. We call these breaks "bio-breaks" because we don't want to assume what someone is doing with that time. Biological needs are most likely, but it could be anything. It's a nice term to use for your break.

The other reason to call these breaks "bio-breaks" is that it gives the audience the thought that they should return right away. Any break in your production runs the risk of losing the audience. By calling the break period a "bio-break" it insinuates that the break is short. You should also be clear with your audience (information that comes from your host is best) about what time to return. The host should state the current time and how long the "bio-break" is scheduled for. This helps everyone sync their time and be back before the next session begins.

The Main Show

Regardless of what type of production you are hosting, there's usually a main stage for the production. This space acts as the livestream and the central environment for the virtual event. From the audience perspective, it'll look familiar to most streams they've experienced. They can choose to make the stream full screen or watch in the inset.

The main show is where you will do the "housekeeping" at the beginning of the broadcast. Make sure you practice the show feature several times before the broadcast to know where the chat, Q&A, and direct messages are. Most virtual event platforms will allow you to duplicate your show from the dashboard, so after you've set up your main stage, you should set up some rehearsals.

It's our advice that you should have one or two "sock puppet" email accounts to register for the event under an alias so you may see what everything looks like from the audience's perspective. In order to ensure a good production, your setup could include several laptops, phones, extra computers, and tablets logged in during your rehearsal. Watching it from every device ensures the streaming experience is operable. This rehearsal also allows you to witness how long the stream delay may be. All VEs use multiple codecs to livestream so there'll always be a delay. It's usually between three and 15 seconds, but it can vary depending on the bandwidth of the attendee.

You should check the following before doing your live show:

- What does it look like when someone is on screen alone?
- What does it look like when a presenter is sharing their deck?
  - Where do they go? Are they still on screen, but minimized? Are they hidden? Is it a split screen?
- What does it look like for an interview set up?
- What does a panel look like?
- What does it look like when a presenter turns off their camera or microphone?
  - Do they disappear like on Zoom? Do they just turn into a black box? Is there a wallpaper displayed?
- Are there alert noises when someone asks a question?
  - Can this be turned off? How does the presenter get the alert?
- What is the lag delay and will it be a distraction to the presenters?

Concurrent Sessions and Breakout Rooms

If you are hosting a conference or a really robust virtual event with different "tracks" for attendees to participate in, you'll likely set up multiple rooms that can stream concurrently. Things can get difficult for a small team if a client or organization is seeking this type of production. Someone on the hosting side *should be* the administrator of the concurrent session or breakout room.

It's easiest if a producer is in the room with the shared sessions as usually the host or emcee of the production gets this time off. The producer's set up usually defaults to invisible and unseen to the audience (if the camera and microphone is off). It's comforting to a presenter or moderator of a breakout room to know that a producer is there. The focus should be on the production, not any issues. In these sessions, typically the presenters are not VE producers but have taken a role of running the room. They should know what buttons **not to push** at any given time.

Some things to think about in a breakout session:

- Remind speakers how to present their decks and how to stop presenting
- If someone is given moderator status, they may have an additional feature on their screen to stop the broadcast at the end of their session.
- Figure out in advance how to keep time for each presenter.
  - Will they use the backchannel? Will the moderator use the microphone?

- Test any audio/video that is part of the deck. Sharing may cause issues with copyright.
- What's the maximum number of panelists that can fit on the screen?
- Does the screen re-sort the speakers if someone turns off their camera and back on? Does it matter?

Poster Sessions, Sponsor Spaces, and Booths

Poster sessions or sponsor spaces are usually nice spaces on the platform that allows for customization and hosting of non-website documents. These rooms are usually for hosting video embeds from social media sites like YouTube or to upload short video clips that are hosted by the platform. If your conference has a poster session, make sure you scope out this feature before you sign up for your license. Some platforms only show links to the hosted content while others display it like an image.

Check the file types that can be hosted as well. Most will host.pdf documents and images, but there will be restrictions on size. If you are hosting a video, there are occasional limits on how many you may post on the screen. Layout is also a concern. While some platforms are customizable with grids and tables, some are just a linear list of items. Your data will likely collect how many attendees clicked or downloaded the posters or sponsor materials, so the setup is really important to the way this page works.

We recommend that you either post an introductory blurb to the top of this page or a short video explaining what this room does and what the attendee will gain from interacting with the hosted objects.

Exhibition-style sponsor spaces are also part of larger platforms. This is when a conference or event would like to provide "booths" for sponsors to talk about their company with attendees. A sponsor exhibition space usually contains a slider or a list or a visual set of icons with interactive features that let people "enter" the booth.

Once inside the booth, usually there is a sponsor on camera who is there to greet attendees. If this is set for large groups, it may use the same screen to share with everyone similar to a Zoom meeting. If this only allows scheduled meetings, it will be a more intimate session. Check on how this feature works before opening this feature to sponsors. There should be no questions that you cannot answer in regard to a sponsor booth—after all, they're helping to pay for your event.

Networking Spaces

Even in the years beyond the pandemic pause, virtual networking is one of the most valuable parts of the virtual event platform. Virtual networking has supplanted many in-person events due to their convenience and accessibility. When investing in a VE platform, the networking features are one of the primary reasons to sign on with a platform.

Networking is an art. By now, most people know how to connect with people virtually, but when the specific directive is to network, some people can get nervous. Some platforms come with several different modalities for networking, but some come with a choice.

Build in ice-breakers or provide themes to discuss in case the networking gets awkward.

- Large meeting rooms
    - These rooms are similar to a Zoom meeting but limited to small groups. Some platforms use a sorting feature that utilizes profile data to connect similar attendees to each other. If this is the case, the profile or registration page should stress the importance of that data when the attendee signs in.
    - Sometimes, a platform may actually say that the hashtags or preferences will be used for the networking feature.
- Small group tables
    - As VE platforms evolve and technology becomes more available, networking features may include virtual tables or organized small group rooms that have themes. These can be made in advance or allow users to come up with their own theme.
    - There are some VE platforms that literally show tables with seats (to visualize how many open spaces remain) and who is in each room. This is more of an intimate networking space and usually a bit more comfortable for attendees because they already have an ice-breaker.
- Speed dating/Matchmaker style
    - These sessions are usually for quick meetings and networking. Usually, these types of sessions are timed and automatically switch to the next person in the queue. Countdown timers are usually visible.
    - In many cases, the platform uses user data to sort people into each room to make a "match" and the conversation is valuable for the attendees.
    - If this is your style of networking, be sure to have the host explain how to use this feature during the housekeeping portion of the show or make a small (and happy) text post that attendees can see.
- Meetings/Private or Scheduled
    - Many VE platforms will provide ways for the attendees to meet with some panelists, sponsors, and experts. There's sometimes a calendar feature that people can click on to schedule a meeting. Please make sure your panelists are aware of this before making this feature available.

- These rooms are usually one-on-one meetings and are especially helpful for sales leads and client meetings.

Gamification

Before we get to data collection, let's talk about event gamification. Basically, all attendees have to use interactive features to operate the virtual event. It does not work automatically just as a conference in real life couldn't automatically teleport you to the keynote stage. Each interaction can be rewarded if you decide to add gamification to the event.

If you do decide that gamification is part of your event, you need to know what the reward may be before you add this feature. What happens when someone wins? Do they get an award? Will you send it to them? Is it digital? Make sure this is very clear before you begin to incentivize the game.

Gamification is when a user is rewarded for **fully** participating in the virtual event. Each room can be assigned a point value and each click or download or sponsor visit can add to their point accumulation. Points may also be rewarded for adding more detail to their profile page ("Add your picture for +10 points!") or for how long they stay within a session ("This session is worth +25 points!").

You can provide a leaderboard that displays attendees who have accumulated the most points. This incentivizes others to "compete" as well. Remind attendees that they are competing against the event, not each other, in order to create a positive environment for the game to be played.

As you may imagine, gamification is reliant on user data, and its actual goal is not to provide an award to the best of the attendees, but rather for you to add a sly way of encouraging attendees to provide you, your organization, or your client with robust sets of user data. The more data the user provides, the better data you will have for follow-ups, sales or marketing leads, and data feedback on how your event operated. Thing of gamification as a behind-the-scenes view of how the platform works from a data perspective.

Check the details of gamification with your VE provider and test the game on your sandbox site before you enable this feature for your VE. Be sure to let people know this is optional and they do not have to play the game within the site. Having a good reward helps explain why they should play anyway.

Data Collection

Data is one of the most important factors in the field of remote media production. The world is digital and data is everywhere. When it comes to collecting data on VE platforms, a very precise conversation must happen between you and the sales and marketing teams and the client. What specifically do they want and why? Is it lead generation? Speaker feedback? Learning outcomes assessment? Audience retention data? These are completely different questions that all have significant data points that can be employed in the collection process.

VE platforms collect data from the first moment someone registers. The amount of registration data is crucial as well. Your registration form should be robust, but as we mentioned earlier, the more that someone has to fill in, the lower the conversion rate. People like streamlined processes or at least a justification for why certain data are being collected.

Important registration data is usually geographic data and organization data. These data points are usually voluntary, and the attendee has to input these in manually. However, many VE platforms do collect IP addresses in their data, but not all licenses permit you to see the data collected from the VE company's perspective.

If your team is interested in lead generation or learning outcomes assessment, time spent in sessions is an important data point. VE platforms usually log user transit across the platform and let you know—with a timestamp—when someone entered a session and left it. Some platforms even show advanced data as to whether the browser tab was switched (meaning the audience member is multi-tasking or distracted) while they were attending the session. Some of this data is very granular and useless but could be important to certain teams.

SURVEILLANCE CAPITALISM

Data collection provides us with the opportunity to talk about surveillance capitalism—the primary method social media platforms use to make profit. At their core, social media platforms are advertising platforms that rely on user-generated content to be sorted into a feed that increases "time spent" on their site. Whether it's Facebook or TikTok or Snapchat, the social part of social media is the use case, but the real purpose is to collect as much information from each user as possible to sell to advertisers all day long.

We used to use the phrase "If you do not pay for it, you are the product," but Harvard Professor Shosana Zuboff says it's often more insidious than that: we are inputs for other products that are then used to try to predict our future purchasing behavior.[14] Nothing is free, and if it is free, that data is being used for advertisers and added to social media algorithms.

This is the digital world we live in. While we are not condoning the tactic, we understand that these systems can only operate at scale with this. Hence why GDPR now exists, and Apple has changed the app store rules to warn users that some apps collect their data.

When it comes to data collection on your virtual event project, be clear with your registrant in some sort of disclaimer text or in the description on the registration form. Your transparency increases trust with the attendee and results in added value for your project. While there has yet to be studies, we believe that your conversion rate will benefit from a clear understanding of what the registrant will get in return for voluntarily adding their data.

The rest of the data on the site you can keep to yourself as it becomes internal data useful for making better production decisions, providing feedback on speakers, and helping you improve your project the next time you produce one.

Certificates

Depending on your production, you may be offering certificates of attendance and/or completion. Before you begin, you need to be very clear about how these certificates are distributed. Many students may ask in advance if this is possible to use for their class or for professional development. Unless you are **absolutely sure** what the institutions want, be as open as possible to the use of certificates. Most VE producers and organizations will give out certificates if they feel the attendee has met an arbitrary requirement like time spent watching the broadcasts or participating in a breakout session. Make these rules clear with any person questioning it and **stay consistent.**

Surveys and Polls

Many, if not all, VE platforms enable polls and surveys. Polls are excellent ways of sharing immediate feedback or interactivity during a live session. You should practice deploying polls before the event because some platforms deploy polls inline during the chat and some are pop-ups. If they are pop-ups, make sure they are not the kind that gets blocked by some browsers.

Surveys are usually deployed before or after an event to gather preliminary data or to provide feedback or generate leads. Many VE platforms have survey software built in, but many organizations or companies opt for third-party survey systems.

Compliance and Accessibility

Accessibility is quite possibly the most important issue of our time. Some VE platforms come with accessibility checks, but most do not. Accessibility refers to how people who may be visually or auditorily impaired may access the virtual event. In addition, virtual platforms are already somewhat inaccessible to those with low Internet literacy or technical difficulties. Unlike television, virtual events require interactivity to operate. It's not like switching a channel on a remote control, there are needs to address to navigate the platform.

Many users with sight impairments may use something called a screen reader. This translates the site to audio and plays it to the viewer. Usually, the most inaccessible part of the platform is the images. On a screen reader, images are read as their file name is alt-text and is not included in the description. Alt-text is part of almost every online website or platform. It allows creators to describe the image to a screen reader user. You should be **as descriptive as possible.** You have to help the user be able to imagine the image or photograph by the words you write.

Some software has now been experimenting with live captioning done by artificial intelligence software. It's mediocre at best, but it is getting better with each new iteration. You should experiment with the accessibility of your platform before you go live to see how accurate the live captioning capabilities are. Zoom happens to have one of the most robust live captioning capabilities, but other platforms are catching up.

Captioning should be part of your post-production process.

Post-Production, Long-Term Hosting and On-Demand

When you sign your licensing agreement with the platform, check to see how long the show will be archived for and whether they continue to charge for new attendees. Most platforms give a month of hosting after your live show and offer long-term hosting packages for your project. We recommend hosting your project on the site for a year.

As we wrote earlier, attendees cost money. The cost of attendees post-live show *may* be an additional cost because they still take up space on the server, though not as much as during the live broadcast. Check with your host provider to see how this works.

On most platforms, your livestreams will be archived soon after the stream ends. On the host side, the livestream is being recorded in their cloud in a streaming format. At the end, it will be processed for on-demand streaming, meaning it will be a slightly different codec than the livestream. You should download the clips and edit them.

Post-production should be included within your workflow. You have control over the on-demand version of the show and may even be interested in submitting the event for an award, so you should clean it up as much as possible.

- If someone had an error with their slide deck, you can use the deck they send you to edit the slides properly.
- If there was a sharing issue (there's always at least one sharing issue), you can eliminate the awkward pauses that occur.
- Occasionally there is a connection issue that makes for an awkward few seconds while you hear the "your mic is off" repeating. This can be edited out.
- Remove transitions that may have taken too long.
- In some cases, you may be able to reframe some speakers if their camera is askew. While this may take some time, it will vastly improve your on-demand experience.
- You should upload your final clips to a company like Rev.com to have the videos professionally captioned. Rev will add the captions directly to the

video and let you edit the contents of the words before you export as a downloadable file.

- Re-upload your clips to the site and double check all videos are in the right place.
- Delete intrusive and inappropriate comments in the chat stream. Some people type issues they are having personally into the chat ("I can't hear you!" or "My screen isn't working" or "Why is there lag?") and when people visit the on-demand of the show, they'll have no idea why those comments are there. Just delete them. No one will miss them.
- But be judicious, remember, you need to be authentic, and too much polishing and cleaning turns your real event into a cold product. Use your judgment.

Warnings to the Wise—Some Important Safety Practices

Trust and safety are one of the fastest-growing parts of online platforms. User safety is of the utmost importance when it comes to making sure you maintain your reputation and your quality of service. While we always strive to make the best possible experience for our audience, there are people that exist to make problems for others. These trolls may have registered under a false name or have decided that today is the day they mess with your project. Most platforms have safety measures built in, but you should ask to be sure there are tools like banning, ejecting, and silencing some users.

Have a discussion with your team before the event to strategize how you will deal with disruptive users.

Here are some things to watch out for:

- **Trolls**
    - A troll is someone who, as Alfred says of the Joker in *Batman,* "just want to watch the world burn." They are incredibly meddlesome and problematic, often finding ways to abuse platforms and say inappropriate things or try to disrupt the flow. Since nearly all platforms disallow camera access for anyone who is not a speaker, odds are the trolling will be in the chat, so keep an eye out for any disruptive behavior.
- **Zoom bombers/Screen bombing**
    - These are users who turn their cameras on with inappropriate imagery or disruptive noise. If they turn up during a virtual event, it's likely in the context of a breakout session or participatory panel. You should know where any tools are to remove or eject a bad user. You should also know how to recover from this in the event it becomes awkward.
    - If a screen bomber appears in a networking event, this can be hard to manage, especially if it occurs during a "speed dating" style of networking. Put a warning on the networking sessions or in the housekeeping to be respectful.

- **Corporate Sabotage**
  - Several times in our experience, we've seen the competition sign up under alias names for a competitor's event. They are easy to spot because they'll usually be asking *very specific* questions to the panelists that may be the intellectual property of the company or questions about costs.
  - Usually, a client will give you a heads up if they feel like saboteurs are likely, but you should be ready to eliminate them or silence them. A moderator can step in to say something along the lines of "we are not going to be covering that today, thank you. Please email ____ for more information."

Getting Good at Putting on a Virtual Show

Making virtual productions is filled with excitement and anxiety. It gets easier each time you put on a successful production, but you'll always likely feel the thrill of making something so many people will see *and* interact with. A lot of people have jumped into the world of virtual presenting and remote media production over the last several, many of whom will continue far off into the future. Whether you were put in a producer position by choice or by company need, it's up to you now to make it work out.

We hope our advice helps you plan your next big event. Make sure to send us an invite!

Notes

1 Burgess, Matt. "What Is GDPR? The Summary Guide to GDPR Compliance in the UK." *Wired UK.* www.wired.co.uk, https://www.wired.co.uk/article/what-is-gdpr-uk-eu-legislation-compliance-summary-fines-2018. Accessed 31 August 2022.

2 "Art. 89 GDPR – Safeguards and Derogations Relating to Processing for Archiving Purposes in the Public Interest, Scientific or Historical Research Purposes or Statistical Purposes." *General Data Protection Regulation (GDPR),* https://gdpr-info.eu/art-89-gdpr/. Accessed 31 August 2022.

3 Ibid.

4 *Vladimir Nabokov Discusses "Lolita" Part 1 of 2.* Directed by JiffySpook, 2008. *YouTube,* https://www.youtube.com/watch?v=Ldpj_5JNFoA.

5 *Children Interrupt BBC News Interview - BBC News.* Directed by BBC News, 2017. *YouTube,* https://www.youtube.com/watch?v=Mh4f9AYRCZY.

6 Labs, Spectrum. *Why Is Trust and Safety Important.* https://www.spectrumlabsai.com/trust-and-safety. Accessed 31 Aug. 2022.

7 *History of PictureTel Corp. – FundingUniverse.* http://www.fundinguniverse.com/company-histories/picturetel-corp-history/. Accessed 31 Aug. 2022.

8 "PICTURETEL GIVES LIVESHARE PLUS SIMULTANEOUS VOICE, DATA." *Tech Monitor,* 7 September 1995, https://techmonitor.ai/technology/picturetel_gives_liveshare_plus_simultaneous_voice_data.

9 Yavorskaya, Galyna. "Webinar History. When the Webinar Was Appeared?" *Webinar Platform MyOwnConference.Com,* 7 August 2017, https://myownconference.com/blog/en/webinar-history/.

10 *25 Webinar Statistics [2022]: Facts About Webinars in the U.S. – Zippia.* https://www.zippia.com/advice/webinar-statistics/. Accessed 31 August 2022.

11 "ON24 Webinar Benchmarks Report Special Edition: Post-COVID Trends." *ON24*, https://www.on24.com/resources/asset/on24-webinar-benchmarks-report-special-edition-post-covid-trends/. Accessed 31 Aug. 2022.

12 "Facebook Live." *Facebook Live | Meta for Media*, https://www.facebook.com/formedia/solutions/facebook-live. Accessed 31 August 2022.

13 Walker. *Through the Looking Glass*. https://www.fourmilab.ch/autofile/e5/chapter2_69.html. Accessed 31 August 2022.

14 Biddle, Sam. "'A Fundamentally Illegitimate Choice': Shoshana Zuboff on the Age of Surveillance Capitalism." *The Intercept*, https://theintercept.com/2019/02/02/shoshana-zuboff-age-of-surveillance-capitalism/. Accessed 31 August 2022.

6

VOICES FROM THE FIELD

The stay-at-home period of the pandemic made us all remote media producers. During that time, there were likely thousands of guides made on Google Docs or on company shared drives, printed, and emailed to colleagues and clients. Many of the guides shared the thoughts that the authors also had during that time, and we added their ideas to this book.

One thing that we discovered by working on this book was the amount of people who were excited to share their unique experiences in virtual presenting. While the text provides a general overview and a guidebook approach to the big issues and the tiny details, the unique perspectives could only be added here, rather than in the subsets or in examples. Some experiences are specific to each event and producer. The stories in this chapter are curated from a series of outreach moments from people we met, learned from, and discussed remote production.

We want you to hear from them as well. This chapter shares some interviews with some talented people that do remote media production as their job or as one of their primary responsibilities. We let them do the talking and gave them the freedom to express themselves and share their stories with you, the reader. We hope you enjoy their tales and adventures in virtual presenting.

Ashesh Satvedi, Director of Video Marketing & Virtual Experiences at Box

Box is a company, created in 2005 by Aaron Levie and Dylan Smith, that makes cloud-based content management and collaboration tools for businesses.

DOI: 10.4324/9781003291718-6

In Your Opinion, What Are the Biggest Issues Facing Remote Media Production?

Certainly, some of the biggest challenges are related to just work working from home. First, working from home has made us just glued to our computer screens, and we're going from meeting to meeting without any breaks in the middle. So, when you are bringing in a remote speaker, knowing that they've been working from home, knowing that this is another thing on their list after many meetings, it's challenging for them to bring that energy to a recording or a live broadcast.

The other challenge is that are you reliant on their Internet access. Internet has been the single number one killer of a lot of these broadcasts. Even if your Internet is great, there is a lot of bandwidth that gets taken up by VPN, security software that's installed from your IT team that causes a lot of bandwidth and processing issues with, especially, live broadcast. We're asking our speakers to join using Chrome or on Zoom, etc., it takes a lot of resources for the computer to process all that and send it over the pipes to the production team.

There is so much from the speaker's home to the production studio that goes in between, that there are so many failure points we are dealing with. Anything could go wrong, and that's what the biggest challenge is. In-person recording or a studio recording, there is so much involved and there is like a big team and it's a heavy production, but in a way it's easier because you can control all of it. Your speaker does not have to worry about anything. They just show up, follow the directions and go. But here we do have to worry about a lot. I'm playing the role of a director a lot of times during our recordings, and we're having to walk our speakers through the process, "this is how you speak," "please don't forget to look at the camera" … At the end of the day, it's still remote and there is only so much you can control.

What Is Unique about Your Workflow, Approach, or Remote Production Methods?

We have a process that most of our speakers now, thankfully, are used to. We have checks and balances of every single thing that goes into production, including the scheduling of the speakers and doing dry runs and rehearsals.

We are making sure that we are not asking our speakers to use tools or software that are way outside of what they've been using on a day-to-day basis. We want to make it as streamlined and as easy for them. We don't make them learn something new just because the production team wants a slightly better quality.

We have tried sending them fancy camera kits or using sophisticated software, and we learned that it took their focus away from the content they needed to present. These are the speakers that we work with often and they know this content inside-out. So, if they're having issues, we could just tell by their facial reactions, the complex production was throwing them off.

So what we are doing now is using software that they use on a day-to-day basis. Then we will do something in post-production to make it beautiful. Our focus is on making them feel comfortable in the delivery of the content, and for them to sound and look natural.

- What "solutions" to managing remote production have you seen suggested or implemented that you are excited about?
- What do you see as the biggest problems facing a switch to remote media production?
- How does remote media production look different 5 years from now?

Can You Give an Example of a Moment or Project Where You Were Stuck or Had a Major Issue Related to Remote Production? What Happened and How Did You Resolve It?

When I've done live broadcast with a studio set up and speakers in-person, we've never had an issue, everything's worked perfectly. When our speakers are remote, on the other hand, we've had a couple of issues. A couple of years ago, we had a very special guest take part in a conversation with our CEO for one of our virtual conferences.

Mid-conversation, the guest's computer just shut down—in the middle of broadcast! My CEO is speaking with that guest and he's like, "what just happened?" The attendees are watching live going, "what just happened?" Thankfully, we put up a slide right away that said, "sorry for the technical issues. We'll be right back."

Internally, my CEO is asking me "are we going to be back online or no?" This is where, as a director, you've got to keep your cool and not freak out. I reassure him that the guest will be right back, when I have no idea if they're going to be back or not, but I need to keep my presenter calm, cool, and confident.

In the end, we made it work and the guest was online after his computer restarted. The beauty of this was that it was the beginning of pandemic, and the online audience was so used to just watching prerecorded content. We saw it in the live chat from the attendees, many saying that it was refreshing for them to see that this is actually live. They weren't complaining that the feed went down. In fact, they felt like that, for a change, they were watching something that feels real.

Of course, I never want that to happen again. Now we learn from it that if something like that happens, you've got to have a plan B, C, and D because anything could happen during a live event.

What Are Some Common Mistakes That On-Camera Presenters Make during Virtual Events?

There are certain speakers that I've seen speak to a live audience very well, but then they would show up on a remotely produced event and they're a completely different person.

They don't feel the energy from the crowd, they don't see the faces in front of them reacting to what they're saying. If they're just staring at their screen or their webcam, it really throws them off.

This is one of the things we try to cover during dry runs, to make sure you're looking at the webcam. It's hard to make eye contact with that virtual audience without looking at your lens, and vice versa—you want to see the crowd but you end up looking away from the lens.

As an attendee, when you're watching that and your speaker is not looking at you, you get distracted easily.

Another mistake that I see our speakers make is not prepping enough for recorded content because they know we can always edit out. Sometimes a speaker might have not rehearsed a written script and you can see the eyes going on the screen left to right. The viewer can clearly tell that they're reading it. I've gotten comments from attendees saying, "Hey, if this was going to be like this, you could have just sent me the notes and I could have read it myself."

What Do You Consider to Be the Best Advice/Leadership You have Provided to On-Camera Talent?

When you're working from home, you're not thinking through your lighting. As a result, a lot of speakers tend to sit in a room with windows behind them. They don't realize how they look and if there's no light in front of them, they're going to look silhouette. A lot of times when we would point that out, they'll put a lamp in front of them and it makes a big difference. Another good tip is for speakers to always keep a glass of water by their side when presenting.

We think because we do this all day and night that that would be just obvious, but it's not obvious to people who aren't full-time producers. Some of the best tips that I have been given were from an expert that helped me prep backstage before an event I was presenting at years ago.

He took me in the greenroom and said, "tell me what you're going to talk about," and so I'd rehearsed my presentation in front of him. Then he had me do it again, and again, and again for 10 minutes straight. Then he said, "now, when you go up on the stage, you run up onto the stage. Don't like just softly, gently walk on the stage." It made a big difference because when you go on with that energy, it's going to flow into what you are saying. A lot of the times when we are speaking, we're just sitting on our chairs and we're not moving much. You might notice that if you're on the phone and you're pacing back and forth in the room, you have so much more energy in that conversation. So sometimes I tell my speakers to stand up, walk around a little, use a standing desk if you can, because when you're using hand gestures and moving even a little bit, that adds energy to what you're saying.

Jeff Miner, Global Business Lead at Google's Creative Works

Google's Creative Works team works with advertisers to create better ads for the platform.

What Is Unique about the Work You Have Done in a Remote Production Environment?

Our team within Google is to help clients make better ads. Now, prior to COVID shutting the world down, we would present to our clients in-person. My creative director, Kim Snow, and I did a lot of meetings together and clients loved our energy and back and forth. And then a little virus called COVID started coming up in the news.

Having to go completely remote, nothing replaced having a person from my team in the room. You can't talk to every single client and there was no scale there. What we really saw was that the slide presentation just doesn't hit in the same exact way.

So we had to figure out something different because we did this one virtual meeting with a client and they were just bored. It was just boring hearing us talk all over video chat. Alternatively, we didn't just wanna send the slide deck. So we just started brainstorming and thought, "what if we actually recorded the presentation in advance and did some nice editing?"

So we took that approach on one client and then about a week after sending it, we just met with them for 30 minutes to answer follow-up questions. In fact, to make us even more prepared, we sent them a form with that video so that they could submit their questions in advance.

The feedback was overwhelmingly positive. The senior brand manager and everyone else on the team really loved the format. Now this was a basic approach, so with continued success, we kept elevation our recorded presentations.

One of the things I loved growing up was old talk shows. I always thought that we could actually communicate our learnings through a talk show format and that we could utilize people's love just like mine of the classic late show format. So we're giving them this format that they're familiar with, we're giving them these references that they love, and we're communicating all of our guidance and learnings in this fun format. So as my colleague and creative director, Kim Snow, would like to say, we're giving the audience their broccoli with the mac and cheese. That is how the Creative Caviar show was born.

How Do You Prep and How Do You Prep Your Fellow On-Camera Presenters?

The first thing I realized is that in addition to authenticity, there's this word that we've been coming back to a lot, which is sincerity. Sincerity is the absence of deceit or hypocrisy. The thing that I think has really worked with us, is that all the on-camera speakers are not being anything but themselves.

When prepping fellow on-camera presenters, I really want to have fun with and lean into exactly who you are. Don't worry about playing to the camera. Don't worry about playing a role, just do *you* within this little playground that we've created and everything else will take care of itself.

The other thing that I feel was important with this is to understand where the viewer is dealing with. There are so many negative things that are happening in our lives when you look at the news for example. I honestly have felt that my interactions in a business perspective have followed suit in a way where there's less excitement. Viewers are more and more cynical.

To combat this, one of the things I wanted to do with these videos is bring a little sweetness and just say something nice about the guests. Is that something that the audience needs to know? No, but it feels nice. That's like the other side of sincerity because we want people to smile while they watch our content.

What Mistakes Did You Make Early on That You've Learned From?

The writing process, a lot of times, is the most difficult for all filmmakers. I really learned that comparing episodes one and two. Spending more time in pre-production in the writing phase and development made the final product so much more crisp and made the production process much easier.

You can do so much in the editing process these days that a lot of times you can clean up most everything, but the human lift to do that is so much more difficult when you haven't put the time in leading up to production. And I think that was my big learning going from episode one, two.

The first thing was, is that I did not write a thorough enough script. I had a good outline and I had the storyboard, but I just needed to think about the words that were being said much more so beyond what I would do for a traditional PowerPoint presentation.

For episode two, I started with a blank piece of paper and I pulled from a ton of different resources, building a real script outline. I wrote every single word that I was planning on saying, that that the guest was planning on saying, and to match the overall storyboard. Then, once we were recording, by the third or fourth take, it's in your memory. The teleprompter is off and you're just going off the cuff. The end result was a video that came together much more organically and efficiently.

Liana Jabs, Digital Project Manager and Digital Producer, Genetic Engineering and Biotechnology News

What's Unique Story That Changed the Way You Produce?

In November 2021, I led the virtual event, mRNA Day for our client, TriLink Biotechnologies. For their 4 hours of content, they wanted two simultaneous "tracks" of presentations and panel discussions. My unique idea was to utilize the client's brand colors to design each track to visually appeal to the audience and keep them engaged with each track—especially if audience members wanted to watch different parts of the tracks and not stay from start to finish. We achieved this by creating Zoom backgrounds, TriLink TriVia, Fun Facts, and Poll Questions in the client's brand colors so that constantly throughout the presentations, the audience would see these fabulous brand colors within each track. This was a breakthrough in our multimedia department because we hadn't yet incorporated such elaborate graphic design and motion graphics in our virtual events, and now we do consistently for every project thereafter because of my initial ideas.

What Was the One Thing You Wish You Knew before You Did the Project above and How Has That Experience Changed Your Future Productions?

I wish I knew how long it would take to create such elaborate motion graphics and how meticulous me and my producers would have to be as we carefully produced each part of the virtual event with the correct colors to ensure proper placement. One wrong move and we would lose the effect we were trying to achieve.

What Went Right? What Went Wrong? What Advice May You Provide to a Reader about How to Better Prepare?

What went right was that the client absolutely loved it and that we had fantastic engagement during the entire event. The client had over 3,000 registrants which were all qualified leads for them to pursue post-event. What went wrong was that the platform wasn't that great and we had to screenshare each video so that we could ensure both tracks were live simultaneously, and we had to deploy the poll questions simultaneously. This was difficult to coordinate because each layer of the tracks was not 100% at the same time, so we had to pay close attention to the first instance of the poll questions on screen to deploy them properly which at one point wasn't completely successful. To better prepare for this, we would have had more support from our platform provider so that we could understand if we were best utilizing its features for such a project like this.

Is Remote Media Production Here to Stay? From Your Specific Experience, What Is the Most Important Thing Future Remote Media Producers Should Know?

Remote media production is absolutely here to stay. The ability for people all around the world to learn from such insightful conversations is a benefit that we didn't know we needed until it happened. Future remote media producers need to know that with more livestreams means more potential for errors that are outside of our control. My previous manager would say often "it's up to the Internet gods now" and we ride by that mantra to ease our day-of-show anxieties knowing full well we did everything possible to assume success and sometimes it isn't completely enough.

Andrea Ranalli, Multimedia Senior Producer and Editor, Founder of InStory

What Is a Unique Story That Changed the Way You Produce? (Translated from Italian)

After the lockdown caused by the 2020 pandemic, I saw my work change. Before then, I worked mainly on narrative and journalism projects, mainly through the production of documentary content shot in developing countries. The end of travel forced us to change our strategy and fortunately through an alliance with another company in Rome, The AMP Audio Service, we were able to sign a collaboration contract with the fashion brand FENDI, supporting it in the production of both content and live and registered for their internal education and training channels.

The main project we worked on with FENDI was the "Webinar Convention" 2021 and 2022, an online event in which the new collection and new business strategies for the season were presented to employees in all offices around the world through a live show broadcast from Palazzo FENDI in Rome. Our production is of about 20 video contributions lasting 3–5 minutes with interviews with the major executives and designers of the brand and also with famous fashion figures in Italy such as the influencer Chiara Ferragni. The live streaming was watched and followed by around 3,500 FENDI employees from all over the world.

What Was the One Thing You Wish You Knew before You Did the Project above and How Has That Experience Changed Your Future Productions?

From this experience, I learned that a production, specifically one with video contributions such as commercials or clips, has longer approval times if done remotely than working in a classic editing room with the customer sitting next to the editor.

Export and upload times and any communication problems and misunderstandings must be considered for each review. We have tried to keep things as simple as possible by adopting Vimeo and Google Drive as material sharing platforms, but in the future we will try to find a platform on the market that allows greater interaction in the review phase.

What Went Right? What Went Wrong? What Advice May You Provide to a Reader about How to Better Prepare?

What went well was that in having to create content between collaborators in Rome, Milan, and Paris, the possibility of working remotely allowed the crews who were making the shots to immediately send the footage to the editors using Google Drive. Given the tight production times, this speed allowed our team to build in extra editing days.

Fortunately, we did not have any major negative experiences or problems, but during the live broadcast, the platform chosen for streaming had a problem and we had to move to the backup platform for about an hour. I admit this caused us a few drops of cold sweat. So maybe the only advice I can give is to not absolutely trust a single technology and be prepared with a backup option.

Furthermore, you must keep in mind that customers do not have great experience of this new way of doing production and we must therefore try to explain to them the technical times behind it before starting the work, especially to avoid creating too optimistic expectations.

Is Remote Media Production Here to Stay? From Your Specific Experience, What Is the Most Important Thing Future Remote Media Producers Should Know?

I believe it is absolutely here to stay, and I believe that the biggest challenge for producers will be to manage communication, specifically with customer requests coming through emails, WhatsApp messages, chats, and so on. These messages are not always perfectly clear and can lead to misunderstandings. My advice is not to forget about direct interaction and to resort when needed to videocall or even simply, phone calls.

Martin Schlesinger, Compliance Analyst at Red Hat

Martin Schlesinger is a compliance analyst, digital marketer, and filmmaker. His previous roles include department management for an Am Law 200 law firm where he led video production, web development, content dissemination, and go-to-market campaigns (https://www.martinschlesinger.com).

What Is a Unique Story That Changed the Way You Produce?

In my previous role, I was the senior video producer for an international corporate law firm. While I had worn the hat of video producer for the decade I'd worked there, it wasn't until 2019 that I stepped into a dedicated video production role. While hiring an in-house video producer is still uncommon for law firms, the law firm where I worked has historically been a little more progressive on this front, as they have an entire in-house marketing department to address any creative, PR, or marketing need a lawyer may have. Most of the video content I edited and produced included webinars, live panel discussions, internal communications, leadership updates, and motion graphic vignettes to promote the law firm's various practice groups and myriad of industry experience across its 19 US offices. Up until the COVID pandemic, I had been traveling to record live footage and editing videos daily in our downtown Raleigh office. COVID changed everything. One by one, law firm offices across the United States closed their doors and told employees to work from home. Nobody knew exactly what to expect. Especially for myself, I was concerned because a big component of my job was traveling over state lines to record interviews, events, panel discussions, and executive updates. Without that, I was left wondering if my role was still critical.

To my surprise, there was an immediate uptick in requests for remote recordings. Lawyers across our US footprint were stuck at home but still wanted to participate in marketing activities and professional development exercises, all of which included video, whether live or pre-recorded. To meet this need, I drafted a how-to guide and checklist for remote recording. This guidance document had gone through various iterations through the years, but with both the pandemic and the immediate need to record remote videos from individuals across multiple states, it was clear this was the time to coalesce and crystallize my production experience and years of coaching talent into a single, digestible resource.

With using only smartphones, lawyers could now record video with high production value. To supplement this initiative, I also created turnkey video production kits that could be shipped out to any location. This kit included a small tripod, lapel microphone, LED desk light, and various adapters to account for different phones and media inputs. The remote video recording guidance and production kits were a boon for jumpstarting remote recording and production. Projects that had been previously paused were now being successfully recorded and produced. Despite the level of detail included in the how-to document, and my direct guidance provided via Zoom calls, there were many hiccups and hurdles.

Here is a list of logistical challenges and learnings I experienced while producing videos remotely:

- Never assume the technical expertise of the talent/subject being recorded. If something can go wrong, it will. Either from a production standpoint, technical standpoint, or both. I often scheduled Zoom calls with video participants to walk through the entire setup before a shoot.
- Play to your subject's strengths. Your subject's previous experience may influence how much time you spend on setup and providing on-camera tips for delivery and body language. If necessary, schedule a call with your subject before the scheduled shoot date to walk through questions, setup, and delivery, and put to ease any concerns they may have.
- Play to your subject's environment. Assess their space to help identify an ideal location before hitting the record button. Lighting, audio, backdrop, and ambient noise are all critical factors.

- Avoid multi-camera setups if your subject will be recording themselves.
- Determine if a video is even needed. Could this be an audio recording instead? If so, native apps such as the iPhone's Voice Memos record better quality audio vs. when recording video.
- In general, you have less control over the quality of the footage you're sent. For each project, allot additional time to fix and clean the footage in order to make it presentable.
- Being a remote video resource, I started receiving video production requests from other teams. Have at your disposal approved, brand-specific templates, title plates, fonts, and any other creative that will reduce your editing time when working across multiple companies, brands, or teams.
- Set expectations with stakeholders on the cost and length of time for any video project. In my experience, the amount of time it takes to produce a finished, polished product (with multiple rounds of edits) takes MUCH longer than many people expect. Use the 10 hours for every minute rule as a foundation.
- Before starting any project, gain a clear understanding of the goals, expectations, and expected outputs from the asking party. If there's uncertainty on the ask or deliverable, that needs to be clarified. If there will be multiple rounds of edits, that should be defined. If there will be multiple stakeholders/approvers, that needs to be taken into account. If b-roll or sound effects need to be purchased, that should be budgeted.
- "What do I wear" is the #1 question I've been asked over the years, and this held true even while remote recording. Expect this question to come up and have a ready-to-go answer.

What Was the One Thing You Wish You Knew before You Did the Project above and How Has That Experience Changed Your Future Productions?

I realize my story involves more than one project, but from the list above, the one thing I wish I knew beforehand would be the last two bullets combined on properly setting expectations. Especially working remote, people are unable to see how hard you're working or the extra time you're spending to create graphics, producing animation, cleaning up video and audio, etc. Overestimate the amount of time needed to edit and deliver a finished product. Crystalize the ask, goals, expectations, and output at the outset, and make sure to get buy-in and sign-off before diving in.

What Went Right? What Went Wrong? What Advice May You Provide to a Reader about How to Better Prepare?

Since you asked, here's a full list of common production "misses" that I experienced while recording and editing video remotely:

- Video was recorded at too low a resolution.
- Video was recorded vertically vs. horizontally.
- Incorrect head room, incorrect look space.
- The camera's zoom function was used, which generally reduces resolution.
- Recorded footage was improperly focused.
- A tripod was not being used, resulting in shaky/unstable footage.
- A volunteer was holding the smartphone/camera to record the subject but anti-shake was turned off or not sufficient.
- Harsh overhead lighting creating shadows on the subject's face.
- Auto-exposure darkened everything because subject was sitting in front of a window.
- Subject was sitting too close to wall or sat in front of a blank wall.
- Subject was using on board mic to capture audio but was sitting too far away, resulting in too much reverb/undesirable signal to noise ratio.
- Subject allowed microphone cable to hang in view of camera.
- Subject was wearing clothing that continually interfered with lapel microphone.
- Subject was sitting too close to an air vent or similar background noise.
- Subject was wearing clothing with stripes, causing a moiré effect.
- Recorded footage was sent directly to email or text, which resulted in a compressed (essentially unusable) file.
- Subject's tone or body language did not properly convey their message.
- Subject looked away from camera before finishing their final statement. Whenever something actually went right, I celebrated with a silent fist pump, then went right back to editing.

Is Remote Media Production Here to Stay? From Your Specific Experience, What Is the Most Important Thing Future Remote Media Producers Should Know?

Remote production is definitely here to stay. From my experience, the most important advice I can give to future remote media producers is this:

Understand the "why"? Why are they making a video? What are they hoping to accomplish? Can their goals be accomplished with video? Who is their audience? Does the message and format make sense for their audience? What is their level of investment in this project? Understanding the "why" unlocks so much potential in achieving goals and fulfilling expectations. Through the process, the subject may question their own original ideas and adjust expectations to match.

Building on understanding the "why" above, understand what your subject is looking to explain. What are they "really" trying to say. Video is a powerful medium because it can convey important information in a visual and digestible format. It's the job of the video producer to summarize and "nuggetize" the most essential information, thereby creating the most impact for the desired audience.

Gemma Toner, Founder and CEO of Tone Networks

TONE Networks is a SaaS platform that companies utilize to engage and retain their female employees that are early to mid-career. TONE works with companies such as Coca-Cola, Comcast, Bank of America, and the Atlanta Braves. The common thread throughout is they all hold common beliefs in gender equity and strengthening their female talent pool.

What Were Some of Your Initial Challenges to Digital Production?

It was a real "test and learn" environment. We had to figure it out as we were going and solicit feedback, which was not at all what we expected. We basically started with videos that were maybe 20 minutes long. We learned that they were way too long and the tone didn't fit. Then we had to keep trying different formats and styles to land where we are today. Which are really short, tight videos with a crystal clear, reliable message where the viewer will know what to expect before clicking "play."

What Are Your Biggest Challenges to Remote Production?

We had all of this great material planned to film in-studio and then we were faced with a huge challenge, when COVID hit, of "How are we going to adapt?" It seemed like every time we tried to get production going, somebody got COVID and we were all on lockdown. So it took a lot of collaboration with our team. I would call friends and experts every now and then and say, "Hey, what are you using?" It started as this cobbled-together system that was far from perfect.

The thing that is probably the most unpredictable is that "last mile" in our connection to the presenter. You can pretty much get to someone's home with enough bandwidth, but that's where the issues often arise. From wherever their modem and router is to wherever that camera is, that can be the biggest challenge. The hardest part is when people are traveling and they are reliant on hotel WiFi. To combat this, we do lots of prep and planning. We've been innovative in finding backup plans and alternative methods of connecting that include backups and redundancy.

How Did You Adapt to Remote Production?

We just had to literally learn this stuff. Our team just jumped right in and said, "Let's just study this and practice." That's how you figure it out. The thing I'm most proud of is that the team really pulled together and figured out how to make it work. There are always surprises because everything changes, nothing stays the same.

There is a new acceptance of remote video from the audience. The beauty in it is that it has become more authentic.

What Do You See for the Future of Remote Production?

We are moving more of our tools into the cloud. This allows for more collaboration and less physical infrastructure. We can prepare more for the unknown by jumping around to different platforms and tools. I think that will continue.

What Advice Do You Have for Remote Producers?

What I try to share with my folks is that you are a better producer when you understand the whole process. You're going to have your own certain superpowers, of course, whether you're a storyteller, a director, or an editor. Wherever you shine, understand where you fit but at least have the knowledge that, if you had to step in, you could at least provide support. Having those rounded skill sets really allows you to have a lot of flexibility and makes the whole team more agile.

What Advice Do You Give to Remote Presenters That Have Little Experience?

I'm personally not comfortable being on camera, but I often have to do it. This is where we need to be authentic and say "You know, this isn't my superpower, but I'm here and I'm going to be myself." Your on-camera talent may not photograph perfectly, or the camera shot may not be what you'd like it to be, but to me, authenticity really comes from what they have to say.

We need to focus on what information our presenters are looking to impart. You've got all these great plans and then there's always something. That's really the nature of technology and the audience has learned to accept that. As producers, we need to accept that too and adapt to it.

How Do You Prepare Your Remote Presenters?

We always try to do a tech call. We'll invest time the week before and it's really a practice run.

These prep sessions let our producing team pick up on those little things like notification sounds. This is an opportunity for our tech team to say "Do you hear that little ding? Can we mute that?" So we're practicing with them. We're looking at the type of computer they have and taking the opportunity to run through the content for them to be comfortable.

If it's a live event, we also get them connected 15 minutes prior, because guess what? People forget! We have to understand that we're not the center of their universe. They've got lots of other things to do and so we take the time to catch our breath, check the tech, the shot, the content, and start out strong.

Welcome to live production, there's always something!

Dave Shaw, Senior Producer Video and Digital Assets, New York Institute of Technology

What Is a Unique Story That Changed the Way You Produce?

A few weeks after COVID hit, we had to make a decision to cancel our [college] in person graduation in favor of a virtual ceremony. This seemed like just another day in office creating another video. The challenge was finding ways to capture high-quality video content while locked down at home. How would we remotely direct? How do we run a teleprompter remotely without delay. Most importantly, how do we put the proper technology together to accomplish all this while making sure the end user can setup and run this on their own. All this, while facing supply issues as the world turned to remote work.

We spent many long days talking with colleagues and friends to find a solution that was not only good for the end user and gave us the high-quality recordings we need but was cost efficient. Using a mobile app that recorded high-quality video to directly to the user's phone, while pushing out a compressed stream that we could see was the solution for recording. This allowed us to both see and hear the recordings and ensure the content was delivered well. Zoom was used for the back-and-forth communication during the recordings. We ran the teleprompter directly on the end user's laptop while controlling their machine directly. Basic ring lights and microphones resulted in decent results and in the end a great event.

What Was the One Thing You Wish You Knew before You Did the Project above and How Has That Experience Changed Your Future Productions?

For many years colleagues and I had been discussing how great it would be to make the flight kits that we could ship, the user could press a couple buttons and do what they needed to. The idea was not a new concept for us, but we never really got far enough on how to execute it. This experience really was the true test to see if something like this would work. The biggest lesson we learned, and not something we really even considered, is we cannot control the Internet speeds of the remote participants. While the files would record to the phone it still took time to upload to the cloud. Users couldn't use the phones for anything else until this was complete. We now have really laid out what the end user will be required to do and book enough time to ensure all things can be accomplished, including the upload, during the session.

What Went Right? What Went Wrong? What Advice May You Provide to a Reader about How to Better Prepare?

This is a loaded question here. I would almost say that everything went right, after everything went wrong. As much as we could be prepared, there were a lot of assumptions made. We thought it would be obvious to charge your phone, charge your laptop, plug in a ring light, have enough storage to record a video, download the app and connect with the link. Once we realized that all these things were not as obvious as we thought, we tweaked the documentation and instructions, and things went a lot smoother. Whenever things like this happen, I always go back to what a professor told us in a news class, "write your story so that a fifth grader would understand." It's sometime very difficult to get out of your element view things from someone else's point of view. Take the time to have a candid conversation with an end user, and good or bad, ask for all their feedback. While you might have taught them a skill and something new, the feedback you get is most valuable. It will make all your future projects easier as you begin to understand the best way to work with these end users.

Is Remote Media Production here to Stay? From Your Specific Experience, What Is the Most Important Thing Future Remote Media Producers Should Know?

I think the remote production is here to stay for some types of production. Every day you see guests on the news from their homes via Zoom. A reporter can go live from their phone from anywhere. You no longer need, or have an expectation, to get a satellite truck out. Presenters that can't attend something in person can now easily still participate. Corporate communications, I think, will still rely on remote production as many companies are still hybrid or remote. The most important thing that I feel future remote producers should know is to understand your subject and take the time to make them comfortable. The one thing I feel is lost with the remote production is the true-face-to face interaction with your subject. When you want to create authentic content, you need to be able to find ways remotely to better connect and make it feel like you are in the room with them, not across the country.

Anastacia Kurylo, CEO, Inform Your Community

As a college professor, author, editor, nonprofit founder, and CEO, Dr. Kurylo has served on the board of five nonprofits, published six books, including two communication textbooks and over 25 articles and chapters, and previously launched a children's business called The Crafty Kids. Dr. Kurylo is dedicated to educating all ages about communication, DEI, and civic engagement. Her nonprofit is called Inform Your Community (https://www.informyourcommunity.org).

What Is a Unique Story That Changed the Way You Produce?

Inform Your Community promotes civic engagement through fun-free events. Five of our six programs are only offered online. Who wouldn't want to craft, watch a movie, or network from the comfort of their own home? We currently host two events a month. People come back to our events because they love the fun programs and because they sincerely want to learn about important issues that matter in an entertaining way. At each event we provide our attendees with entry level pre-partisan information on one topic they want to know more about such as immigration, LGBTQ Pride, Restorative Justice, remote learning and working, food waste, and invisible disability. Our motto is "Fun Today. Change Tomorrow."

For example, for our children's crafting event celebrating small businesses attendees made their own storefront magnetic playset including choosing a name for their company while we discussed the importance of small businesses for local communities. We mail the craft kits to families before the event for free and never charge an entrance fee. I remember attending a cooking event online during the pandemic where they sent all the ingredients for free in advance. I was so happy when I received the cute kit and it added to the excitement and, ultimately, fun of the event. After also attending several cooking events online that required you to be ready to cook with your own ingredients, I saw the value for Inform Your Community in sending the kits in advance for establishing goodwill, for inclusivity, for branding, and so on. Imagine the excitement of the kids when they see all the goodies in that kit—felt, foam, and wood pieces as well as fabric flowers, alphabet stickers and so much more! Sending materials in advance of an event is a good model, if also a costly one for an organization, which makes us that much more reliant on donations to keep our events free.

What Was the One Thing You Wish You Knew before You Did the Project above and How Has That Experience Changed Your Future Productions?

Just like throwing a party, hosting a fun online event relies on a lot of people and I underestimated this. As a 501(c)(3) nonprofit organization, Inform Your Community started with four volunteers and in 2 years has grown to have nearly 20 volunteers. We rely on our volunteers and donors to help us continue to offer free registration, free craft materials, and free shipping. When I founded the organization, I anticipated the need for donations but had no idea how much our amazing volunteers would be integral to our growing quickly! Many people may assume that online events don't require a lot of work, but they definitely do. To make our programs a success we are always looking for more donors, volunteers, sponsors, and partners as well as experts to help us with our curriculum.

What Went Right? What Went Wrong? What Advice May You Provide to a Reader about How to Better Prepare?

Personality can enhance or detract from the content of an event. We have been successful at keeping the energy up and engaging with attendees. We are committed to inclusivity, so we work hard not to treat all attendees as if they are the same. For our events we introduce our pronouns, describe what we are wearing for those who may be visually impaired, and make sure live transcription is available for those with auditory impairments. My advice would be to debrief right after every event when the details are fresh in your mind. That's how we have learned to improve our future events in these and other ways.

Is Remote Media Production Here to Stay? From Your Specific Experience, What Is the Most Important Thing Future Remote Media Producers Should Know?

As people feel more comfortable socializing as they did in pre-pandemic times, the traditional webinar will no longer be a preferable form of communication. Having said that, online experiences that are unique and fun will be desirable. We can't undo the last few years or go back in time. We have made advancements in our comfort with online socializing, and we will no doubt continue to enjoy online events when these are offered in enjoyable ways. The major difference now is that people know what a good online event is like.

Robb Montgomery Is an American Mobile Journalism Educator Based in Berlin

Robb is the author of *Smartphone Video Storytelling* and *Mobile Journalism* textbooks and the chair of the Mobile Journalism Awards competition. His documentaries have been awarded top prizes at global film festivals and he trains journalists for CNN, Reuters, *The New York Times*, Journalism Co UK, Mediacorp, Radio Free Europe, *Hindustan Times*, Middle East Broadcasting Network, Channel News Asia, BILD, InterNews, and VRT public broadcasters. His certificate courses (hosted by the Smart Film School) are used by journalism schools and media organizations worldwide.

What Is a Unique Story That Changed the Way You Produce?

The Pandemic hit the Mobile Journalism Awards right about the time we were making plans to host several cinema screening events where we would showcase the winning documentaries in several different countries. With travel and indoor meetings suspended, our nonprofit was offered a game-changing donation from the CEO of Filmocracy. Paul Jun donated his company's high tech virtual Film Festival tech to Visual Editors, NFP to use at no charge. With this virtual meeting space, we could recreate many of the social and theatrical aspects of a real Red Carpet event. The tech platform Filmocracy offers us is way ahead of a Zoom or Teams-style wrapper. We could host up to 800 people for our awards show and we also used it run a Mobile Journalism Workshop a few months later. The virtual auditorium space is beautifully laid out as a large room with dozens of tables and chairs where participants can gather and chat with tablemates. It is such a friendly environ, and they have upgraded their platform to offer more creative show productions. See visuals here: https://www.visualeditors.com/mobile-journalism-workshop/

From my side, I was able to produce this from my tiny video studio in Berlin where I already had live-to-tape equipment, but no live switcher or sound board. To enable live camera switching by the show host, (me!) I also added a Stream Deck Companion and a Korg NanoKontrol2 Midi to USB control surface. These allow me to program dedicated buttons to hit while running the Mobile Journalism Awards broadcast.

What Was the One Thing You Wish You Knew before You Did the Project above and How Has That Experience Changed Your Future Productions?

This project allowed me to also use the upgraded live studio to produce dynamic, multi-camera, video lectures for students, training workshops for reporters and produce a large inventory of fresh training tutorials for the Smart Film School. Videos that are professional that they need, little to none post-editing. This has been a game-changer.

What Went Right? What Went Wrong? What Advice May You Provide to a Reader about How to Better Prepare?

You don't have to do all of the tasks (host, technical director, show designer, talent booker, judge wrangler, comms, etc.) as a solo operator. I am a little insane and also running a nonprofit that has a tiny budget. If you do try this, you need to be prepared to invest a lot of time programming your shots with macros and your show graphics, and rehearsing. Sort out how you will live switch when you also have live guests to manage to bring into the show. How will you keep the audience entertained while you do it all?

Is Remote Media Production Here to Stay? From Your Specific Experience, What Is the Most Important Thing Future Remote Media Producers Should Know?

Yes, this experience has rewired how I use my studio to teach and present the Mojo Awards. We will probably use the Smart Film School platform for the Mobile Journalism Awards as it has been upgraded with similar virtual tools to make a global screening event possible. This is important to us with the added benefit of us managing registrations, rather than trying to kludge that together with a third party. The customer relationship needs to be first party.

7

CONCLUSION

There was a small whoosh, a click, and a whir as the VHS tape was put into the VCR. The machine was attached with a wire that had three plugs on each end—video, audio left, and audio right. It was plugged into the television set in the middle of the room. The TV was a big screen, 32 inches! It was nearly as deep as it was tall and sat on a nice piece of furniture. It was the centerpiece of the room, and it was one of the few portals to visual entertainment that you had around the house. The tape in the VCR was a recording of an educational seminar taped a few weeks previous at your corporate headquarters.

The video was uneventful though educational and you remember your parents watching it through glazed eyes. It was just a wide shot of a conference room and when each leader spoke, the camera slowly zoomed into them, settling on a medium close-up. Holding a microphone wired to the camera, each presenter spoke directly into the camera, occasionally looking at their notes or their colleagues for reaction. Several parts were interesting, so you watched your parents rewind the tape, occasionally overdoing it and they spent a few minutes finding the point they left off. When it was done, the tape was rewound to the beginning, ejected, and put back into the sleeve.

For nearly two decades, this seemed like the best it was going to get. Then one day your friend introduced you to mini-DV. A small form factor tape that fits into unimaginably small cameras. The audio was better, the image was crispy, and the footage was digital. You learned how to record seminars and instead of one camera, set up a three-camera shoot. The footage was still stored on tape, but now you could digitize the footage and edit it on your computer. You just got an amazing program called Final Cut and wanted to remove some mistakes and edit between the angles. By the end of the week, you had a great show put together

DOI: 10.4324/9781003291718-7

and you exported it into a dot-m-o-v file and uploaded it to your company's server.

It felt like overnight that tapes disappeared. First, cameras were put into your cellphone and then your phone became smart. You can record anywhere you wanted, the devices were more accessible, and a new storage system was making it easier to transfer footage. It felt weird at first because the storage was on very small chips that were called secure digital cards and they held whole gigabytes of space on something that was the size of a Ritz cracker. It was a far cry from the days you held a 3.5-inch floppy disk that barely even held 1.5 megabytes. The biggest difference in your workflow was the spare time! When you shot on tape, it would take the same amount of time to digitize it as it took to record—now it's just drag and drop.

The storage sites on the web like YouTube and Vimeo were only the beginning of the next stage. You could comment, share, and even re-edit other people's work. It was storytelling at another level. The realm of live remote broadcasting was once only that of news agencies with huge microwave dishes on their vans. One day you were in the park and there was someone just standing there with their phone livestreaming to a site. You can see on the screen little hearts appearing as they spoke to their virtual audience. It was an entirely new world of presenting and it was all on one device. While more people were getting involved in video storytelling and virtual presenting, it was still not fully proliferated.

Cameras were everywhere, presenting was everything, technology was smaller, quality was higher than ever!

In March of 2020, everything changed forever. On the guidance of health professionals and caring colleagues and educators, we isolated away from each other. To connect and see our loved ones, our students, our co-workers, we turned on the cameras we've had for the last several years. We spoke to the screens, looking just below the tiny lenses on our phones and our laptops. Eye contact was weird, but we made do because it was better than nothing. And just like that, we knew we had to create the next paradigm of work, meetings, events, learning, connecting, and networking. Collectively we did it! But there were no guides, just a desire to make things work.

One day, after you were done with your Zoom call, you wandered into the basement and found your parents' old VHS tapes. In a blue sleeve, you see something funny and pull the tape out. It says on the printed label: "Corporate Workshop, 1987." Underneath it the words, in blue pen, it says "Friends, ER, Frasier." It'd been taped over at some point, the corporate workshop lost to history.

In just 40 years, everything changed and in each iteration of remote media production, we learned to adapt. The tools are nearly the same, but the method is different. We relied on professionals to create our media. We would watch tapes, not make them. Now we produce, direct, present, and distribute all ourselves.

What comes next?

The Future of Virtual Presenting

The first thing that most people say when you ask people what they believe will be around the corner is virtual reality, the "metaverse," and immersive environments. The futuristic look of the headsets and the 3D spaces are visually attractive and present a feeling that the future is already here. While we agree that immersivity is the future, there is still a large barrier to entry to headset-based experiences.

As of this writing, Meta is investing billions in their metaverse projects, hoping to get users to join them in the avatar worlds. In the meantime, virtual event companies continue to see growth and Zoom, Microsoft Teams, WebEx, and Google Meet are part of so many people's everyday lives. It's far more likely that we'll lean into virtual presenting from this angle over the next decade, but we should still discuss what comes next.

Platforms of the Future

The next era of virtual event platforms may well engage with avatars and virtual reality technologies. Aside from Meta's Metaverse, Spatial (spatial.io), Engage VR (engagevr.io), AltSpaceVR (altvr.com), and Virtway (virtway.com) among others, have already staked claim to the next generation of virtual meeting spaces. Each product respectively focuses on a different aspect of the upcoming metaverse environments.

Metaverse environments could mean a few things, so we'll try to clear it up. In nearly every aspect, we already inhabit immersive virtual spaces in our mediated lives. Social media is already an immersive environment. When we participate in social media, we use both the technology and our brains to keep connections, communicate, and share information on these platforms. Even when we watch tv, we put ourselves in immersive settings—almost 90% of us watch multiple screens while we consume media.[1] But the metaverse *is* technically different. The metaverse (named after a dystopian technology in Neil Stephenson's 1993 *Snowcrash*) is intended to be a goggle-based virtual environment where you connect with other users wearing a headset.

The virtual reality headset is not a new technology. The Cyberia team we mentioned in the book developed headset-based virtual reality in 1989 from technologies developed in the 1960s. The latest iteration, brought back into popularity by the Oculus Rift and HTC Vive, has much in common with their 1990s predecessors. VR is still two, tiny monitors with convex lenses right near your eyes to give stereo panoramic views. VR engages in visual differential to make sure you don't get sick. Like car tires when you make a turn, each tire moves at a different speed. In the headset, there are minute differences between each display to make it look smooth.

When we put on a headset to use virtual reality, we are immersed almost immediately, and our senses are overwhelmed by the digital environment. Other users in the VR space seem more personal as their movements represent their actual body movements and they can look around. The authenticity of VR is part of the success of the technology. In addition, choosing an avatar to represent yourself in virtual reality is as authentic as your physical presentation. In a world where you can design the avatar, the choices you make represent a presentation of self far more creative than reality. VR avatars have been helpful to the LGBTQ+ community and those who identify as non-binary.

At this point, VR-based virtual events are still somewhat a novelty because of access, not because of technology. VR is an exclusive technology, prioritizing those with money to afford the gear, binocular color vision, and mobility. Not everyone can get a hold of a headset for VR-based events, so you may exclude some audience members. Further, VR-based events have a risk factor in terms of trolling, abuse, and poor behavior. Throughout the history of VR, people have been subject to abuse in the virtual space as users in the guise of an avatar have groped or forced themselves on other users without their permission.[2]

On the other hand, many of these immersive platforms have incredible amounts of extra features that benefit from the three-dimensional space. Having networking events where you can interact with human avatars and "take up space" in the digital world gives a sense of realism that two-dimensional platforms cannot duplicate well. Good immersive environments may put users in virtual theatres and around networking tables. A speaker may have the opportunity to give a talk through their web camera and see human-like figures in the crowd, giving a better sense of how many people they are speaking to.

If you are interested in adopting a metaverse, VR, or immersive virtual event platform, you can test the environment on apps like VR Chat in advance to get a sense of how low-stakes VR operates. When you are meeting with the platform's salespeople or demonstrators, ask questions about access and exclusion and trust and safety. The more you plan for the sake of the audience, the better your production.

Future Features

One of the largest downsides of our current digital environment is its siloed experiences. Apps are their own unique communication system within your digital appliance. If you are on WebEx, you cannot use the camera for other features on the computer. The features of FaceTime do not match that of Zoom. The user interface on a browser-based platform is usually incompatible with app-based products.

Someday, we may be able to work with cross-platform communication and calling. This is fairly unlikely given the competitive nature of the companies involved, but the more we normalize video communication, it might be something that comes about through regulation. It would be extremely convenient to answer Zoom calls in FaceTime or join a virtual event through software we are already familiar with. Rather than training your KOLs on new platforms each time, the future may hold a possibility where any camera will sync with the software in use. A camera bridge would be quite a jump forward for access.

In some ways, we may already be on the way to this solution with the advent of augmented and mixed reality. Whereas VR is about immersion and digital environments, AR and MR enhance the physical world with digital interactions. Augmented reality is when digital objects are overlaid on physical space using a camera lens. The most common and most well understood AR product is Pokémon Go, the mobile app that allows users to catch small fantasy characters overlaid in your own environment through the lens.

Mixed reality on the other hand is a bit bulkier. With MR, you wear a headset similar to a VR headset, but you can see through it. MR headsets have cameras that scan the physical environment and enable the digital objects on screen to scale to the physical space you are occupying. It could be a benefit for virtual event and webinar platforms to incorporate AR or MR so you can present in your room but see everyone else who is there with you.

There are some interesting approaches to AR and MR in the form of devices that use cameras in tandem with projection. The short-lived Amazon Glow was a children's communication and learning toy that integrated cameras, video screen, and a projector. The device projected a game or book onto the table while a camera detected hand gestures or objects. Unfortunately, the Glow was discontinued after a year. A similar device by Osmo enhances physical objects with animation and colors on a tablet screen, without a projector.

Going back to the authenticity chapter about your setting, an AR/MR environment would allow more of your space to be useful in your presentation method. You can arrange your setting knowing that more of your appearance will be transmitted to the audience. AR and MR technologies still have access issues like VR, but the cross-platform communication could be useful for bridging the presentation divide.

Finally, we're also seeing new technologies in immersive spaces that movie studios and television series have already adopted that may have a purpose in remote media production and virtual events. Studios interested in replacing some of the intense visual effects may use more practical backgrounds and have reintroduced the concept of matte paintings in the form of high-resolution video walls.[3] Using game engines (like the ones to make video games), high-resolution video walls provide an immersive experience for the actor to see the setting in which the action takes place. (In contrast to the imagination necessary with green screen settings.)

FIGURE 7.1 Wrap around high-resolution video walls as seen at the National Association of Broadcasters Convention 2022

In the future, these immersive settings may be just the right environment for hybrid events. The walls act as both the presentation spaces as well as an interactive device. Because the camera motion tracks the background, the audience at home always sees the conformed version of the production and the level of production value increases incredibly. At the moment, this hardware is pricey, but with the costs of flatscreens coming down and the access to game engines increasing, hybrid digital and virtual events with immersive settings may be around the corner.

Tech within Reach

New technologies are born every day for virtual presentation. The history of technology is biased (heck, so is history), and hasn't always performed well for those who are not capable of using the technology the way the technologists intended. An example that gets brought up quite often in tech responsibility circles is the story of the Xbox 360 Kinect camera. The Kinect camera was a stereo lens camera that mapped users in their space so they could play immersive action or sports games on the Xbox console gaming system. The big downside of the camera was that it originally had an incredibly difficult time detecting dark skin tones.[4]

When technology is developed, it sometimes lacks diversity in its process. There are biases and blind spots in nearly every technology that exists. While the

Kinect incident occurred in 2010, "techno-racism" continues to occur even with newer technologies.[5] From face-detection software on your iPhone to face-tracking for focus on Zoom, the camera does a better job with light-skinned people. The history of tech has bias based on mostly white and male dominance.

There are new technologies working hard to change the way systems have worked. One of the highlights is the Lumina camera (getlumina.com). Lumina is an artificial intelligence (AI) driven camera for face follow and autofocus, but most importantly has real-time color correction for different skin tones. Whereas Black skin used to appear too dark, Lumina's technology analyzes the lighting and illuminates each user to be presented most photo-realistically.

AI-driven cameras will become far more available over the next several years and are designed to take a lot of the guesswork out of focus and lighting. In a hybrid world, a good image with a good camera is indispensable. On the topic of cameras, there is also the issue of eye contact. AI cameras are good at motion tracking and making sure your eyes are placed in the frame correctly, but most cameras are still above the screen and as a result, above the eyes of the recipient on screen.

Center Cam (thecentercam.com) is an interesting technology that attempts to solve the eyeline issue. Simply put, Center Cam is a web camera on a small unobtrusive boom. You can adjust the lens to be directly in front of the person on screen and match the lens to their eyes. By positioning the camera in the center of the monitor, the appearance that you are constantly making eye contact with the person on the other side becomes more evident.

The field of telehealth could benefit from a technology like Center Cam so patients feel as though doctors and health practitioners feel more personal and connected. Telehealth boomed during the pandemic but will likely continue to be a percentage of the health industry for the rest of our lives.[6] Telehealth reduces unnecessary visits to the ER and allows for non-physical treatment to be administered by the doctor themselves. Doctors do their best to make eye contact and using a technology like Center Cam can make their jobs a bit better.

Another technology that seems to be making its way into people's lives is more interactive features like physical mute buttons, ring lights with temperature controls, and low-level luminance for the back of the laptop. These technologies are all available now and represent the tech industry's interest in increasing quality and continuing the support of the hybrid world.

Being There, Virtually

For the first time in its nearly 20-year history, Facebook lost users in February 2022.[7] Aside from Meta's shock, it signaled that we are now going to go through a shift to the next iteration of social media use and experience a new paradigm of virtual presenting and remote media production. This book was conceived because we saw that people were continuing to create new ways of meeting, presenting, and networking in the virtual worlds outside the old systems—which includes "traditional" social media like Facebook.

Every person we spoke to about remote media production and virtual presenting said they are experimenting with new ways to produce successful projects. Additionally, nearly everyone had at some point created their own guides to help colleagues, co-workers, presenters, students, and experienced speakers learn how to navigate the digital world. We listened and we tried to collect all the points into one place. The goal of a guidebook like this one is to help you focus on the project and the quality of the work, not sit there and type out Google Doc guides to send out.

We hope that you are the one who will develop the next big platform for virtual presenters to interact with. One way or another, we're entering a new world of connectivity and are inspired by all the new ways we'll use our authenticity to connect with others meaningfully. Perhaps we'll be in the audience when you are presenting on screen, or we'll meet in a networking booth on a virtual event platform.

Thanks for reading! We're looking forward to your success!

Notes

1 Anderson, Nate. "88% of Americans Use a Second Screen While Watching TV. Why?" *Ars Technica*, 26 Dec. 2019, https://arstechnica.com/gaming/2019/12/88-of-americans-use-a-second-screen-while-watching-tv-why/.

2 Cohen, Jamie. "Researchers Have Warned About Harassment in the Metaverse for Decades." *OneZero*, 22 Feb. 2022, https://onezero.medium.com/researchers-have-warned-about-harassment-in-the-metaverse-for-decades-c66c6293bced.

3 Cohen, Jamie. "The Future of Cinema Is Video Games, Just Not the Way You Think." *Medium*, 29 Apr. 2022, https://newanddigital.medium.com/the-future-of-cinema-is-video-games-just-not-the-way-you-think-b6a664099b76.

4 Diaz, Sam. "Tech Racism? Will Dark-Skinned Gamers Have Trouble with Kinect's Facial Recognition?" *ZDNET*, https://www.zdnet.com/article/tech-racism-will-dark-skinned-gamers-have-trouble-with-kinects-facial-recognition/. Accessed 2 Sept. 2022.

5 Karimi, Faith. "People of Color Have a New Enemy: Techno-Racism." *CNN*, https://www.cnn.com/2021/05/09/us/techno-racism-explainer-trnd/index.html. Accessed 2 Sept. 2022.

6 Pearl, Robert, and Brian Wayling. "The Telehealth Era Is Just Beginning." *Harvard Business Review*, 1 May 2022. *hbr.org*, https://hbr.org/2022/05/the-telehealth-era-is-just-beginning.

7 Dwoskin, Elizabeth, et al. "Facebook Loses Users for the First Time in Its History." *Washington Post*. www.washingtonpost.com, https://www.washingtonpost.com/technology/2022/02/02/facebook-earnings-meta/. Accessed 2 Sept. 2022.

GLOSSARY

This glossary is provided to quickly define terms we are using in the context of this book.

Agency Your self-motivated actions and intentions in a situation where you can make your own choices. We also use the term to describe organizations like advertising agencies.

Broadcast General term for anything media that is distributed to many people simultaneously, whether the audience is known or not.

Codec Shortened portmanteau of code and decode. A codec is a digital system that encodes a signal into something digital portable (like a file) and also allows it to be decoded for viewing in real time.

Encryption Converting anything into code that requires a key to convert back. Codecs may be used to encrypt data as well.

Ethernet A protocol for the transfer of information, usually carried over a series of wires and connected via a pin that can be attached to a modem or a computer or a wall outlet.

Feed A general space for a community to see the flow of information transactions happening during an event or on social media.

GDPR The European Union's General Data Protection Regulation is a set of privacy laws established in the EU to regulate the flow and archiving of user data and privacy.

HD/SD High definition refers to a video product with a resolution of higher than 1280×720 pixels and standard definition is anything with lower than a 860×480 pixel resolution.

HDMI A high-definition multimedia interface is a plug for the output and input of video signal from a camera or television. Be aware that one-way HDMI cables exist.

ISO Isolated camera recording. If you are shooting a multiple camera production and recording each camera independently for later post-production use, you are using an ISO.

Keynote Keynote is usually the speech at the beginning or end of a conference day that sets the tone for the event. A keynote speaker is usually chosen as the main event and can speak to the subject naturally and authentically as they are likely the main figure in the field of that event's theme. When planning an event, consider your keynote speaker before marketing begins.

KOL Key opinion leader. KOLs are usually sources and/or experts in their respective fields who can speak to the theme of an event without additional stress. KOLs draw audiences for events.

Livestreamer Livestreamers are people who have made their careers broadcasting themselves in realtime as they add commentary to other clips, video games, or from location-based events. Livestreamers usually make their income from endorsements or sponsorships.

Multidirectional Video Platform Cloud-based video hosting platforms that allow users to broadcast to their audience while allowing simultaneous communication from the audience back to the streamer. This is often in the form of chat, comments, Q&A, "likes," and sometimes allowing viewers to broadcast their video into the production.

Platform A proprietary space for a company where information is created, exchanged, shared. This can refer to any number of virtual event software products to social media sites.

Playlisting Creating a timed experience for simulive productions where you play one clip directly after another creating the feeling that cameras are switching or acts are changing rather than different clips are playing.

Post-production Editing, rebuilding, or re-ordering footage that is stored on a hard drive. Productions that are created and shown later are considered post-produced projects.

Pre-recorded A part of an event where the footage was captured well in advance of the airtime. Usually pre-recorded clips are labeled pre-recorded so audience members know the information cannot be interacted with in real time.

Resolution The number of pixels in the image that enables a screen to present higher quality images.

RTMP Real-time messaging protocol. This is a standard protocol used for streaming video over the internet.

Simulive A fully produced webinar that is aired at a later date, but may include real time question and answer sessions or a live chat with the KOL or experts.

Store and Forward Video is recorded on the local device and uploaded either simultaneously while recording or afterward to a remote server location or cloud destination.

Streaming A codec-based transmission of video that rapidly converts footage into a format that can be distributed to many people at once with little delay over the internet. This includes everything from Zoom to webinars to Netflix.

The Cloud A cute term for a massive number of servers and hard drives all over the planet that store data.

Trust and Safety A growing industry that encourages proactive approaches to the success of human connections on social media, event platforms, and applications.

vMix vMix stands for "vision mixer." It is Windows-based software that allows switching between multiple inputs, cameras, video files, and has integrated audio mixing. It is commonly used in live streaming scenarios because it can be installed on a laptop and allows the user to switch, stream, and record.

VPN Virtual private network. Enables encryption over a private network or allows for access to servers outside your region to access sites unavailable within your region due to regulations.

YouTubers Video bloggers who have become creators and producers that are well recognized on the YouTube platform. Other terms for YouTubers are creators or vloggers. Most YouTubers make their income from subscribers and view counts as well as endorsements and sponsorships.

REFERENCES

25 Webinar Statistics [2022]: Facts About Webinars in the U.S. – Zippia. https://www.zippia.com/advice/webinar-statistics/. Accessed 31 Aug. 2022.

Abadi, Mark. "The Classic Advice to Dress for the Job You Want Has a Major Flaw, and It Could Make a Job Interview That Much Harder." *Business Insider*, https://www.businessinsider.com/dress-for-job-you-want-advice-flaw-2018-11. Accessed 30 Aug. 2022.

Anderson, Nate. "88% of Americans Use a Second Screen While Watching TV. Why?" *Ars Technica*, 26 Dec. 2019, https://arstechnica.com/gaming/2019/12/88-of-americans-use-a-second-screen-while-watching-tv-why/.

Antibodyody Antibody Song – Raven the Science Maven. Directed by Dr. Raven the Science Maven, 2020. *YouTube*, https://www.youtube.com/watch?v=KBpQg6JMxSc.

Antonelli, William. "What's a Good Internet Speed? How to Upgrade Your Internet Setup to Fit Your Needs." *Business Insider*, https://www.businessinsider.com/guides/tech/what-is-a-good-internet-speed. Accessed 30 Aug. 2022.

"Art. 89 GDPR – Safeguards and Derogations Relating to Processing for Archiving Purposes in the Public Interest, Scientific or Historical Research Purposes or Statistical Purposes." *General Data Protection Regulation (GDPR)*, https://gdpr-info.eu/art-89-gdpr/. Accessed 31 Aug. 2022.

Ashworth, Boone. "How to Host a Virtual Watch Party." *Wired*. www.wired.com, https://www.wired.com/story/how-to-host-a-virtual-watch-party/. Accessed 30 Aug. 2022.

Biddle, Sam. "'A Fundamentally Illegitimate Choice': Shoshana Zuboff on the Age of Surveillance Capitalism." *The Intercept*, https://theintercept.com/2019/02/02/shoshana-zuboff-age-of-surveillance-capitalism/. Accessed 31 Aug. 2022.

Burgess, Matt. "What Is GDPR? The Summary Guide to GDPR Compliance in the UK." *Wired UK*. www.wired.co.uk, https://www.wired.co.uk/article/what-is-gdpr-uk-eu-legislation-compliance-summary-fines-2018. Accessed 31 Aug. 2022.

Call, Megan. *Neuroplasticity: How to Use Your Brain's Malleability to Improve Your Well-Being.* http://accelerate.uofuhealth.utah.edu/resilience/neuroplasticity-how-to-use-your-brain-s-malleability-to-improve-your-well-being. Accessed 30 Aug. 2022.

Children Interrupt BBC News Interview – BBC News. Directed by BBC News, 2017. *YouTube*, https://www.youtube.com/watch?v=Mh4f9AYRCZY.

Cohen, Jamie. "Researchers Have Warned About Harassment in the Metaverse for Decades." *OneZero*, 22 Feb. 2022, https://onezero.medium.com/researchers-have-warned-about-harassment-in-the-metaverse-for-decades-c66c6293bced.

Cohen, Jamie. "The Future of Cinema Is Video Games, Just Not the Way You Think." *Medium*, 29 Apr. 2022, https://newanddigital.medium.com/the-future-of-cinema-is-video-games-just-not-the-way-you-think-b6a664099b76.

Diaz, Sam. "Tech Racism? Will Dark-Skinned Gamers Have Trouble with Kinect's Facial Recognition?" *ZDNET*, https://www.zdnet.com/article/tech-racism-will-dark-skinned-gamers-have-trouble-with-kinects-facial-recognition/. Accessed 2 Sept. 2022.

Dwoskin, Elizabeth, et al. "Facebook Loses Users for the First Time in Its History." *Washington Post*. www.washingtonpost.com, https://www.washingtonpost.com/technology/2022/02/02/facebook-earnings-meta/. Accessed 2 Sept. 2022.

Ellsworth, Phoebe C., and J. Merrill Carlsmith. "Effects of Eye Contact and Verbal Content on Affective Response to a Dyadic Interaction." *Journal of Personality and Social Psychology*, vol. 10, no. 1, 1968, pp. 15–20. *DOI.org (Crossref)*, 10.1037/h0026385.

"Facebook Live." *Facebook Live | Meta for Media*, https://www.facebook.com/formedia/solutions/facebook-live. Accessed 31 Aug. 2022.

"Feel like a Fraud?" Https://Www.Apa.Org, https://www.apa.org/gradpsych/2013/11/fraud. Accessed 30 Aug. 2022.

Ford, Paul. "The American Room." *The Message*, 14 July 2016, https://medium.com/message/the-american-room-3fce9b2b98c5.

Fowler, J. H., and N. A. Christakis. "Dynamic Spread of Happiness in a Large Social Network: Longitudinal Analysis over 20 Years in the Framingham Heart Study." *BMJ*, vol. 337, no. dec04 2, Dec. 2008, pp. a2338–a2338. *DOI.org (Crossref)*, 10.1136/bmj.a2338.

Frier, Sarah. *No Filter: The Inside Story of Instagram*. Simon & Schuster, 2020.

Goffman, Erving. *The Presentation of Self in Everyday Life*. 1. Anchor Books ed., rev. Ed, Anchor Books, 1990.

Gorman, James. "ON LANGUAGE; Like, Uptalk?" *The New York Times*, 15 Aug. 1993. *NYTimes.com*, https://www.nytimes.com/1993/08/15/magazine/on-language-like-uptalk.html.

History of PictureTel Corp. – FundingUniverse. http://www.fundinguniverse.com/company-histories/picturetel-corp-history/. Accessed 31 Aug. 2022.

Joseph, Stephen. *Authentic: How to Be Yourself & Why It Matters*. Piatkus, 2019.

Karimi, Faith. "People of Color Have a New Enemy: Techno-Racism." *CNN*, https://www.cnn.com/2021/05/09/us/techno-racism-explainer-trnd/index.html. Accessed 2 Sept. 2022.

Labs, Spectrum. *Why Is Trust and Safety Important*. https://www.spectrumlabsai.com/trust-and-safety. Accessed 31 Aug. 2022.

"ON24 Webinar Benchmarks Report Special Edition: Post-COVID Trends." *ON24*, https://www.on24.com/resources/asset/on24-webinar-benchmarks-report-special-edition-post-covid-trends/. Accessed 31 Aug. 2022.

Pearl, Robert, and Brian Wayling. "The Telehealth Era Is Just Beginning." *Harvard Business Review*, 1 May 2022. *hbr.org*, https://hbr.org/2022/05/the-telehealth-era-is-just-beginning.

"Picturetel Gives Liveshare Plus Simultaneous Voice, Data." *Tech Monitor*, 7 Sept. 1995, https://techmonitor.ai/technology/picturetel_gives_liveshare_plus_simultaneous_voice_data.

"Psychology to Grin About: The Benefits of Smiling and Laughter." *UWA Online*, 6 June 2019, https://online.uwa.edu/news/benefits-of-smiling-and-laughter/.

Raindrops. Directed by Tyler Oakley, 2007. *YouTube*, https://www.youtube.com/watch?v=pIdT_tIPomw.

Reeves, Richard. "The City Politic: The More Things Change..." *New York Magazine*, 22 Jan. 1973, pp. 8–9.

Rushkoff, Douglas. "Act as If You're Really There." *OneZero*, 16 Mar. 2020, https://onezero.medium.com/act-as-if-youre-really-there-3e6e38dc4d1a.

Seppälä, Emma, et al. "Research: Why Breathing Is So Effective at Reducing Stress." *Harvard Business Review*, 29 Sept. 2020. *hbr.org*, https://hbr.org/2020/09/research-why-breathing-is-so-effective-at-reducing-stress.

Spector, Nicole. "Smiling Can Trick Your Brain into Happiness—and Boost Your Health." *NBC News*, https://www.nbcnews.com/better/health/smiling-can-trick-your-brain-happiness-boost-your-health-ncna822591. Accessed 30 Aug. 2022.

Thompson, Matt. "Five Reasons Why People Code-Switch." *NPR*, 13 Apr. 2013. *NPR*, https://www.npr.org/sections/codeswitch/2013/04/13/177126294/five-reasons-why-people-code-switch.

Vladimir Nabokov Discusses "Lolita" Part 1 of 2. Directed by JiffySpook, 2008. *YouTube*, https://www.youtube.com/watch?v=Ldpj_5JNFoA.

Walker. *Through the Looking Glass*. https://www.fourmilab.ch/autofile/e5/chapter2_69.html. Accessed 31 Aug. 2022.

Wu, Tim. *The Master Switch: The Rise and Fall of Information Empires*. 1st ed, Alfred A. Knopf, 2010.

Yavorskaya, Galyna. "Webinar History. When the Webinar Was Appeared?" *Webinar Platform MyOwnConference.Com*, 7 Aug. 2017, https://myownconference.com/blog/en/webinar-history/.

Zanten, Boris Veldhuijzen van. "There Were 17,000 YouTubes Before YouTube." *TNW | Boris*, 28 Oct. 2013, https://thenextweb.com/news/17000-youtubes-youtube.

INDEX

For Product Safety Concerns and Information please contact our EU representative GPSR@taylorandfrancis.com
Taylor & Francis Verlag GmbH, Kaufingerstraße 24, 80331 München, Germany

www.ingramcontent.com/pod-product-compliance
Ingram Content Group UK Ltd.
Pitfield, Milton Keynes, MK11 3LW, UK
UKHW022020180926
475701UK00005B/950
* 9 7 8 1 0 3 2 2 5 7 7 7 8 *